AFRICAN AMERICANS
AND THE
FIRST AMENDMENT

SUNY Series in African American Studies

John R. Howard and Robert C. Smith, editors

African Americans and the First Amendment

The Case for Liberty *and* Equality

TIMOTHY C. SHIELL

Published by State University of New York Press, Albany

For information, contact State University of New York Press, Albany, NY
www.sunypress.edu

Library of Congress Cataloging-in-Publication Data

Names: Shiell, Timothy C., author.
Title: African Americans and the First Amendment : the case for liberty and equality / Timothy C. Shiell.
Description: Albany : State University of New York Press, 2019. | Series: Suny series in African American studies | Includes bibliographical references and index.
Identifiers: LCCN 2018045644| ISBN 9781438475813 (hardcover) | ISBN 9781438475837 (e-book) | ISBN 9781438475820 (paperback)
Subjects: LCSH: African Americans—Civil rights. | Freedom of speech—United States.
Classification: LCC KF4757 .S525 2019 | DDC 342.7308/508996073—dc23 LC record available at https://lccn.loc.gov/2018045644

10 9 8 7 6 5 4 3 2 1

This work is dedicated to all the people who exercised their freedom of speech, assembly, association, press, religion, and petition to promote racial equality, to those who are doing so, and to those who will do so in years to come.

CONTENTS

PREFACE

Courts in the United States have made bold statements about the significance of freedom of expression for more than 100 years. Consider three examples:

> Freedom of speech and press have always been supposed to be the very cornerstone of Anglo-Saxon democratic institutions.[1]

> If there is any principle of the Constitution that more imperatively calls for attachment than any other, it is the principle of free thought—not free thought for those who agree with us but freedom for the thought that we hate.[2]

> Freedom of thought and speech . . . [are] the matrix, the indispensable condition, of nearly every other form of freedom.[3]

In the 1960s, Harvard University law professor Thomas Emerson expressed a scholarly consensus that free speech is not the only social good but is essential to achieving the others (such as public order, justice, equality, and moral progress). Therefore, these other values must be pursued by regulating action, not expression.[4] In that same era, the First Amendment values of freedom of religion, free press, free assembly, and the right to petition were widely recognized as essential to the African American struggle for equality culminating in the successes of the civil rights movement. David Hudson Jr. writes, "the First Amendment played a crucial role in the epic struggles of the civil rights movement of the 1950s and'60s when Dr. Martin Luther King, Jr. and countless others engaged in sit-ins, protests, marches and other demonstrations to force social change."[5] Hudson quotes many other First Amendment experts to indicate a consensus on this conclusion, including Jack Greenberg, director-counsel of the NAACP Legal Defense and Educational Fund from 1961 to 1984; Robert O'Neil, director of the Thomas Jefferson Center for the Protection of Free Expression; Robert Richards, founding director of the Pennsylvania Center for the First Amendment at Pennsylvania State University; and journalism professors Linda Lumsden and Margaret Blanchard.

This civil rights era consensus on the importance of free speech and the consonance of free speech and racial progress has been fractured because of two main factors. First, progress in racial equality seemed to stagnate and even regress in the 1970s and 1980s. Second, hate speech incidents, especially at universities and colleges, have been attracting significant scholarly and public attention since the late 1980s. Legal scholars began to challenge the idea that the First Amendment is our first freedom and supports racial progress. Owen Fiss wrote "the firstness of the First Amendment appears to be little more than an assertion or slogan."[6] An increasing number of scholars began to advocate broad bans on hate speech that curtailed existing free speech rights, which they believed were necessary to make more gains in racial equality. For example, Richard Delgado and Jean Stefancic recommended universities enact speech codes punishing "severe personal insults," including insults based on body shape or poor parking ("you idiot, why did you take up two spaces?") and insults based on race, gender, or sexual orientation ("you fag, you're going straight to hell").[7] Alexander Tsesis proposed laws that prevent "disparaging stereotypes from ingraining themselves in the social conscience" and prohibit charismatic leaders from "harnessing racist, xenophobic, and anti-Semitic ideologies to further discrimination and achieve ruinous objectives" regardless of whether these expressions pose any direct or immediate threat of harm.[8] Catharine MacKinnon proposed a revival of the long-abandoned bad tendency test and the group libel doctrine to punish offensive speech.[9] Mari Matsuda argued that members of dominant groups should be banned from using hate speech against members of nondominant groups, but members of nondominant groups should not be similarly restricted.[10] The idea that liberty and equality are in fundamental conflict has attracted substantial attention,[11] and surveys show widespread support for censorship of offensive expression.[12] Some have gone further to argue that disrupting, shutting down, or violently opposing offensive expression is justified.

This book argues that First Amendment values, particularly freedom of expression, have been—and continue to be—essential allies in the struggle for racial equality and justice. Liberty and equality can and do conflict in some cases, but these values are not in *fundamental* conflict. This distinction has important implications. The misconception that they are in fundamental conflict has been detrimental to the cause of racial equality in many important ways. Rather than urge greater restrictions on expression, advocates of racial equality and justice should remain committed to robust free speech rights and exercise that right vigorously. The argument is laid out in four chapters.

Chapter 1 demonstrates the role First Amendment values (not law)—especially free speech—played in racial progress from the colonial era to the 1930s. I use the phrase "American apartheid" to refer to this era, in which a pervasive system of legal, political, economic, and social inequality was imposed by whites on African Americans and was supported by restrictions on speech, press, assembly, petition, and religion. Likewise, the denial of equality supported the denial of liberty. Yet the defiant exercise of liberty (First Amendment values) against the status quo inequality played a crucial role in the racial progress that was achieved. The chapter focuses on African Americans but also addresses other groups to demonstrate the long reach of the oppression of equality and suppression of liberty. Some important milestones covered include the slave clauses in the US Constitution, the Cherokee Nation Cases, the abolitionist movement and *Dred Scott* decision, and the series of Supreme Court decisions from the 1870s to the 1890s deconstructing Reconstruction and civil rights laws. Even when slavery was outlawed, African Americans remained targets of organized terror and victims of systemic social, economic and political subordination, especially but not exclusively in the Jim Crow South. Inequality was buttressed by restrictions on liberty. There was extensive censorship of and mob violence directed at African Americans and other minorities, labor activists, political dissidents, and free thinkers. The strong First Amendment legal rights we know today did not begin to develop until after World War I persecution of dissenters and its concomitant condemnation of "radical immigrants." The US Supreme Court finally used the First Amendment in 1931 to protect free speech (*Stromberg v. California*) and free press (*Near v. Minnesota*) from state suppression.

Chapter 2 supports the conjunction of liberty and equality through an examination of Angelo Herndon's pivotal case, culminating in the Supreme Court decision *Herndon v. Lowry* (1937). Herndon, a black communist, was arrested in Atlanta, Georgia, for inciting insurrection during the Great Depression under a law originally enacted as an anti-abolitionist, anti–slave revolt statute. Despised by many for the color of his skin and his political beliefs, Herndon found legal support from a determined fringe organization. Even when he lost at trial, on appeal to the Georgia Supreme Court and in the US Supreme Court in 1935, his struggle for justice continued. His plight attracted national and international attention and support, and his lawyers found a new basis to pursue his freedom. This time he won at trial but lost again on appeal to the state supreme court. In a stunning turnaround, the US Supreme Court found in his favor in 1937. It was the first time the court protected a black man's speech and the first time it struck down a Southern speech restriction. Herndon's case is commonly recognized as an important First Amendment decision, but it was more than that. It was a critical step in the civil rights movement, a milestone in the debate over race-neutral versus race-conscious strategies, and a paradigmatic example of the use of mass politics and mass protest to advance liberty and equality. Herndon's victory was the first time black dissent (free speech) and black legal equality were upheld together as the law of the land.

Chapter 3 continues the argument through a study of the symbiotic relationship of First Amendment values and the civil rights movement from the *Herndon* decision to the 1970s. The vigorous assertion of and exercise of First Amendment values was an intentional and essential component of advances in civil rights; likewise, the movement to attain civil rights was integral to the expansion of First Amendment legal rights. Harry Kalven Jr. suggested in his 1965 book *The Negro and the First Amendment*, the African American struggle for equality won back First Amendment rights for all citizens in the 1960s that communists had lost for us in the 1950s. Liberty and equality were widely understood to be fundamental allies. Attention is given to the role of international criticism of American apartheid in the expansion of civil rights and to key organizations, especially the National Association for the Advancement of Colored People (NAACP). The final section addresses US Supreme Court Justice Thurgood Marshall, whose devotion to First Amendment values (especially freedom of expression) and racial equality is a paradigm of the view this book defends.

Chapter 4 concludes the argument by refuting the post–civil rights era challenge to the alliance between liberty and equality, namely, the idea they are in fundamental conflict. When substantive equality remained out of reach for most African Americans in the 1970s and 1980s, combined with a national spotlight on hate speech in employment and education, scholars and activists began to break from the "essential allies" tradition and increasingly argued that strong First Amendment protections were an obstacle and a threat to racial equality. Their solution? Weaken First Amendment protections by reviving dubious legal justifications for censorship—the bad tendency test, fighting words, and group libel—and applying new justifications, such as hostile environment harassment. The chapter begins with a review of attempts to censor hate speech beginning in the late nineteenth century and transitions to the judicial decisions that rejected broad hate speech bans and upheld narrowly drawn restrictions on speech. A section is devoted to the very popular but fatally flawed international argument urging the United States to join an "international consensus" enforcing broad hate speech bans. The chapter concludes with powerful evidence demonstrating (1) the idea that liberty and equality are in fundamental conflict has undermined the pursuit of racial equality, and (2) liberty and equality are fundamentally allied through their shared opposition to orthodoxy and commitment to inclusion and participation. Robust First Amendment values and legal rights remain essential to advocating racial equality.

Contemporary defenders of the alliance of liberty and equality should acknowledge three important points. First, we are still far from a postracial egalitarian society. African Americans and other minorities and marginalized groups still face significant discrimination and obstacles from education to economics.[13] Second, targeted and pervasive hate speech takes a psychological and physical toll, and the costs are not shared equally.[14] Third, robust First Amendment values and law cannot guarantee continued progress in racial equality and justice. Nothing can guarantee this progress. However, the preponderance of evidence shows African Americans (and other historically marginalized groups) have benefited greatly and continue to benefit from the vigorous use of First Amendment values and these values have greatly benefited from and continue to benefit from the pursuit of equality. The struggles for equality and robust freedom of speech, press, assembly, petition, and religion are intertwined. The best path forward is to stay focused on liberty *and* equality.

ACKNOWLEDGMENTS

In writing *African Americans and the First Amendment*, I benefited from the advice and assistance of many people and organizations. My carpool partner, Bob Zeidel, provided almost daily feedback on book-related ideas and arguments. Jim Turk, director of the Ryerson University Centre for Free Expression, sent valuable comments on all chapters. University of Wisconsin–Stout students Kailey Dresel, Stacie Koziol, Olivia Krueger, Shane Miller, Dillon Quest, and Zipporah Turnbull offered many suggestions that improved the manuscript. I had many conversations about the subject with my wife, Carolyn Shiell, and my son, Ethan Shiell, provided valuable editorial help. A UW-Stout Faculty Research Grant provided release time from teaching in spring semester 2017 that enabled me to write chapters 2 and 3. Several sections of chapter 4 draw on information from my earlier book, *Campus Hate Speech on Trial*, first published by University of Kansas Press in 1998 and republished as a second, revised edition in 2009. Series editors John R. Howard and Robert C. Smith, and two anonymous reviewers provided significant recommendations that enabled me to polish the arguments and better integrate the themes of the book. Finally, I thank Senior Acquisitions Editor Michael Rinella and SUNY Press staff Rafael Chaiken, Jenn Bennett-Genthner, and Kate Seburyamo for their roles in bringing the book to life, and Laura Poole for excellent copyediting.

Campus Hate Speech on Trial, Second Edition, Revised published by the University Press of Kansas, © 2009. www.kansaspress.edu. Used by permission of the publisher.

CHAPTER 1

American Apartheid

Power concedes nothing without demand.
It never did and it never will.

—Frederick Douglass[1]

Liberty and equality have been closely interconnected throughout American history. This is true in both a negative and a positive sense. In the negative sense, the denial of liberty supported the denial of equality and vice versa. White-controlled government and private interests in the United States denied African Americans equality in political, economic, educational, and social spheres and suppressed their liberty by restricting their rights to speak, publish, assemble, petition, and worship. Denials of equality and liberty are two sides of the same coin—a coin that came up "heads, I win; tails, you lose." This was American apartheid.[2] Yet the connection also existed in a positive sense: the exercise of liberty supported equality and vice versa. Even when liberty and equality were heavily restricted by law—especially to people of color—during American apartheid, to the extent greater racial equality was achieved, it was essentially tied to the exercise of First Amendment liberty values.

To be sure, this era is too long and complex to provide more than just an overview in one chapter, so here I focus on the most significant legal developments regarding liberty and equality with some attention to extralegal aspects to support major themes. The chapter addresses liberty and equality in three suberas: colonial history, the Antebellum era, and post–Civil War to the 1930s. This examination reveals that progress in racial equality was painful and slow and fell far short of substantive liberty and equality. However, it also demonstrates a symbiotic relationship between liberty and equality that contributed significantly to the progress that did occur. African Americans and their allies used the First Amendment values of free speech, religion, the press, assembly, and petition to advance racial equality, and in turn, advances in racial equality led to greater legal protections for African American liberty. In effect, an irresistible force managed to budge an immovable object. Why? As will be explained in more detail in chapter 4—liberty and equality promote greater inclusion and participation and oppose orthodoxy.

THE COLONIAL ERA

The first Africans to arrive on continental US soil were slaves of Spanish colonists in Georgia in 1526, the Tampa Bay area in 1528, and St. Augustine in 1565.[3] The Africans who arrived in the English Jamestown colony in 1619 became indentured servants,[4] but by 1636 only whites could be indentured servants.[5] Enslavement of African Americans—and Native Americans—was widely practiced prior to its legalization in, for example, Massachusetts (1641), Connecticut (1650), Virginia (1661), Maryland (1663), New York (1664), and New Jersey (1664). As early as 1688, a few colonists opposed slavery,[6] and English judicial decisions against slavery beginning in 1705 culminated in the 1772 *Somerset* case freeing all existing English slaves.[7] The decision did not apply to the American colonies.

The details of the oppression of slaves varied according to the nationality of the colonizer, the geographical location of the colonial outpost, the colony's demographics, the prevailing modes of economic production, and the operation of the Atlantic slave trade affecting overall quantity, sex ratio, and geographical source of the slaves.[8] It is beyond my present purposes to join the debate on whether racism led to slavery, slavery led to racism, or they commingled to produce the resulting system.[9] The salient fact for my purposes is when the United States was founded in 1776, both racism and slavery were firmly in place. Slavery was legal in all thirteen colonies, and white supremacy was assumed even by the white minority who opposed slavery.

Freedom of speech and press were severely curtailed for colonists and slaves in the colonial era. The English Parliament Licensing Order of 1643 and Licensing Act of 1662 required government approval of publications until the laws' repeal in 1694, but censorship in the colonies predated these laws and continued after their repeal. Consider a few examples. The first US printer—Stephen Day of Cambridge, Massachusetts—was arrested and paid a £100 bond pledging not to further offend officials only four years after opening his press in 1639.[10] Massachusetts had licensers of the press from 1662 to 1755. Virginia forbade printing between 1682 and 1729. The first newspaper, *Boston's Publick Occurrences Both Forreign and Domestick*, began in 1690 but was out of business four days later after offending the governor.[11] Because criticisms of public officials or material considered immoral or blasphemous were punishable, hundreds of colonists were required to recant offensive speeches or writings, were expelled from the community or colony, or worse.[12] The long arm of colonial censorship was a forgotten part of history until Leonard Levy's *Legacy of Suppression* was published in 1960.[13] Levy's "discovery" of extensive colonial censorship, considered radical and revisionist in 1960, is now orthodoxy.

To be sure, colonists criticized and satirized government institutions, policies, and authorities, but they did so at great peril because speech that had a "bad tendency" was illegal.[14] Expression was not protected if it undermined authority, order, or morality. Many successful prosecutions claimed that a newspaper editor committed criminal libel (sedition) merely by criticizing a colonial official. Although the jury famously acquitted John Peter Zenger after his lawyers argued that truth was a defense against criminal libel in *Crown v. John Peter Zenger* (1735), true statements deemed seditious continued to be punished.[15] Truth as a defense against charges did not become law until after the colonial period. The New York legislature was first to pass such a law in the aftermath of *People v. Croswell* (3 Johns. Cas. 337 NY 1804).[16]

Colonial government also curtailed freedom of religion. Since slaves were chattel, their ability to worship was subject to the whims of their masters. For free men, freedom of religion primarily consisted of the legal right of a local majority Christian denomination to exclude, oppress, or even kill others.[17] For example, the Puritan Church received state tax money and punished nonconformists with fines, whippings, prison, banishment, or hanging. Although the Anglican church in Virginia permitted non-Anglicans to worship as they chose, they were banned from public office, restricted to specific meeting houses or locations, and forced to pay taxes to support the Anglican church. The Anglican church also was established by law in Maryland, South Carolina, North Carolina, Virginia, Georgia, and metropolitan New York. Localized majority-rule religious establishments existed in Massachusetts, Connecticut, New Hampshire, and Vermont. Catholics in Massachusetts could hold public office only after renouncing the pope. The colonial textbook (*New England Primer*) and its 1800s replacement (*McGuffey's Readers*) framed all knowledge around a Protestant worldview.[18]

In sum, liberty and equality in the colonial era were predominantly the privilege of white, propertied, Protestant males. African Americans, free or enslaved, had little liberty or equality.

INEQUALITY IN THE ANTEBELLUM ERA

The colonists' break from English rule resulted in few immediate improvements in liberty or equality for most African Americans, but the winds of change began to stir. There were approximately half a million slaves at the founding of the United States, most living in the South, where they composed about 40 percent of the population.[19] The Declaration of Independence adopted by the Continental Congress on July 4, 1776, boldly proclaimed "all men are created equal"; this did not mean all men (or women) had equal legal rights or liberties. The new nation's hero and first president, George Washington, owned slaves from age eleven to his death in a state with a 40 percent slave population and only 1 percent free blacks. He was raised to believe in white superiority and black people as mere chattel, but he came to believe slavery ought to be gradually abolished and was the only founding father who owned slaves to free them.[20] Thomas Jefferson considered slavery a moral depravity that violated natural law and rights and was the greatest threat to the survival of the new nation, yet he also believed in white superiority and the impossibility of free whites and free blacks living peacefully together.[21]

The 1790 Naturalization Act restricted citizenship to free white men, but a growing consensus in the North against slavery led states to adopt policies gradually abolishing slavery.[22] Over time, abolitionists convinced northerners that slavery conflicted with biblical teachings, had debilitating and dehumanizing effects on the slave owner, violated the natural law of individual liberty, and led to murder, robbery, lewdness, and barbarity. Delaware's constitution (1776) outlawed the importation of slaves, but not slavery itself. Vermont's constitution (1777) freed male slaves over age twenty-one and female slaves over eighteen. Pennsylvania (1780) freed the future children of existing slaves. Slavery was abolished in Massachusetts in 1783 by judicial interpretation of the state's constitution. New Hampshire (1783), Connecticut (1784), Rhode Island (1784), and Maine (1789) passed laws gradually ending slavery. The Northwest Ordinance (1787) outlawed slavery in the territory but permitted the recapture and return of fugitive slaves.

Few Southerners were convinced by moral arguments, and there was a strong economic component to the divide over slavery.[23] This division led to three compromises in the 1789 US Constitution, replacing the 1781 Articles of Confederation and Perpetual Union. The "slave clauses" did not explicitly establish or justify slavery but implicitly acknowledged it. The Three-Fifths Clause in Article 1, Section 2, Clause 3 stated: "Representatives and direct

Taxes shall be apportioned among the several States which may be included within this Union, according to their respective Numbers, which shall be determined by adding to the whole Number of free Persons, including those bound to Service for a Term of Years, and excluding Indians not taxed, three fifths of all other Persons." This was a compromise between Northerners, who didn't want slaves to count in determining political representation, and Southerners, who wanted slaves to count as whole persons. The deadlock was resolved by including taxes. The North thereby limited the political impact of slaves in the census count, and the South limited their federal tax liability. The Slave Trade Clause in Article 1, Section 9, Clause 1 stated, "The Migration or Importation of such Persons as any of the State now existing shall think proper to admit, shall not be prohibited by Congress prior to the Year one thousand eight hundred and eight, but a Tax or duty may be imposed on such importation, not exceeding ten dollars for each person." This clause permitted existing states with slaves to continue the slave trade without federal interference for twenty years with only a concession to a potential tax. The sunset provision and non-application to new states combined with leaving the option for a state to ban slavery within its own borders to satisfy Northern and Southern interests. The Fugitive Slave Clause in Article 4, Section 2, Clause 3, stated, "No person held to service or labour in one state, under the laws thereof, escaping into another, shall, in consequence of any law or regulation therein, be discharged from such service or labour, but shall be delivered up on claim of the party to whom such service or labour may be due." This avoided establishing slavery as a constitutional right (the persons involved were held to service or labor under state law) and provided no enforcement mechanism (which satisfied Northern interests); however, it recognized a slave owner's state-sanctioned property right in a slave (which satisfied Southern interests).

After the Revolutionary War, the free black population increased slightly in the South because a few owners freed slaves who fought against the Crown. For example, prior to the war, 1 percent of blacks lived free in Virginia; after the war, 4 percent lived free. The continuation of slavery as a dominant mode of labor in the South meant that most African Americans continued to lack even the most basic forms of liberty and equality. Slave codes varied by state, but typically slaves could not legally marry, be educated, carry a gun, assemble without a white person present, conduct any business without the consent of their owner, preach, keep dogs or stock, or cultivate land for personal use. A slave who used abusive or provocative language toward a white person was subject to a maximum of thirty-nine lashes.[24] Slaves worked on plantations and in pottery mills, textile centers, iron mills, dockyards, and more. They had no legal right to freedom of religion but were not forced to become Christians, as were slaves in many other New World countries, because from "colonial times through the first decades of the nineteenth century most southern slave owners feared Christian slaves would become unruly servants or might even demand freedom and equality."[25] By the 1830s and 1840s, Southern slave owners came to believe, as an Alabama judge put it, "religious instruction, properly directed, not only benefits the slave in his moral relations [but] also enhances his value as an honest, faithful servant and laborer."[26]

The existence of free blacks in the South was a thorn in the side of the white establishment. Freedmen were a living refutation of white supremacist ideology and increased slave discontent. Thus, when the number of free blacks in the South doubled to 260,000 between 1820 and 1860 and interracial sex threatened white purity, the white establishment defined "black" in broader terms and began to enforce a rigid black-slave white-free dichotomy with restrictions on emancipation; systems of registration, taxation, and guardianship; forced expulsions; and "voluntary" enslavement. The repression was successful: by the 1850s, free blacks in the South "had nowhere to go."[27]

African Americans in Northern states suffered legal, political, and social inequality through law, social norms, and mob violence. Indiana passed a law expatriating free blacks and prohibiting the entrance of new ones; Illinois, Iowa, and Delaware excluded blacks from the militia, public schools, and testifying against a white person.[28] Northern states customarily enforced segregation on stagecoaches, steamboats, and trains, which led an English observer to comment there were "two nations—one white and another black—growing up together within the same political circle, but never mingling on a principle of equality."[29] Most states did not allow black men to vote, although there were exceptions and changes over time.[30] For example, in 1821 New York placed a $250 property requirement on black men at the same time it dropped most property requirements for white men. Pennsylvania allowed black men to vote until stripping them of that right in 1838. Rhode Island disenfranchised black men in 1822 but returned the right to vote after the so-called Dorr Rebellion in 1843. Massachusetts granted black men the right to vote in the 1780s and never changed course. According to Christopher Malone, the voting changes resulted from changes in the economics of racial conflict, political race affiliation, and racial coalitions.[31] White supremacy in the North was also enforced by mob violence. John Hope Franklin and Elizabeth Brooks Higginbotham observe, "Riots, murders, the destruction of churches, schools, and orphanages occurred in the Mideast and the Northeast."[32]

African Americans were denied educational equality by law, social norms, and mob violence. Slave codes in the South typically prohibited blacks from attending school or even reading and writing.[33] Free blacks in the South had worse education than those in the North. For example, in 1850 about 1,500 of 2,000 black children attended school in Boston, whereas fewer than 300 out of 6,500 did in Louisiana, and only 40 out of 22,000 in Virginia; in 1860 about 33 percent of black children were schooled in the North but only 4 percent were schooled in the South.[34] The situation was only slightly better in the North. The first African Free School was not founded until 1787 in New York, and it did not receive public funding until 1824. A school for black girls in Canterbury, Connecticut, had to struggle through attempted arson and uses of a vagrancy law to prosecute students from out of state.[35]

The example of Boston is illuminating. Boston schools initially included blacks, but black parents petitioned for separate schools as early as 1787 because of widespread harassment of their children by white teachers and students. Their petition was denied by the state legislature, so a private segregated school was established in 1798. Eventually, black children were admitted only into segregated primary schools on Belknap and Sun Court Streets; beyond primary grades, they were admitted only to the segregated Smith School. By the 1840s, black parents petitioned for integrated schools because of prejudice resulting from segregated schools and objections to paying tax dollars to support public schools their children could not attend. Their petitions were rejected, so Benjamin Roberts brought the first suit in the nation against "separate but equal" practices on behalf of his daughter, Sarah. Charles Sumner, an outspoken white abolitionist, and Robert Morris, one of the first African American lawyers, argued that the Massachusetts constitution and state laws were color-blind, and the racially segregated schools were thus illegal. In a decision foreshadowing the future "separate but equal" doctrine of the US Supreme Court, the Massachusetts Supreme Court rejected their argument. *Roberts v. City of Boston*, 59 MA 198 (1850), held that the policy was adopted and enforced in a legally sound manner and separate education was equal. Any resulting racial prejudice "is not created by the law, and probably cannot be changed by the law."

The role the US Supreme Court would play in legal disputes over liberty and equality was unclear. A democracy can function without judicial review (the ability of a court to overturn primary legislation),[36] and the power of the Supreme Court to strike down congressional acts was a matter of contention.[37] The US Supreme Court first addressed the constitutionality of an act of Congress in *Hylton v. United States*, 3 US 171 (1796), when it upheld a federal tax on carriages for conveying people. Seven years later it struck down an act of Congress for the first time. *Marbury v. Madison*, 5 US 137 (1803), unanimously held the Judicial Act of 1798 was unconstitutional because it extended the jurisdiction of courts beyond the limits established in Article III of the Constitution.[38] In defending the right of the court to nullify federal legislation, Chief Justice John Marshall emphasized that the absence of judicial review meant an act of Congress would be constitutional just because Congress passed it, not because it fulfilled the requirements of the Constitution. This negates the foundation of all written constitutions. Second, the Constitution grants judicial power to all cases arising under the Constitution, and this power can only be fulfilled if the court can nullify an act of Congress violating the Constitution. Third, judges are required to take an oath to uphold the Constitution. They could not keep this oath if they refused jurisdiction on a case alleging an act of Congress violated the Constitution. Finally, the Constitution declares itself the supreme law of the land and only those laws consistent with the Constitution are also law.[39]

Marbury is one of the most important Supreme Court opinions. By 2014, the Court had invalidated 176 acts of Congress.[40] Yet as we shall see, throughout American apartheid the court frequently exercised that power to uphold racial inequality and restrict civil liberty. Even in those rare cases—such as the Cherokee Nation cases addressed next—in which the Court ruled in favor of a racial minority, other factors mitigated or negated its impact.

Colonists also enslaved Native Americans, often for export to other colonies to prevent them from escaping to familiar territory. Some Native tribes—including the Cherokee—kept war captives as slaves or enslaved others as a means of benefiting from or assimilating to "white ways."[41] Because slave records usually did not indicate race, there is no reliable estimate of the overall numbers of Native American slaves.[42] South Carolina was an exception. Its 1708 population of 9,580 included 4,100 African American slaves and 1,400 Native American slaves.[43]

The Cherokee Nation, whose territory encompassed land in eight Southeastern states, began to lose land to colonists in the late 1700s through land disputes, violence, and war. The climax came in 1828 when the Georgia legislature passed laws annexing Cherokee land; abolishing their government, courts, and laws; and establishing a process for confiscating their land and redistributing it to whites. The federal executive branch refused to protect the Cherokee from the state's assault, so the tribe petitioned the US Supreme Court to strike down the laws. They argued that they were a foreign nation subject to treaty with and action by the federal government alone according to the Constitution's Treaty Clause, Article 2, Section 2, Clause 2.

The Cherokee Nation lost. *Cherokee Nation v. Georgia*, 30 US 1 (1831), held the Supreme Court had no jurisdiction because Indian nations within US borders were not "foreign nations."[44] Rather, they were "domestic dependent nations" in a "state of pupilage" resembling that of a "ward to his guardian." The court disregarded the merits of their plea, and the tribe was subject to the oppressive state laws despite Chief Justice Marshall's observation that "if courts were permitted to indulge their sympathies, a case better calculated to excite them can scarcely be imagined."[45] In other words, the court would address only "what the law is," not "what the law should be," and the court determined what "the law" is by identifying the original meaning of the phrase "foreign nation." Whether this provided substantive justice or fairness to the Cherokee was irrelevant.

A second legal case involving the Cherokee was already in progress. In 1825, Congregationalist missionary Samuel Worcester and his family moved from Vermont to live with the Cherokee. He taught the Gospel and the English language, helped establish the first Native American newspaper (the *Cherokee Phoenix*), and assisted tribal leaders in defending their rights against white encroachment. To stop people like Worcester, Georgia banned non-Indians from Indian land without a license from the state in 1830. In an "early instance of religiously based civil disobedience and dissent,"[46] Worcester and ten other white people wrote a newspaper article opposing the law and intentionally got themselves arrested for residing on Indian land without a license. All were convicted. Nine accepted pardons. Worcester and one other refused the pardon to appeal their conviction.

In a stunning reversal from its 1831 decision, the Supreme Court held in *Worcester v. Georgia*, 31 US 515 (1832), that the Cherokee Nation was a foreign nation subject to agreement only with the federal government, not individual states. The Georgia law was unconstitutional. Why did the court reverse itself? There is evidence the justices regretted their earlier decision. Justice Joseph Story, for example, wrote to his wife on March 4, 1832: "Thanks be to God, the Court can wash their hands clean of the iniquity of oppressing the Indians and disregarding their rights."[47] Yet no such language appears in the decision. Instead, the court defended its new view about the legal status of the Cherokee with an analysis of the legal relationships, especially treaties, between the tribe and colonial, federal, and state governments, including Georgia. Rather than look only to the text of the Constitution or the intentions of the framers, the Court looked more broadly into the history of the relationships and, in ruling that indigenous peoples were subject only to federal control, struck a blow against the states' rights doctrine that has played a pivotal role in our nation's history.[48]

Tragically, the Cherokee legal victory was purely symbolic.[49] Enforcement was in the hands of the Executive Branch of government, and Presidents Andrew Jackson and Martin Van Buren continued the practice of removing tribes to "Indian Territory" west of the Mississippi. Thousands of Cherokee died during their forced removal from 1836 to 1839.[50] Abolitionists recognized the common plight of African Americans and Native Americans. Lewis Perry notes, "virtually every antislavery reformer who withdrew from the gradualist colonization movement in favor of immediate abolitionism linked this radical step to disgust at Jacksonian Indian policy."[51] A graphic example: the masthead of the influential abolitionist William Lloyd Garrison's publication *The Liberator* depicted participants in a slave market trampling Indian treaties.

Women were denied liberty and equality, too.[52] Unmarried women had more rights than married women, but they still could not vote, lacked equal employment and education opportunities, and more. A married woman lost virtually all legal rights due to the English common law doctrine of coverture.[53] For example, married women had a right to a lifestyle consistent with her husband's status and property she owned prior to marriage remained hers, but she could not sell or otherwise dispose of that property herself.[54] At the nation's founding, New Jersey was the only state to allow women (who met property requirements) to vote but rescinded that right in 1807. The constitutions of Wyoming (1869) and Utah (1870) granted women suffrage, but women in Utah were disenfranchised by the Edmunds-Tucker Act (1887) in which Congress annulled numerous state laws stemming from Mormon practices and authorized seizure of church assets to use for public schools as a threat to make Mormons accept the ban on polygamy. Women did not gain the right to vote generally until the Nineteenth Amendment was ratified in 1920. States gradually reduced coverture from the mid- to the late nineteenth century, but the US Supreme Court did not rule it unconstitutional until *Kirchberg v. Feenstra*, 450 US 455 (1981), struck down Louisiana's "Head and Master" law giving husbands sole control of marital property.

Here, too, abolitionists saw the connection between illiberty and inequality, and liberty and equality. For example, Harriet Beecher Stowe, author of the famous abolitionist novel *Uncle Tom's Cabin*, observed in an 1869 speech that the condition of women under coverture was in many respects like the condition of

African Americans.[55] Stowe was arguing against both sets of inequalities, and her opponents understood the link as well. Opponents of the Civil Rights Act of 1866 objected to increased equality and liberty for African Americans on the basis it would lead to increased equality and liberty for women, too. In other words, they considered it bad enough to grant equal rights to former slaves, but to grant them to married women was even worse.[56] Frederick Douglass, the escaped slave who became a celebrated orator, author, and politician, took the link further in advocating equal rights for blacks, women, Native Americans, and immigrants.[57]

SUPPRESSION OF CIVIL LIBERTY IN THE ANTEBELLUM ERA

Government authorities and vigilantes continued to suppress free speech, press, assembly, petition, and religion after the nation's founding.[58] One of the most important examples is the Sedition Act. Just seven years after the Bill of Rights was ratified, the Federalist Party, led by President John Adams, passed the Alien and Sedition Acts of 1798, creating restrictions on immigration (Naturalization Act), dangerous noncitizens (Alien Friends Act), noncitizens from a hostile nation (Alien Enemies Act), and citizens critical of government (Sedition Act). They claimed the laws were needed to prevent the French Revolution from spreading to our shores. The Democratic-Republican Party, led by Thomas Jefferson, objected to the Sedition Act. They believed it violated the Constitution's free speech clause and would be used for political purposes to persecute critics of the Federalists. They were right: high-profile political prosecutions under the Sedition Act indicted fourteen people and convicted ten.[59] Fortunately, popular backlash contributed to a Democratic-Republican victory in the 1800 elections, and the new regime let the Sedition Act lapse, freed those still serving sentences, and repaid fines.

The legislative lapse of the Sedition Act did not mean speech, press, assembly, petition, and religion were free from government suppression. First, none of the legal cases involving the Sedition Act reached the Supreme Court, and the lower courts that heard the cases—including three with Supreme Court justices "riding circuit"—upheld its constitutionality.[60] Second, *Barron v. Baltimore*, 32 US 243 (1833), unanimously held the Bill of Rights—including the First Amendment—applied only to acts of Congress.[61] The Court reasoned that constitutional limits only apply to states where expressly stated, and the Bill of Rights did not expressly state their application to state government. The decision left states free to restrict civil liberties as they saw fit within the limits of their own constitution. Third, the Supreme Court was minimally protective of speech in the few cases involving acts of Congress it considered. Its initial First Amendment case, *Anderson v. Dunn*, 19 US 204 (1821), held that the power of Congress to punish contempt of Congress was limited to "the least possible power adequate to the end proposed," but it did not identify any limits or requirements regarding the content of the speech Congress could consider contempt.[62] Fourth, the bad tendency test continued to be used to punish unpopular speech and criticisms of government. There were convictions for criticism of President Jefferson in 1804,[63] a sheriff in 1811,[64] and an 1824 case involving blasphemy.[65] The bad tendency test was used to punish political dissent as late as *Gitlow v. New York*, 268 US 652 (1925), and *Whitney v. California*, 274 US 357 (1927). Finally, even if the criticism of government was true, one could still be found guilty of seditious libel. Massachusetts, for example, did not pass a law allowing truth as defense against sedition until 1855.[66] The Supreme Court did not explicitly prohibit sedition laws until *New York Times v. Sullivan*, 376 US 254 (1964).[67]

Consider African American publications. The first black copyrighted publication was *A Narrative of the Proceedings of the Black People during the Late Awful Calamity in Philadelphia* (1794). It argued for respect, freedom, and equal citizenship. The first black newspaper—just one of nearly 900 newspapers in the nation at the time—was *Freedom's Journal*, launched in New York in 1827 as an avenue for black expression and response to racism. There was virtually no Antebellum black press in the slave-holding South. The *Daily Creole* in New Orleans published for a short time circa 1856 but was pressured by whites to oppose abolitionism. In the North, about forty black newspapers published prior to the Civil War, but they suffered from frequent changes in ownership or bankruptcy due to financial difficulties related to white disinterest or antagonism, low black literacy rates, a social justice agenda not motivated by profitmaking, and low advertising revenue.[68] Before the Civil War, the black press often focused on uplifting messages to blacks rather than criticisms of racism and inequality to avoid antagonizing whites or inciting mob violence.[69] Some did advocate abolitionism—such as Frederick Douglass's *North-Star* and *Frederick Douglass' Paper*—and some blacks wrote for *The Liberator*. But "radical" black writings—such as David Walker's *An Appeal to the Coloured Citizens of the World* in 1829 urging black readers to fight their oppression and convince white Americans to abandon the evil institution of slavery—faced government and vigilante suppression. In Charleston and New Orleans, distributors of Walker's book were arrested, and harsh penalties were enacted for its circulation in other places.[70] Georgia announced an award of $10,000 to anyone who could hand over

Walker alive and $1,000 to anyone who murdered him. Walker died mysteriously just a few months later.[71]

Freedom of religion continued to be suppressed. New York's constitution banned Catholics from public office. In Maryland, Catholics (but not Jews) had civil rights equal to Protestants because the state had a substantial Catholic population. Connecticut did not disestablish the Congregationalist Church until it adopted a constitution in 1818, and Massachusetts did not disestablish the Congregationalist Church until 1833. Public schools continued their Protestant bias. *McGuffey's Readers* replaced the *New England Primer* but continued to preach a Protestant world-view.[72] The Civilization Act of 1819 provided funds for only Protestant missionaries to convert Native Americans. Public schools continued to require devotional reading from the King James Bible (KJB) and other Protestant religious observances. Protestants battled over whose interpretation of the KJB to require in public schools until they found a common foe in the 1820s to 1840s: Irish and German Catholic immigrants. Protestant leaders publicly supported Protestant teachers and KJB reading in public schools as a means to convert Catholic children.[73] Public school textbooks included blatantly anti-Catholic references.[74] Catholic children in public schools who refused to engage in reading the KJB or other Protestant observances were punished—often by beating or caning—or were expelled from school, a practice that continued in some states into the twentieth century.[75] When Catholics protested the discrimination, violent Protestant mobs often retaliated.[76]

The law upheld religious discrimination in public schools.[77] The First Amendment offered Catholics (or any other religious minority) no protection. *Permoli v. Municipality No. 1 of New Orleans*, 44 US 589 (1845), held the "constitution makes no provision for protecting the citizens of the respective states in their religious liberties; this is left to the state constitution and laws."[78] Protestant bias in public schools was so pervasive that it was a shock when the Ohio Supreme Court ruled in *Board of Education v. Minor*, 23 Ohio 211 (1872) that the Cincinnati school board could lawfully choose not to require KJB reading. Wisconsin was the first state to ban Protestant devotional KJB reading in public schools in *State ex rel Weiss v. District Board*, 76 WI 177 (1890). The US Supreme Court did not ban devotional Bible reading in public schools until *Abington v. Schempp*, 374 US 203 (1963).

Abolitionism was the most significant movement uniting liberty and equality. The antislavery movement became the nation's lightning rod when it expanded dramatically in the 1820s and 1830s and began to include free blacks and runaway slaves and demand an immediate end to slavery rather than gradual abolition.[79] Patrick Rael provides an excellent account of famous and lesser-known African Americans who contributed to this effort despite the obstacles against them and shows how the "universalist" appeals they developed are still invoked in contemporary struggles for racial justice.[80] States and the federal government went to great lengths to suppress the antislavery message.[81] Southern states restricted and later banned antislavery speech and press with draconian penalties, including the death penalty,[82] and demanded that Northern states follow suit.[83] When abolitionists flooded the mail with newspapers and pamphlets, defenders of slavery failed to convince Congress to ban abolitionist speech and press, but they succeeded in getting the Post Office to censor the US mail[84] and Congress to impose a gag rule on abolitionist petitions. Although Northerners eventually rejected legal censorship of abolitionism when they realized it was a denial of their own liberty,[85] significant legal actions and mob violence against abolitionists still occurred in the North.[86] Abolitionists were threatened, beaten, and even killed.[87] Perhaps the most famous abolitionist martyr was Elijah Lovejoy, a minister and newspaperman who had three abolitionist presses in St. Louis destroyed by mobs before he was killed by gunfire defending his fourth press in Alton, Illinois, in 1837. Rather than suppress abolitionism, Lovejoy's death sparked widespread protests and increased support for the end of slavery.

The divide over slavery led to a series of hotly debated political compromises as new states were admitted. The Missouri Compromise (1820–1821) admitted Missouri as a slave state and Maine as a free state to maintain the balance in the Senate. The Compromise of 1850 admitted California as a free state and left slavery to the voters in New Mexico and Utah, but it also included the Fugitive Slave Act, strengthening requirements to return escaped slaves. The Kansas-Nebraska Act of 1854 further inflamed passions by repealing the Missouri Compromise so Kansas voters could make it a slave state to balance Nebraska as a free state. The demand that abolitionist speech be protected—argued especially by the Liberty Party, the Free Soil Party, and eventually the Republican Party—grew louder. Finally, the US Supreme Court leaped into the scalding cauldron with a decision many legal scholars consider its worst.[88]

Dred Scott was a born a slave in Virginia but lived and worked in Illinois (a free state) and Wisconsin (a free territory). Assisted by abolitionists, Scott sued for his freedom in Missouri state court in 1846, appealing to legal precedents in other states that granted slaves freedom under similar conditions. He lost in the state courts, so he sued in federal court in 1853 and appealed negative decisions all the way to the nation's highest court. It was the sixth time the Supreme Court rejected a slave's petition for freedom,[89] and a big loss for African Americans. *Dred Scott v. Sandford*, 60 US 393 (1857), held the Missouri Compromise of 1820 to be unconstitutional since the Fifth Amendment protects the rights of slave owners, and neither enslaved African Americans nor free blacks descended from slaves could be citizens or entitled to any protections of citizenship. Chief Justice Roger Taney, writing the 7–2 majority opinion, ruled that the authors of the constitution considered blacks inferior beings, unfit to associate with the white race—so inferior they had no rights that whites were bound to respect. Moreover, he claimed that granting Scott's petition would have disastrous consequences:

> For if [African Americans] were so received, and entitled to the privileges and immunities of citizens, it would exempt them from the operation of the special laws and from the police regulations which [the slave states] considered necessary for their own safety. It would give to persons of the negro race, who were recognized as citizens in any one State of the Union, the right to enter every other State whenever they pleased, singly or in companies, without pass or passport, and without obstruction, to sojourn there as long as they pleased, to go where they pleased at every hour of the day or night without molestation, unless they committed some violation of law for which a white man would be punished; and it would give them full liberty of speech in public and in private upon all subjects upon which [a slave state's] own citizens might speak; to hold public meetings upon public affairs, and to keep and carry arms wherever they went. And all of this would be done in the face of the subject race of the same color, both free and slaves, and inevitably producing discontent and insubordination among them, and endangering the peace and safety of the State.[90]

Taney and others hoped the *Dred Scott* decision would put an end to the national conflict over slavery. It did not. It prompted the economic Panic of 1857 and intensified the abolitionist movement and Southern ambitions to extend slavery to the free territories. The decision merely threw fuel on the flames that exploded into the Civil War.

When the Civil War began, Northern censors turned their attention from abolitionists to critics of President Abraham Lincoln and the war.[91] Prior to the war, Republicans had criticized Democrats for endorsing the right of Southern states to ban abolitionist speech and for its complicity in mob actions against abolitionists in Northern states.[92] The Republican Party 1856 presidential slogan was, "Free Speech, Free Press, Free Men, Free Labor, Free Territory, and Frémont."[93] Once the war began, the Republican government attempted to control war news with restrictions on newspaper correspondents, the telegraph lines, and the mail; arrests of newspaper editors; and restraint of the press.[94] Congress passed a law prohibiting speech counseling resistance to the draft, and Lincoln's suspension of the writ of habeas corpus (a judicial mandate for the government to bring a prisoner before the court to determine whether the detention is lawful) enabled the military to arrest and indefinitely detain citizens for disfavored expression even where civilian courts still operated. The military conducted mass arrests of war dissenters in border states and regulated news to troops to control elections and took control of border state governors. Many dissidents were threatened, persecuted and assaulted; even churches joined in by inspiring members to abuse the "treasonous."[95] In 1864, congressional Republicans attempted to expel Peace Democrats Benjamin Harris (MD) and Alexander Long (OH) for speaking in Congress against the war. Thomas Carroll summarizes: "A brief glance through the Civil War history will convince one that the rights of individuals were considerably abridged, and no adequate remedy existed in many cases."[96] In sum, legal protections for First Amendment values were little recognized for whites in Antebellum America and not at all for blacks.[97] Yet exercising First Amendment values still contributed toward at least some progress in racial equality.

INEQUALITY IN THE POST–CIVIL WAR ERA

Prosecuting the war led to considerable changes in the role and power of the federal government and president, the structure and nature of the economy, and more. These changes led the Supreme Court toward a new understanding of the Constitution in which they continued to refrain from imposing First Amendment protections on state actions but began to impose liberty of contract protections on the states.[98] As the focus on liberty of contract and continuing denial of First Amendment values played out, the "haves" got cake with icing, the "have nots" got bread, and African Americans got stale crumbs.

Union victory in 1865 led to passage of the Reconstruction amendments. The Thirteenth Amendment (1865) abolished slavery and nullified the *Dred Scott* decision. The Fourteenth Amendment (1868) guaranteed all citizens due process and equal protection of the law and barred states from violating citizen privileges and immunities. The Fifteenth Amendment (1870) prohibited discrimination in voting rights based on "race, color, or previous condition of servitude." Sadly, the Reconstructionist ambition to provide greater equality for freed slaves and their descendants—despite some initial progress—largely went unfulfilled as its policies and practices were deconstructed.[99]

In the immediate aftermath of the war, there was little done to help freed blacks. The Southern economy was devastated by the war, so former slaves had little or no economic opportunity. Congress established the Freedmen's Bureau in 1865 to assist former slaves and displaced whites, but the agency was abandoned when Congress didn't renew its authorizing legislation, due to objections to its expansion of federal authority. Moreover, when the postwar Congress began its session, the unrepentant South sent an host of former Confederate politicians and military leaders, including the former vice president, six Cabinet officials, fifty-eight representatives, and four generals. Former confederates took control of state government and enacted "Black Codes" to continue white domination of the freed slaves. South Carolina outlawed interracial marriage, established compulsory apprenticeships for black children beginning at age two, upheld unwritten contracts providing the black "servant" with food and clothing but no salary, and prohibited blacks from engaging in any business without an annual license (which few could afford).[100] Black people were convicted of petty offenses to "apprentice" them to white landowners to pay off the fine. Mississippi blacks were not permitted to own or lease farmland. Laws allowed white employers to "apprentice" black orphans and children who lacked "proper parental support," but not white youth.

The Reconstruction era began in 1866 when the "radical" Republicans gained enough seats to overcome vetoes by President Andrew Johnson to abolish the ex-Confederate-led state governments and Black Codes, establish Reconstruction state governments, and send 20,000 federal troops to enforce these changes. With ex-Confederates banned from voting and black men now voting, 16 African Americans were elected to Congress, over 600 were elected to state legislatures, and hundreds more were elected to local offices.[101]

Consider the example of Robert Smalls from South Carolina. Smalls first gained national attention in 1862 when he freed himself, his crew, and their families from slavery by commandeering a Confederate ship to run the US blockade. His example led President Lincoln to accept African American soldiers into the army and navy, and Smalls was present at as many as seventeen major battles. In 1864, his eviction from a streetcar for refusing to give up his seat to a white passenger led a coalition of reformers to persuade the Pennsylvania legislature to ban racial discrimination in public transportation.

After the war, Smalls became a successful businessman in Beaufort, founded the Republican Party of South Carolina, helped found and fund a black newspaper, and won election to the South Carolina state legislature and the US House of Representatives. As Reconstruction was deconstructed, his political roles declined, but Smalls served as a federal customs collector until 1913 and died in 1915. His legacy lives on through many memorials; for example, his name was given to forts, warships, and roads, and his home was designated a National Historic Landmark.

Defenders of American apartheid, the "Redeemers," retaliated violently against Reconstruction. In 1867 the Ku Klux Klan spread through the South, terrorizing and murdering blacks and white sympathizers. Federal and state efforts to squelch the Klan only led to the formation of more violent groups such as the Pale Faces, Knights of the White Camelia, and White Brotherhood. A reign of terror employing threats, intimidation, whipping, lynching, and even armed insurrection befell the South. These last two techniques deserve further discussion.

During the height of lynching between 1889 and 1918, more than 2,500 African Americans were lynched by white mobs, often in front of crowds who would take home pieces of the victim as souvenirs.[102] Between 1877 and 1950, more than 4,000 black men, women, and children were lynched for such "offenses" as walking behind a white woman, attempting to quit a job, reporting a crime, or organizing sharecroppers.[103] Local newspapers provided graphic details, including horrific descriptions of torture, and the Southern press "was extremely creative when it came to providing moral, if not legal, justification for the action of lynch mobs."[104] Southern editors who opposed lynching faced mob violence themselves.[105] Republicans in Congress tried to pass a federal law against lynching, but the Southern Democratic voting bloc consistently prevented its passage.

White supremacists also conducted armed insurrections. The Wilmington, North Carolina, massacre provides one example. On November 10, 1898, after two years of vitriolic anti-Reconstruction rhetoric, white supremacists invaded Wilmington with the support of many white churches to end the successful political fusion of white Lincoln Republicans and blacks in a city that was half African American. A Gatling gun was brought to town, and a mob of thousands went on a killing and burning spree. As many as sixty people were killed, the only black newspaper in the state was destroyed, elected black officials (including the biracial mayor) were chased from town, black property was confiscated, and a new white supremacist mayor and city council were installed. More than 2,000 blacks left the city in the wake of the violence.

The Supreme Court supported the reign of terror and deconstruction of Reconstruction in a series of decisions. *Blyew v. United States*, 80 US 581 (1872), freed two white Kentucky men who murdered four members of a black family (two young girls survived). The dying son crawled to neighbors and identified the two perpetrators, but Kentucky law prohibited black testimony against whites. Authorities took the case to federal court. The all-white jury from a neighboring county found the two men guilty and sentenced them to hang. On appeal, the Supreme Court freed the men because it held that state law prohibited black testimony against whites and dead victims have no rights to protect under the Civil Rights Act.[106] The court again turned a blind eye to racist violence when *United States v. Harris*, 106 US 629 (1882), held the federal government could not prosecute vigilante lynching under the Civil Rights Act or the Fourteenth Amendment.

Arguably, the most devastating ruling was *Slaughter-House Cases*, 83 US 36 (1873). The cases concerned a group of slaughterhouses dumping offal upstream from New Orleans that caused repeated cholera outbreaks and other hazards. After several unsuccessful attempts to deal with the problem, the city convinced the state legislature to grant an exclusive franchise to the Crescent City Live-Stock Landing and Slaughter-House Company in 1869 to ensure animal slaughtering was done at an appropriate location. Opponents of the law filed federal lawsuits, claiming it violated the Privileges and Immunities Clause of the Fourteenth Amendment. Crescent City victories in all the lower court decisions were upheld 5–4 in the Supreme Court decision consolidating the lawsuits. The court majority held that the authors of the Privileges and Immunities Clause intended to protect only former slaves and to protect only federal rights violated by state law. Plaintiffs lost because they were not former slaves and the state law did not violate any federal right. The decision was significant because it protected Jim Crow state laws from lawsuits appealing to the Privileges and Immunities Clause. The *Slaughter-House* holding on this clause remains in force "even though the history of the amendment makes plain its objective was to impose the federally adopted civil rights upon the states."[107] When the Supreme Court began striking down Jim Crow state laws in the twentieth century, it was via the Due Process and Equal Protection Clauses of the Fourteenth Amendment; however, that approach has been problematic because substantive due process was not part of the original meaning of those clauses.[108]

United States v. Cruikshank, 92 US 542 (1875), "finished the job of gutting the Privileges and Immunities Clause by explicitly holding it did not incorporate the First or Second Amendments as to the states."[109] The case involved white Democrats in Louisiana who murdered black voters in election violence. They were convicted of violating the right to freedom of assembly and the right to keep and bear arms under the Due Process Clause and Enforcement Clause of the Fourteenth Amendment. The Supreme Court ruled that these clauses applied only to state action, not private action. Thus, black victims had to rely on state protection . . . protection everyone knew states did not provide. *Cruikshank* has never been overturned.[110]

Republicans responded to *Cruikshank* with the Civil Rights Act of 1875, the last of seven civil rights laws passed between 1866 and 1875.[111] The law established the right to "full and equal enjoyment of the accommodations, advantages, facilities, and privileges of inns, public conveyances on land or water, theaters, and other places of public amusement; subject only to the conditions and limitations established by law, and applicable alike to citizens of every race and color, regardless of any previous condition of servitude." Premised on the Enforcement Clause of the Fourteenth Amendment, it enabled black people who were denied equal accommodation by private businesses to sue in federal court. However, the US Supreme Court ruled 8–1 in the *Civil Rights Cases*, 109 US 3 (1883), that the Civil Rights Act of 1875 was unconstitutional. Congress did not pass new civil rights legislation for eighty-two years.

The deconstruction of Reconstruction by Southern state governments was abetted by a nefarious political compromise, further Supreme Court decisions, and mob violence. Democrat Samuel Tilden won the popular vote in 1876 and had 184 electoral votes to the 165 electoral votes of Republican Rutherford B. Hayes, but Southern Democrats offered to give 20 disputed electoral votes—and thus the election—to Hayes on the condition that 20,000 federal troops were withdrawn from the South. The deal was done, and when federal troops were withdrawn in 1877, Reconstruction governments were toothless. Frank Latham writes, "During the next thirty years, the Southern white set out to control or get rid of the Negro by a combination of fraud, trickery, threats, and violence."[112] The black vote was suppressed by devious tactics, such as moving polling places far from their homes, closing ferries on election days to prevent them from getting to polling places, organizing abusive and violent whites to guard the polls, and simply not counting their votes when cast. The Supreme Court continued its pernicious habit upholding racial inequality. *United States v. Reese*, 92 US 214 (1876), held that a white Kentucky magistrate could lawfully refuse to register a black man from voting in a municipal election because Section 3 of the Fifteenth Amendment did not repeat Section 2's protections for race, color, and previous condition of servitude. This loophole allowed states to deny blacks the vote based on "administrative preliminaries," such as poll taxes, literacy tests, grandfather clauses, and restrictive residency clauses.[113] Finally, white supremacists who murdered blacks and sympathetic whites were acquitted in sham trials.[114] The combination of legal and illegal tactics decimated the black vote. In Louisiana, the black vote shrank from 130,334 in 1896 to only 1,342 in 1904.[115] In Alabama, there were 180,000 registered black voters in 1896, but only 3,000 registered in 1900.[116] In South Carolina, 67,000 fewer votes were cast in its 1936 election compared with its 1876 election even though the state's population had doubled and women had the right to vote in 1936.[117] The combination of racial politics, court decisions, and racial violence gave white supremacists control of Southern state government.[118]

The Supreme Court also denied liberty and equality to African Americans and others by upholding antimiscegenation laws in *Pace v. Alabama*, 106 US 583 (1883). Antimiscegenation laws were first enacted in the colonial era—for example, New York in 1638 and Maryland in 1664—and forty-one states eventually had them.[119] Most states banned white–black relations, but twelve also banned white–Native American relations, fourteen prohibited white–Asian relations, and nine included "Malays." Arizona updated its law in 1931 to include "Hindus." In his 1951 analysis, James Browning attributes the laws to a white desire to maintain economic and social advantages and avoid supposed unnatural and deplorable results of mixed-race offspring.[120] Southern courts explicitly endorsed the latter justification.[121] These laws also served broader ideological, anti-immigrant, and patriarchal purposes.[122]

The epitome of Reconstruction deconstruction was the de jure "separate but equal" doctrine that coexisted with de facto separate and unequal practices. The travesty began when *Hall v. DeCuir*, 95 US 485 (1877), struck down a Louisiana law requiring racially integrated vehicles in interstate travel on the basis that the law was an unreasonable burden on interstate commerce. The *Hall* decision prompted Tennessee to become the first state to enact a law segregating the races in first-class railroad cars in 1881. Thereafter, every Southern state (except Missouri) passed laws separating the races on trains and in railroad waiting rooms between 1887 and 1907.[123] *Plessy v. Ferguson*, 163 US 537 (1896), chiseled the doctrine in stone when it upheld Louisiana's Separate Car Act of 1890. A group of prominent blacks, creoles, and whites opposed to the law arranged a test case. Homer Plessy, a man legally classified as black despite being seven-eighths white, was recruited to board a whites-only car operated by the East Louisiana Railroad, which also opposed the law because it required them to purchase more rail cars. A sympathetic detective was hired to arrest Plessy for refusing to leave the whites-only car under the statute (rather than under some other law, such as vagrancy). Plessy lost at every level. The Supreme Court ruled 7–1 that separate accommodations did not place any "badge of inferiority" on blacks and that "separate but equal" accommodations fulfilled the requirements of the Fourteenth Amendment. Even the lone dissenter in *Plessy*, Justice John Marshall Harlan, who argued for a "color-blind" Constitution, pronounced the white race dominant "in prestige, in achievements, in education, in wealth and in power" and "will continue to be for all time."[124] The Northern white press virtually ignored the *Plessy* decision; the Southern press applauded it; only the black press criticized it.[125] The Court upheld the separate but equal doctrine in two more cases.[126]

African Americans vigorously resisted the separate but equal doctrine but had little immediate success. Blair Kelley provides an excellent account of many brave people and organizations who struggled and litigated against segregated public transport prior to the *Plessy* decision as well as the street boycott movement in twenty-five Southern cities following the decision.[127] The Mobile *Daily Register* commented in 1903, "In every city where it has been found advisable to separate the races in the street cars the experience has been the same. The negroes . . . have invariably declared a boycott."[128] The boycotts produced only minor temporary setbacks for segregation because by then the Jim Crow system was "in bulk and detail as well as effectiveness of enforcement comparable with the [slave] codes of the old regime."[129] In a rare dissent, a prominent South Carolina newspaper editorial offered a reductio ad absurdum argument against segregated railroad cars:

> If there must be Jim Crow cars on the railroad, there should be Jim Crow cars on the street railway. Also on all passenger boats . . . Jim Crow waiting saloons at all stations and Jim Crow eating houses.... There should be Jim Crow sections of the jury box, and a separate Jim Crow dock and witness stand in every court and a Jim Crow Bible for colored witnesses to kiss . . . a Jim Crow section in county auditors' and treasurers' offices.... Perhaps, the best plan would be . . . [to establish] two or three Jim Crow counties.[130]

Unfortunately, Southern whites adopted rather than rejected the extreme segregation parodied by the editorial. African Americans suffered pervasive discrimination and segregation from birth to death in a system that white supremacists lauded as a "return to sanity" and "final settlement." As a result, "American blacks could not look for protection in their nation's law or courts . . . [and] there was rampant violence in the form of lynching and race riots."[131] In 1919 alone, there were twenty-six white race riots against blacks. Chauncey DeVega notes, "White riots and pogroms against Black Americans are a fixture of American history" largely ignored by modern education and media and forgotten by the white American public.[132]

The fact that accommodations were not equal eventually provided a legal chisel to chip away at the separate but equal doctrine. Educational inequality was the key. The Morrill Act established public land grant colleges for whites in 1862, but not for blacks until 1890; black colleges were denied equal funding.[133] In 1898, Florida spent twice as much per student on white education as on black education; in 1900 a black-majority county in Mississippi spent $22 per white student but only $2 per black student.[134] In *Cumming v. Board of Education of Richmond County*, 175 US 528 (1899), the Supreme Court upheld a Georgia district policy providing a high school education only for whites—not equal education, not even separate education! The governor of Mississippi summed up the Southern attitude when he declared that money spent on education of African Americans was an "positive unkindness" because it "renders [the Negro] unfit for the work which the white man has prescribed, and which he will be forced to perform" and "will not be allowed to rise above the station which he now fills."[135] The president of Georgia Institute of Technology stated, "When the colored race all become skilled bricklayers, somebody will have to carry the mortar. When they all become plumbers, who are going to be the helpers, the men who carry the tools? When they become scientific farmers, who are going to be the laborers? Are Southerners, we Southern whites? No. We have settled that question long ago."[136] In 1937 a Maryland commission found that twenty-four times as much was spent on white higher education than on black higher education, only one of the four black colleges was accredited, and the state provided education in law, medicine, dentistry, and pharmacy only to whites.[137] Nathan Margold's research proving that segregated facilities were never equal underpinned the successful lawsuits by the National Association for the Advancement of Colored People (NAACP) demanding equal facilities for black students. The first legal victories desegregated state university law schools in *Murray v. Pearson*, 169 MD 478 (1936), and *State ex rel. Gaines v. Canada*, 305 US 337 (1938). These initial victories were largely symbolic given the widespread practice of segregation and massive resistance to integration.

The illiberty and inequality suffered by blacks in the post–Civil War period was suffered by others. The Supreme Court upheld an Illinois law banning women lawyers in *Bradwell v. Illinois*, 83 US 130 (1873), and upheld the denial of women's right to vote in *Minor v. Happersett*, 88 US 163 (1875). As noted already, most states sought to maintain "white purity" by banning marriage or sexual relations between whites and nonwhites. The Supreme Court denied citizenship to Asian Americans in *Ozawa v. United States*, 260 US 178 (1922), and *Toyota v. United States*, 268 US 402 (1925). It upheld the right of schools to allow only whites in *Lum v. Rice*, 275 US 78 (1927). Chinese Americans endured legal discrimination and mob violence.[138] The California Supreme Court barred them from testifying against whites in *People v. Hall*, 4 CA 399 (1854). The federal government banned Chinese immigration through the Chinese Exclusion Act (1882). The California Alien Land Law (1920) prohibited the Chinese from owning land. The California Supreme Court outlawed segregated San Francisco schools in *Tapes v. Hurley*, 66 CA 473 (1885), but the state legislature responded by passing a law allowing segregated schools for "Mongolians." Racial segregation in California public schools was legal until five Mexican American fathers won an appeal to integrate Orange County schools in *Mendez v. Westminster*, 161 F.2d 774 (9th Cir. 1947) (en banc) (1947). *Mendez* was the first judicial victory for public school integration in the country. The US Supreme Court ruled immigrants from India were ineligible for naturalized citizenship since they were not white in *United States v. Bhagat Singh Thind*, 261 US 204 (1923). After the Mexican-American War (1846–1848), hundreds of Mexicans living in annexed areas were lynched.[139] Despite a treaty guaranteeing them full and equal rights with whites in the newly acquired US territories, "Between 1850 and 1880, most of the vast territories claimed by Mexicans in California had been confiscated by whites by a variety of legal strategies and most Mexicans reduced to poverty and marginal status.... Similar patterns of confiscation . . . took place in New Mexico and Texas."[140]

California was admitted as a free state in 1850, but Native Americans there remained subject to the existing system of forced labor until 1863. Chinese and Mexican miners were required to pay a "foreign miners tax" not required of white miners. The land west of the Mississippi promised to Native Americans was taken by white settlers and railroads with government approval as Native Americans were relegated to reservations in undesirable areas and forced to adopt white religion, language, education, and customs. White leaders openly declared Native Americans "varmints" incapable of civilization who should "die off."[141] Abraham Lincoln signed the Homestead Act in 1862 allotting 160 acres to any white settler who could pay $1.25 and cultivate it for five years, and Congress granted another 100 million acres to railroads, resulting in the loss of millions of acres of Native American territory and forced relocation to reservations. In 1871, Congress passed the Indian Appropriations Act, ending the "nation" status of Indian tribes.

In the rare cases where the Supreme Court upheld some form of racial equality, the victory was largely symbolic. *Strauder v. West Virginia*, 100 US 303 (1880), struck down state laws excluding blacks from serving on juries; states got around this by requiring jurors to be voters (upheld in *In re Wood*, 140 US 278 [1891]) and disenfranchising blacks through poll taxes, literary tests, and other means (also upheld by the Supreme Court[142]). *Yick Wo v. Hopkins*, 118 US 356 (1886), held that a law racially neutral on its face but applied in racially prejudicial manner violated the Equal Protection Clause, but the Court ignored this reasoning when considering Jim Crow laws. *Truax v. Raich*, 239 US 33 (1915), struck down Arizona's statute requiring at least 80 percent of any establishment's employees be qualified electors or natural-born citizens but left private employers free to discriminate based on race or ethnicity. *Buchanan v. Warley*, 245 US 60 (1917), struck down a Louisville zoning ordinance to protect white property rights to sell rather than black rights to buy,[143] and it was effectively negated by *Corrigan v. Buckley*, 271 US 323 (1926), upholding racially restrictive housing covenants.

The primary Supreme Court decision that advanced racial equality was *Moore v. Dempsey*, 261 US 86 (1923). In that case the court first used the Due Process Clause of the Fourteenth Amendment to overturn "Southern racial justice." *Moore* reversed the mob-dominated trial convictions of black plaintiffs alleged to have murdered a few whites in an Arkansas race riot while overlooking roving bands of white vigilantes and federal troops who murdered hundreds of blacks in retaliation.[144] *Moore* had lasting significance because the Court gradually expanded its use of the Due Process Clause to uphold federal intervention into racist state laws and actions.

To be sure, a few African Americans defied the odds to attain success in business, politics, education, and more. Such success was rare because "blacks were not only denied a place on the ladder of economic opportunity but were kicked off the ladder."[145] They were barred from most industrial jobs, unions, and retail jobs and were forced to find work largely as unskilled laborers or strikebreakers. Cities zoned "vice" activities to black neighborhoods, which created illegal economic opportunities for blacks and left their communities devastated by crime. The only legal economic upside to segregation was that from 1900 to 1930 it produced a "golden age of black business" because urban black entrepreneurs had a segregated black clientele.[146] A collection of articles edited by

Cecilia Conrad, John Whitehead, Patrick Mason, and James Stewart provides more details and analysis of the meager economic conditions and opportunities blacks endured throughout American apartheid (and into the twenty-first century) and the benefits racial inequality afforded whites.[147] For example, the top 1 percent of wealth holders in the South during the Antebellum era were typically rural planters reliant on slave labor; the wealth denied slaves between 1790 and 1860 is estimated to be in the billions or even trillions (in 1983 dollars); even nonslave-owning whites in the South were better off than Northern black laborers.[148] Things changed little when sharecropping replaced slave labor in the Reconstruction era, and the rationale remained the same, namely, "childlike and improvident" blacks could not survive without white control. Black sharecroppers were kept in perpetual debt to white lenders who charged outlandish interest rates on the loans the sharecroppers needed to farm. "Sweet benevolence at 30 percent interest rates."[149] When rural blacks sought better opportunities in Southern cities and the industrial North, they found only slightly better conditions because they typically got the least desirable jobs and were paid less than their white counterparts.[150]

It is important to recognize that the Supreme Court's deference to state Jim Crow laws was at odds with its activism in striking down state economic restrictions as infringements of individual property rights or invalid exercises of police power.[151] Joseph William Singer frames it thus:

> If maximum-hours laws violated property rights, why did not the intrusive regulatory system known as Jim Crow similarly unconstitutionally interfere with the right to control one's property? . . . Jim Crow laws required businesses to segregate and, in the case of trains, to provide expensive duplicative services. Perhaps Jim Crow laws could be understood as merely supporting the right of businesses to serve customers in a segregated manner. This interpretation needs to suppress the fact that Jim Crow laws not only forced businesses to segregate, but imposed substantial costs on businesses that could not easily afford to provide two entirely separate—and equal—services. Perhaps instead, the Jim Crow laws were understood to enhance property rights by protecting the rights of white customers to eat and sleep in an all-white environment. Yet to understand Jim Crow laws in this way, one must turn the baseline on its head, defining the basic property right in question as belonging to the white customer desiring access rather than to the business seeking to control access to its premises.[152]

A doctrinally consistent Court would have struck down segregation laws because they violated liberty of contract. Their inconsistency invites us to conclude, as Derrick Bell argued, that maintaining white supremacy was the only thing the Court thought was more important than liberty of contract.[153]

In sum, Reconstruction was short-lived and resulted in limited progress. Slavery was over, but African Americans still were denied basic forms of political, legal, economic, and social equality. Leland Ware comments, "By the beginning of the twentieth century, the equality rights established by the Fourteenth Amendment were, for all practical purposes, nullified in the former Confederate states. In other regions of the nation, public policy and private practices excluded African-Americans from schools, neighborhoods, public accommodations, and all but the most menial occupations."[154]

SUPPRESSION OF CIVIL LIBERTY DURING THE POST–CIVIL WAR ERA

From the end of the Civil War to the 1930s, the government and vigilantes continued to suppress unpopular speakers and ideas. There were isolated minor judicial victories for civil liberties,[155] and a few scholars argued for stronger civil liberties,[156] but in practice courts deferred to the police power doctrine.[157] The denial of liberty applied to "radicals" and "free thinkers,"[158] and especially to African Americans. Nat Hentoff observes that after the federal troops were withdrawn from the South in 1877, blacks had practically no right of expression at all.[159] Some recognized the connection between illiberty and inequality. William Carter Jr. notes that "legally sanctioned silencing of opposition to slavery and racial subordination was a central feature of the slave system that the Thirteenth Amendment's framers sought to dismantle."[160] Representative James Ashley of Ohio stated during debate on the amendment, "[slavery] has for many years defied the Government and trampled upon the national Constitution, by kidnapping, mobbing, and murdering white citizens of the United States guilty of no offense except protesting against its terrible crimes."[161]

Consider the black press. Patrick Washburn points out black newspapers led the fight for black equality even though they were "operating against a background of continual inequalities for blacks and a white America that routinely, and sometimes fiercely and illogically, fought the granting of any new rights."[162] After the Civil War, increasing black literacy and continuing white neglect of black interests and racist portrayals of black people led to a rapid expansion in black newspapers.[163] As many as 575 black publications had begun by 1890, but most failed due to financial difficulties. Publications influenced or funded by Booker T. Washington downplayed black inequality and illiberty, but others were more outspoken. For example, the *Memphis Free Speech*, owned by Ida Wells, crusaded against lynching until white mobs destroyed her paper and press and threatened to lynch her and the editor.[164] Wells moved away and bravely continued her cause. The first commercially successful black newspaper, the widely influential *Chicago Defender*, is another example. Its demands for black liberty and equality led white vigilantes to confiscate issues, murder two of its Texas distributors, and murder a black schoolteacher in Texas for publishing an article in it about a lynching. State and local governments also suppressed the black press. The state of Tennessee and numerous towns across the South passed laws making it illegal to read or distribute a black newspaper, and an Arkansas judge issued an injunction prohibiting distribution of the *Chicago Defender*.[165] In 1921, Mississippi enacted a law making it a misdemeanor to publish anything favoring equality between whites and blacks.[166]

The federal government suppressed black newspapers and periodicals as well as those supporting progress in racial equality. In 1918 the postmaster revoked the second-class mailing privileges of the New York–based socialist monthly magazine *The Messenger* for pointing out the hypocrisy of expecting black support for the war when they were treated as second-class citizens,[167] and in 1919 a Virginia newspaper lost its mailing privileges for the same reason.[168] Under the Espionage Act, the editor of the *San Antonio Inquirer* was convicted for printing a similar letter to the editor after the conviction and execution of black soldiers involved in a Houston riot who were defending a black woman sexually assaulted by a white policeman.[169] The perceived threat posed by the black press led the federal government to conduct extensive and largely secret investigations from 1917 into the 1950s.[170]

Censors targeted labor activists and political dissidents, too. From 1897 to 1904, union membership increased from 447,000 to 2,072,700, and the number of American Federation of Labor (AFL)–affiliated internationals climbed from 58 to 120.[171] By 1917 there were more than 600 socialist publications.[172] Nearly 4,500 labor strikes occurred just in 1917.[173] Defenders of the economic and political status quo responded. *Spies v. Illinois*, 123 US 131 (1887), upheld death sentences for the speech of the leaders of the Industrial Alliance in the wake of the 1886 Haymarket riot. Socialist Party members leading street gatherings were convicted of breaching the peace and were denied the right to parade in Massachusetts, Georgia, Minnesota, Michigan, California, and Colorado.[174] An anarchist was convicted for distributing a pamphlet opposing compulsory vaccinations.[175] In 1880 anarchist editors were hanged in Illinois, and an anarchist newspaper was suppressed in New York.[176] The "Red Scare" following World War I led to the Department of Justice Palmer Raids in 1919 and 1920 using warrantless searches, denial of due process, and "clear cases of brutality" as standard tactics to arrest more than 10,000 labor and socialist organizers for their political views.[177] Postmasters denied favorable second-class mailing privileges to union publications.[178] Members of the Industrial Workers of the World (IWW, known as "Wobblies") were prosecuted for their speech and assembly.[179] Hundreds of Wobblies were arrested or beaten by vigilantes for supporting workers' rights and opposing US entry into World War I.[180] The Wobblies invented the "free speech fight" as a political tactic, and virtually all of the state criminal syndicalism statutes (laws punishing speech that advocates any unlawful act as a means of reform) passed from 1917 to 1920 targeted the Wobblies.[181] Although labor supporters were guilty of violence in some cases, peaceful labor organizing efforts and strikes often met with illegal tactics and violence from anti-union vigilantes, private security agencies, police, the National Guard, and the US Army.[182] In 1917, the *New York Post* was excluded from the mails because it had endorsed a socialist candidate.[183] Noted author Upton Sinclair was arrested for attempting to read the First Amendment at a union rally, and American Civil Liberties Union founder Roger Baldwin was arrested for illegal assembly for reciting the text of the First Amendment in a public setting. The US Supreme Court did its part to suppress labor unions when it ruled that states could not ban "yellow dog" contracts (in which employees are required to promise not to join a union) in *Adair v. United States*, 208 US 161 (1908), and ruled an employee could be fired for being a union member in *Coppage v. Kansas*, 236 US 1 (1915).

Dissident women were also suppressed. Suffragettes were arrested and imprisoned.[184] In one of the most publicized instances, between June and November 1917, more than 200 suffragettes from twenty-six states were arrested while parading with signs outside the White House, hoping to convince President Wilson to endorse women's right to vote.[185] Maude Malone was convicted of disorderly conduct when she refused to stay silent when told to do so by the chair of a public political rally.[186] Women who spoke or wrote about birth control, venereal disease, or equal rights were suppressed. Officials suppressed Margaret Sanger's publications on birth control, venereal disease, and working women.[187] As a child, Sanger witnessed firsthand the majority's reaction to unpopular speech when she was pelted with fruit and blocked as she accompanied her father and Robert Ingersoll, "the Great Agnostic," to a public lecture.[188] Officials used the anti-obscenity Comstock Act (1873) to prosecute women who provided sex-related medical information or advocated birth control or "free love."[189] Authorities arrested anarchist and free thinker Emma Goldman approximately forty times, "sometimes for speeches made, sometimes for speeches planned, and sometimes just for being Emma Goldman."[190]

The list goes on. The Salvation Army was a frequent victim of police power and got mixed results in court decisions.[191] Free thinker Charles B. Reynolds was convicted of blasphemy for a satirical pamphlet circulated in Morristown, New Jersey.[192] Public property was not considered a venue for free speech, so the US Supreme Court upheld the conviction of a preacher for speaking without a permit in the Boston Commons in *Commonwealth v. Davis*, 167 US 43 (1897). All public assemblies were banned within certain areas in Detroit and Los Angeles. The Supreme Court upheld the conviction of an editor of an article advocating nude bathing in *Fox v. Washington*, 236 US 273 (1915), and ruled that motion pictures were not protected expression in *Mutual Film Corporation v. Industrial Commission of Ohio*, 236 US 230 (1915). In Chicago, police served as movie censors, determining which films were morally acceptable.[193] In 1908, the mayor of New York closed all 500 movie houses in the city for being immoral.[194]

Criticizing a politician was risky business. States used criminal libel statutes to convict critics of government officials, and incumbent politicians used civil libel law to recover sizable judgments against critics.[195] In 1891 William Lamb was convicted of libel for running an ad critical of a local politician,[196] and in 1902 Pennsylvania enacted a law criminalizing criticism of state officials.[197] Between 1871 and 1900, there were more than 200 criminal libel actions in state courts.[198] In 1928 alone, Boston banned sixty-eight books.[199] According to Michael Gibson, more than sixty cases involving some aspect of freedom of expression reached the US Supreme Court between 1791 and 1917; however, they are "examples of how the Constitution's guarantees of free speech and a free press should not be interpreted."[200] Gibson also points out that unpopular speech was silenced by mob violence, economic and social threats, lack of resources, and rules of judicial procedure.[201]

Censorship reached its zenith during World War I and its aftermath as state and federal courts joined the country's hysteria over the war and immigration.[202] The US Supreme Court upheld convictions for subversive speech in *Schenk v. United States*, 249 US 47 (1919), *Frohwerk v. United States*, 249 US 204 (1919), *Debs v. United States*, 249 US 211 (1919), *Abrams v. United States*, 250 US 616 (1919), *Schaefer v. United States*, 251 US 466 (1920), *Pierce v. United States*, 252 US 239 (1920), and the previously mentioned *Gitlow* (1925). The Court upheld postal restrictions on socialist newspapers in *Milwaukee Social Democratic Pub. Co. v. Burleson*, 255 US 407 (1921). Louise Edward Ingelhart reports there were more than 1,900 sedition prosecutions and 800 convictions;

the postmaster refused mailing privileges to more than 100 publications, including 50 socialist newspapers.[203] The exception was *Meyer v. Nebraska*, 262 US 390 (1923) in which the court overturned a state law banning foreign language instruction. Only a few lower court judges upheld a free speech claim.[204] Vigilantes assaulted, tarred and feathered, and otherwise harassed those who spoke against the war or war policies.

Freedom of religion continued to be denied. Religious segregation of African Americans was nearly universal throughout the country into the 1940s.[205] Religion for blacks in the postslavery era differed from the Antebellum era only insofar as in the postslavery era white denominations followed the "separate but equal" mentality of organizing black churches into synods or presbyteries separate from white ones, whereas previously whites kept slave churches under the direct control of white synods or presbyteries.[206] Government and vigilantes persecuted members of the Church of Jesus Christ of Latter-day Saints (Mormons). Vigilantes tarred and feathered their founder and leader, Joseph Smith, in 1832; murdered seventeen Mormons after the Missouri governor issued an executive order to exterminate or drive Mormons from the state in 1838; and destroyed their press and murdered Smith and his brother in Illinois in 1844. The Supreme Court banned polygamy in *Reynolds v. United States*, 98 US 145 (1878) and the Edmunds-Tucker Act (1887) annulled Mormon-inspired state laws regarding women's right to vote, polygamy, child inheritance, the use of sectarian materials in public schools, and authorized seizure of church assets to intimidate the church into abandoning polygamy. The act was upheld by the Supreme Court in *Late Corporation of the Church of Jesus Christ of Latter-Day Saints v. United States*, 136 US 1 (1890). Jews did not fare as badly as did African Americans, Native Americans, or Asians,[207] but they faced religious discrimination throughout American apartheid.[208] As their population expanded in the early to mid-1800s due to immigration from Central Europe and exploded during immigration from Eastern Europe in the late 1800s and early 1900s, anti-Semitism contributed to immigration restrictions and led to private discrimination, for example, exclusions from hotels and housing, quotas at colleges, and racial violence and intimidation.[209]

In sum, it can be argued that civil liberty had even less legal protection in the post–Civil War era than in the Antebellum era because the federal government joined state and municipal governments and vigilantes in suppressing speech, press, assembly, petition, and religion. Judicial decisions rejected legal enforcement of First Amendment values and rarely even had a dissenting opinion.[210] There were isolated exceptions upholding free speech, but most often, "in the eyes of the courts, the miniscule claims of rights by individuals failed to compare favorably when weighed against the good of the entire commonwealth."[211] Vigilante mobs often targeted outspoken blacks and "radicals" with threats and violence. To the extent that free speech existed, it was primarily a moral ideal, a value we aspired to rather than one that was legally enforced.

Yet citizens continued to demand liberty and equality.[212] Theodore Schroeder, who served as secretary of the Free Speech League for much of its brief existence, championed free speech as a matter of principle, even defending people with whom he disagreed.[213] Legal scholar Roscoe Pound proposed government regulation be limited to time, place, and manner restrictions,[214] and Ernst Freund maintained that mere advocacy should not be restricted.[215] Justice Louis Brandeis, appointed to the US Supreme Court in 1916 despite his Jewish heritage and progressive views, wrote powerful dissents advocating greater freedom in the World War I First Amendment cases. Justice Oliver Wendell Holmes Jr., who penned the legendary "free speech for the thought we hate" motto, began joining Brandeis's dissents. In the 1920s, Zechariah Chafee Jr. became the leading First Amendment scholar writing extensively and persuasively on behalf of stronger First Amendment protections. The ACLU was founded in 1920 to defend First Amendment rights. The NAACP was founded in 1909 "to ensure the political, educational, social, and economic equality of rights of all persons and to eliminate racial hatred and racial discrimination," and began developing sophisticated educational and legal strategies to support equality and opportunities for African Americans. By 1918 the NAACP's publication *Crisis* had a monthly circulation of 100,000, and by 1921 the organization boasted 400 branches.[216] Organizations promoting worker rights, most importantly the AFL, were gaining members and advocates. The movement for women's suffrage led to ratification of the Nineteenth Amendment in 1920. The US Supreme Court finally applied the First Amendment to state action in *Gitlow* in 1925. Although it upheld the statute in *Gitlow*, it went on to strike down state restrictions on speech in *Fiske v. Kansas*, 274 US 380 (1927), *Stromberg v. California*, 283 US 359 (1931), and *Near v. Minnesota*, 283 US 697 (1931).

CONCLUSION

Throughout American apartheid, the government, organizations, individuals, and mobs restricted and denied African Americans (and others) liberty and equality. Black people lacked both formal and substantive equality in politics, law, economics, and social life. The US Supreme Court played a significant role in denying civil and economic liberty to blacks.[217] In 1920, racial constraints applied to virtually every aspect of black life across the nation.[218]

Dissent against the status quo was suppressed with federal, state, and municipal laws, judicial decisions, police power, and vigilante mobs.[219] From the founding of the nation to the Civil War, the constitutional understanding of the First Amendment prevented Congress from restricting these civil liberties but left state governments and vigilantes free to suppress dissent. From the Civil War to the 1930s, federal courts increasingly focused on enforcing economic rights against the states while neglecting First Amendment rights, so the federal government joined the states and vigilantes in suppressing racial, ethnic, and religious minorities, women, laborers, the poor, political dissidents, and others advocating social, political, legal, economic, or educational change. A black man in the South who spoke freely might well be arrested, assaulted, or murdered by white vigilantes. If arrested, he was consigned to the not-so-tender mercies of white police, witnesses, lawyers, judges, and juries. If "things went south" as they did in the Elaine (Arkansas) Massacre of 1919, it was considered justice if no blacks were lynched, even if hundreds were killed by white vigilantes and the mass trial of accused blacks was a mob-dominated sham.[220]

Alexis de Tocqueville, the French aristocrat whose study of the United States published as *Democracy in America* in two volumes (1835 and 1840) became a classic of American political thought, maintained that liberty and equality were the fundamental values driving the democratic wave building around the globe. Individual freedom along with equality before the law and social equality struggled against a long history of authoritarianism and social caste. Although Tocqueville believed the United States was "an immense and complete democracy" and that greater liberty and equality were inevitable, he recognized liberty and equality could conflict and that whites ruled blacks and Native Americans tyrannically. Tocqueville opposed slavery on moral, religious, and economic grounds, but he also believed "it is impossible to foresee a time when blacks and whites will come to mingle and derive the same benefits from society."[221] Despite the tremendous obstacles, we shall see that Tocqueville was right about the inevitability of greater liberty and equality and wrong about the impossibility of racial progress. The symbiotic advances in liberty and equality achieved both in the worst of times and in better times derive from the fact that they aim at greater inclusion and participation as well as opposition to orthodoxy—ideas we explore in more detail in chapter 4. Progress was achieved because African Americans and their supporters never stopped exercising First Amendment values to demand greater liberty and equality. The gains in formal and substantive equality that occurred were due largely to the use of speech, press, assembly, petition, and religion to argue the justice and morality of their cause. Exercising these values in the pursuit of racial equality and justice often involved considerable personal peril. Courageous men and women risked and sometimes lost reputations, friendships, fortunes, freedom, and even their lives as they spoke out against oppression and struggled for greater liberty and equality through nonviolent resistance, active civil disobedience, education, religion, and the legal process.[222]

Thus, rays of hope broke through the storm clouds of oppression and censorship. African Americans and white sympathizers were educating the public and setting new legal precedents. A handful of activists, lawyers, and scholars were pushing the legal system to rethink the meaning and scope of First Amendment law. Historically disadvantaged groups were organizing and proselytizing to enhance their legal, political, economic, and social interests. But would the US Supreme Court and American public explicitly endorse black liberty and equality? The crucial test case, the ordeal of Angelo Herndon, is next.

CHAPTER 2

A Pivotal Case

> The greatest tragedy is to live placidly and safely and to keep silent in the face of injustice and oppression.
>
> —Angelo Herndon, *Let Me Live*

Angelo Herndon faced the wrath of the white Southern legal establishment from 1932 to 1937, one of the most turbulent economic and political eras in US history. The year he was arrested, the Dow Jones Industrial Average hit its lowest point of the Great Depression with an estimated 25 percent unemployment nationally and 50 percent unemployment for African Americans.[1] Twenty million people sought public and private relief assistance. In some cities, whites demanded blacks be fired from jobs and replaced with unemployed whites. Racial violence increased, especially in the South. Black women endured near slave labor conditions working as domestic servants. Criminal syndicalism statutes, police power, private security, and vigilantes tried to crush labor and political unrest. Protesting workers were killed in Dearborn, Michigan; the US Army forcibly dispersed World War I veterans demanding a promised war bonus; and a farmers' revolt began in the Midwest. Republican President Herbert Hoover insisted the country just needed to wait out the bad times. As a result, Democrat Franklin Roosevelt won in a presidential campaign that reversed long-term voting trends and rearranged political party alliances. Roosevelt's New Deal transformed the nation's economy and the role of the federal government in the economy, although the benefits to blacks were largely denied until communists and the Congress of Industrial Organizations committed to their cause. Fascism took hold in Europe and found support in the United States. International tensions increased around the world.

In the tumultuous 1930s, Herndon—described by constitutional law scholar Paul Finkelman as "every white southerner's nightmare"[2]—became a lightning rod. His first trip to the US Supreme Court resulted in a loss on a technicality, but his victory on the merits in his second trip is recognized as an important First Amendment case. But Herndon's ordeal was more than that. It was also a pivotal point in uniting the struggles for African American equality and liberty, a vital moment in the debate between race-neutral and race-conscious strategies, and an enduring example of mass politics and protest. It was the start of a "Second Reconstruction" and, in effect, serves as a case study in the alliance of liberty and equality through their mutual commitment to greater inclusion and participation and opposition to orthodoxy.

THE SETTING

Eugene Angelo Braxton Herndon was born the fifth of seven children in a poor black family living near Cincinnati, Ohio, in 1913. His father died of miner's pneumonia when Angelo was nine. His mother, limited to work as a maid, was unable to provide for the whole family. Age thirteen Angelo went to work in the coal mines, and the next year he moved with his brother Leo to Birmingham, Alabama, to work for the Tennessee Coal, Iron and Railroad Company. He became a communist after hearing a white labor organizer advocate racial cooperation in the class struggle. At just seventeen years old, Herndon became a labor organizer for the Communist Party USA (CPUSA) amid the 1929 stock market crash and onset of the Great Depression. He attended the National Unemployment Convention in Chicago; helped organize an Anti-Lynching Conference in Chattanooga, Tennessee; and worked with Southern sharecroppers as part of the CPUSA "Black Belt" initiative.

Given the era's intolerance for unpopular speech, especially from blacks, Herndon "accumulated arrests, beatings, lynch threats, and local publicity, but apparently not many recruits."[3] After one arrest in Birmingham in 1931, he was kept in the mental ward of the county jail for eleven days, then brought in a cage to a judge who dismissed him after questioning with a note "to get a job" with the local leader of the Ku Klux Klan. When Herndon did not leave town, he was arrested again and beaten.[4] The CPUSA sent him to Atlanta in 1932, hoping he would have more success.

Herndon was out of the frying pan and into the fire. Atlanta was undergoing serious racial tension during the worst year of the Great Depression, and local authorities were determined to crush any sign of political insurgency by poor whites or blacks. Their determination was especially intense given the recent publication of *Georgia Nigger* by white journalist John Spivak. Spivak's account of the brutal conditions black prisoners suffered in Georgia penal system led to a US Senate order to conduct an immediate investigation. In late June 1932, Fulton County closed its relief agencies and proposed sending all the unemployed to work on farms. On June 30, an anonymous flyer demanding immediate relief for the unemployed was distributed in poor black and white neighborhoods. The next morning, nineteen-year-old Herndon, who had organized three CPUSA meetings and recruited five members, was one of the leaders of a peaceful march of approximately 400 blacks and 600 whites to the county court building. The biracial approach was intentional: the anonymous leaflet urged biracial unity in the fight against "the bosses" as the only way to make gains. Such a biracial public protest was virtually unthinkable in the Jim Crow South. As John Hammond Moore puts it, "Atlanta whites were so desperate that they followed the leadership of a Red, Yankee black boy."[5] When the protesters arrived at the court building, county officials separated the marchers by race, thereby allowing the whites to talk to the council but turning the black people away. The next day officials released $6,000 to feed the 23,000 people in Atlanta dependent on the relief system.

The white establishment could not let this demonstration go unpunished, especially when a second flyer (written by Herndon) appeared in early July that "bragged of the $6,000 obtained for relief, asked the whereabouts of thousands more which authorities claimed were being saved by salary cuts, and emphasized 'the bosses' had been shocked at the sight of Negro-white unity."[6] Blacks and poor whites organizing together was unacceptable to the white establishment, even if their common interest was to avoid starvation. Atlanta police put a watch on the post office because the anonymous flyers had included a post office box number. On July 11, they arrested Herndon when he picked up mail at the postal box. They took him to his apartment, seized all his books and pamphlets as evidence, and jailed him without bail on suspicion of committing a crime. A booklet titled *The Communist Position on the Negro Question*, advocating a southern "Black Belt" with a black majority as an autonomous communist state, drew special attention.

On July 21, a white lawyer and two black lawyers sought Herndon's release. The judge ordered the police to either secure an indictment in twenty-four hours or release him. Prosecutors charged Herndon with incitement to insurrection under section 56 of the Georgia Penal Code: "Any attempt, by persuasion or otherwise, to induce others to join in any combined resistance to the lawful authority of the State shall constitute an attempt to incite insurrection." This section was derived from an 1830s law passed to squelch abolitionists and slave rebellion. After the Civil War, the statute was updated to eliminate references to slaves but remained focused on preventing uprisings among freed slaves. Prior to Herndon's case, this section had only been invoked three times.[7] In 1868, John T. Gibson, a black preacher, was convicted but released on appeal because the Georgia Supreme Court interpreted the law to criminalize only insurrection and attempted insurrection, not incitement to insurrection. In 1871 the legislature added incitement to insurrection to section 56. In 1916 the statute was used to prosecute William Pollard, the leader of a streetcar workers' strike. Pollard was convicted but did not serve any sentence, and charges were dropped in 1919.[8] In 1930, six people—two white men, two white women, and two black men—were indicted for incitement to insurrection due to their CPUSA activities and literature; they avoided trial through various legal challenges and by leaving the state. Herndon was not so fortunate. The all-white grand jury indicted him, even though the indictment listed the alleged crimes as occurring on July 16, a time when Herndon was in police custody.

Herndon accepted legal representation from the International Labor Defense (ILD). The ILD was founded in 1925 under the auspices of the CPUSA, although the ILD also included noncommunists. William Patterson, the black secretary of the ILD, hired two inexperienced black lawyers—Benjamin Davis Jr. and John Geer—to defend Herndon because more experienced white lawyers refused to assist. This made Davis and Geer the first black lawyers to handle a major civil rights case in the South. The prosecutors—John Hudson and T. J. Stephens—were prominent white lawyers who continually focused the all-white jury's attention on the defendant's race by using racist epithets despite the defense objecting and the judge reluctantly ordering the term "defendant" be used to refer to Herndon. The prosecution also repeatedly appealed to the jury's sexual racism in describing Herndon's political acts as black sexual aggression against white women. Their tactics included waving a copy of *Redbook Magazine*, one of the pieces of literature claimed to show Herndon's intention to incite insurrection along with the *New York Times* and other publications, proclaiming, "Look at the red cover of this magazine.... Is that proof enough?"[9] To top it off, the prosecution demanded the death sentence. Herndon, a poor black communist targeted by the powerful and wealthy white establishment, expected to be hanged.

The racial divide during the trial was evident. The white judge, Judge Wyatt, was known to use "the law with respect to Negroes like a butcher wielding a knife to kill a lamb."[10] Herndon's attorneys argued the absence of black jurors not just in this case but from all juries in Atlanta in living memory created an unfair trial, but Wyatt dismissed this complaint. Several white jurors turned their backs to black lawyer Ben Davis and refused to listen to his summation. Unfazed, Davis went on to read a description of a lynching from one of Herndon's pamphlets that caused a spectator to faint and pointed out the hypocrisy of prosecuting Herndon for organizing a peaceful interracial hunger march while authorities ignored lynching and other racial oppression.[11]

Davis and Geer focused their legal strategy on two cornerstones. First, the evidence against him was flawed. For example, the prosecution's main witness admitted he did not have personal knowledge of any of Herndon's alleged crimes, and a professor called as a witness testified that most of the literature Herndon possessed was available in Emory University's library. Judge Wyatt dismissed the professor's testimony as irrelevant. Second, they framed the case as an attack on the working class, black and white, which also was the strategy Herndon used when he took the stand. Herndon talked about the suffering of poor blacks and whites and the biracial aims of the CPUSA, observing how the white establishment pitted poor whites against blacks to prevent them from uniting against the status quo. He was under no illusion his argument would succeed, but he hoped to at least be executed as a martyr for a cause: "You may do what you will with Angelo Herndon.... You may succeed in killing one, two, even a score of working-class organizers. But you cannot kill the working class."[12]

In closing, the prosecution urged jurors to remember Herndon's goal was to "attack [our] homes, take our property, rape our women, and murder our children."[13] The defense urged jurors to defend the Bill of Rights and Constitutions of the United States and Georgia and ignore the prosecution's diversionary racist tactics. Judge Wyatt instructed the jury that the mere possession of insurrectionist literature was not criminal; the evidence must show that immediate serious violence against the state of Georgia was to be expected or was advocated. On January 18, 1933, after just two hours of deliberation, the jury found Herndon guilty but recommended mercy: eighteen to twenty years on the prison chain gang rather than the death penalty. Anne Emmanuel notes that the guilty verdict was a foregone conclusion: the only reason it took the jury two hours to deliver its verdict is that two jurors held out for the death penalty.[14] The jury's "mercy" was less noble than it might sound. John Spivak, who wrote the exposé on the horrific conditions black prisoners in Georgia endured, pointed out:

> The 18 to 20 year sentence . . . means only one thing: it means a death sentence. In collecting material for "Georgia Nigger," I examined most of the available records of the police commission. I found no record of

> any prisoner on the chain-gang . . . who lived more than 10 years. Besides the fiendish tortures which are inflicted on prisoners and under which many die in agony, the prisoners are forced to work under a killing pace.[15]

Only one newspaper in Georgia, the Macon *Telegraph*, protested the decision.[16] Davis and Geer filed a motion for a rehearing, but it was denied by Judge Wyatt.

With Herndon in prison, Davis and Geer appealed to the Georgia Supreme Court. In May *Herndon v. The State*, 178 GA 832 (1934) upheld the conviction on the basis that the insurrection need only be capable of success at any time. It did not need to occur or even be imminent. If the state "were compelled to wait until the apprehended danger became certain, then its right to protect itself would come into being simultaneously with the overthrow of government."[17] Mark Tushnet summarizes the Georgia Supreme Court's view: "The Black Belt was ripe for revolution, secession through self-determination was a realistic possibility, and it could only happen violently."[18] The decision inspired a new wave of communist witch hunts in Atlanta that only subsided when overzealous police completely botched a case.[19]

When the Georgia Supreme Court denied a rehearing in September 1934 (*Herndon v. The State*, 178 GA 597 [1934]), Herndon's lawyers appealed to the US Supreme Court. Herndon was released on a massive $15,000 bail and took a train to New York with two of his attorneys and two railroad detectives because the KKK had threatened to murder him.[20] Fortunately, Herndon arrived safely in New York and joined the CPUSA and other supporters, such as the American Civil Liberties Union, in a publicity blitz on his behalf. In Atlanta, the provisional and interracial Committee for the Defense of Angelo Herndon was formed. The ILD successfully made the case a national and international cause célèbre highlighting the "oppressive nature of 'southern justice' for black Americans."[21] An April 10, 1935, a *New Republic* editorial proclaimed, "Few cases in American jurisprudence have been of greater importance than the appeal of Angelo Herndon." He spoke to audiences around the country, such as the National Student League at Harvard University. White liberals helped fund his defense.[22]

The prominent civil liberties attorney Whitney North Seymour of New York agreed to argue Herndon's case before the Supreme Court on the condition that it rest solely on free speech grounds. He maintained that section 56 violated the First Amendment because it failed to meet the "clear and present danger" test announced in *Schenk v. United States*, 249 US 47 (1919). Moreover, because it failed to define *insurrection* clearly, it allowed for prosecution of people (like Herndon) who were merely advocating on behalf of a legal political party and advocating doctrines that could be read in libraries. For the prosecution, Fulton County assistant solicitor J. Walter LeCraw claimed the appropriate test was the "dangerous tendency" test used by the court in *Gitlow v. New York*, 268 US 652 (1925); but his main argument was that the constitutionality question had been raised too late to be a proper ground for appeal.

The Supreme Court voted 6–3 to uphold Herndon's conviction on a technicality in *Herndon v. Georgia*, 295 US 441 (1935). Justice George Sutherland wrote for the majority and held that the Court had no jurisdiction because the question of the constitutionality of the statute—even though it had been raised twice—had not been raised "properly." The first time the defense questioned the constitutionality of the statute was during the original trial, and the second time was in their appeal for a rehearing to the state supreme court. The Court held these two instances did not count because the trial court had overruled the original challenge and it was not raised in the initial appeal for a rehearing to the state supreme court. Since the US Supreme Court was hearing the appeal of the state supreme court's denial of rehearing and that decision did not address the constitutionality of the statute, there was no question for the US Supreme Court to hear.

In stark contrast to his majority opinion in *Powell v. Alabama*, 287 US 45 (1932), Justice Sutherland did not address the racist dimensions of Herndon's case. *Powell* was the first of the Scottsboro Boys cases in which racial injustices in the Southern legal system were the focus in the legal narrative and the basis for the court overturning state action. Sutherland's neglect of the racist dimensions of Herndon's case also conflicts with the attention the Supreme Court gave to racial injustice in two other Scottsboro Boys cases—*Norris v. Alabama*, 294 US 587 (1935), and *Patterson v. Alabama*, 294 US 600 (1935)—that were decided only a month before *Herndon v. Georgia*. One cannot help but wonder about this inconsistency. Kendall Thomas asks, "The racial implications of Herndon's arrest and trial were clear. In the Scottsboro cases, the Supreme Court had placed weight on the racial dimensions of Southern political and legal culture. Were these issues irrelevant to the outcome in *Herndon v Georgia*?"[23]

In dissent, Justice Benjamin Cardozo (joined by Louis Brandeis and Harlan Stone) argued that the majority used flawed reasoning and ignored relevant facts. Another case, *Carr v. State*, involving two Georgia Supreme Court decisions, was moving through the legal process along with Herndon's case.

Carr v. State, 176 GA 55 (1932) (*Carr v. State* I) was issued several months before Herndon's trial. In that case, the court held that section 58 (addressing only the distribution of insurrectionist literature) could sustain a conviction at a weaker standard (the bad tendency test by which virtually any expression deemed "dangerous" could be found criminal) than the clear and present danger test. No one involved in Herndon's original trial thought *Carr v. State* I was relevant to his case. Indeed, the trial judge had instructed the jury to use the clear and present danger test. Thus, any federal question that might have arisen in virtue of that decision was unasked. *Carr v. State*, 176 GA 747 (1933) (*Carr v. State* II) was issued after Herndon's original trial and conviction but before his appeal. In this case, the state supreme court upheld its earlier decision but rejected the clear and present danger standard. Herndon's lawyers now recognized the relevance of the Carr decisions, but under the procedural rules of Georgia criminal law, they could not move for a new trial, move for an arrest of judgment, or raise the question in appeal because it had not been raised in the jury trial. Thus, Herndon never had a chance to raise the federal question in a "proper" way! The Court was demanding that Herndon's lawyers should have known at his original trial that the state supreme court would later reject the clear and present danger test. Also, the Court was expecting his lawyers to raise the point at his original trial even though Judge Wyatt instructed the jury to use the clear and present danger test. Confusion over the legal standard for protected speech was not isolated to Herndon's case.[24]

Herndon v. Georgia was widely condemned in the national press. The *New York Post* called it "a mass of shabby technicalities" in a May 22, 1935, editorial.[25] *The Nation* condemned it as "a final seal of approval on one of the most indefensible examples of class justice so far recorded in this country."[26] It was also protested in law journals. For example, a note on recent cases published in the *University of Pennsylvania Law Review* decried the court's distressing decision as "assiduous in avoiding a decision."[27]

Herndon's lawyers moved for a rehearing, and his supporters renewed the publicity blitz. By this time the ILD had started its Popular Front strategy pursuing alliances with liberal organizations rather than branding them "class traitors." Newspaper and magazine columnists, the National Bar Association, the NAACP, the Methodist Federation for Social Service, prominent religious figures, and others took up Herndon's cause. The Supreme Court denied his appeal with only the comment "rehearing denied" in October 1935, *Herndon v. Georgia*, 296 US 661 (1935). Before Herndon returned to Georgia to begin his sentence, New York Congressman Vito Marcantonio pledged to keep his cause alive in the US House of Representatives; a black alderman in Paris vowed to rally the whole of France to his cause; and a Manhattan rally attended by thousands, including famous authors, religious leaders, and labor leaders, took the "Angelo Herndon oath" to support him.[28]

On October 28, 1935, Herndon—accompanied by attorney Elbert Tuttle and journalist Joseph North—surrendered to authorities to begin serving his sentence. Tuttle served Sheriff James Lowry a writ of habeas corpus claiming that Herndon's imprisonment was unconstitutional. The judge in Herndon's new trial, Hugh Dorsey, was a former governor notorious for his role as prosecutor in the trial of Leo Frank. Frank, a "Yankee Jew" factory superintendent, was convicted of murdering a thirteen-year-old female employee, kidnapped from prison, and lynched by an anti-Semitic mob when the governor commuted his death sentence to life in prison.[29] This time, Herndon was represented in trial court by his US Supreme Court counsel. To the surprise of many, Dorsey ruled that section 56 was unduly vague and therefore unconstitutional. Of course, the state appealed and the Georgia Supreme Court upheld Herndon's conviction primarily by reference to its earlier decision. That meant Herndon's appeal now went back to the US Supreme Court.

Herndon v. Lowry (1937)

Two years after Herndon's unsuccessful 1935 plea, the same nine justices of the US Supreme Court heard the same lawyers for the defense and prosecution argue their cases—except this time the court was hearing the case on its merits. It was the first time the Supreme Court reviewed a sedition statute from the South, the first time it reviewed a sedition conviction for an African American, and "the first time [it faced] the possibility that an American citizen might be hanged or electrocuted for nothing except expressing objectionable opinions or owning objectionable books."[30] The outcome was far from clear.

In *Gitlow v. New York*, 268 US 652 (1925), the majority applied the First Amendment to a state restriction on speech for the first time in US history while upholding Gitlow's criminal anarchy conviction for publishing a socialist article. The Court ruled that speech specifically outlawed by legitimate statute is subject to the (less protective) bad tendency test; however, speech not specifically outlawed by legitimate statute was subject to the (more protective) clear and present danger test. Since the New York criminal anarchy law was a legitimate statute and specifically outlawed socialist publications, Gitlow's speech was subject to the bad tendency test, and given its bad tendency (in the opinion of the Court), the conviction was upheld. Georgia's section 56 appeared to be a legitimate statute, but it did not specifically outlaw Herndon's communist pamphlets or organizing activities. This suggested the clear and present danger test, more protective of speech, ought to apply even though the Georgia Supreme Court said it did not. That would still leave open the question of whether his expression constituted a clear and present danger, and the World War I decisions using the clear and present danger test were uniformly hostile to subversive speech. Not good for Herndon.

Fiske v. Kansas, 274 US 380 (1927), vacated the conviction of Industrial Workers of the World (IWW) organizer Harold Fiske under the state criminal syndicalism law because the state's application of the law to him violated the Due Process Clause of the Fourteenth Amendment. Fiske failed to get due process because the only evidence offered by the state to support his conviction was the preamble to the IWW constitution, but the preamble did not advocate force or violence as a means of political or economic change. Fiske's arrest and conviction were an "arbitrary and unreasonable" enforcement of the law. The decision reinforced the Court's commitment to due process but did not overturn the state's syndicalism law or clarify the line distinguishing protected and unprotected speech. Still, the *Fiske* decision offered Herndon the hope the court might free him on due process grounds.

Whitney v. California, 274 US 357 (1927), offered Herndon little hope. The Court unanimously upheld a state criminal syndicalism law making it a crime to be a member of an organization that advocates the commission of crimes as means to political change and its application to Anita Whitney. The majority invoked the clear and present danger test but asserted that Whitney's speech was not protected because it was "inimical to the public welfare, tending to incite crime, disturb the public peace, or endanger the foundations of organized government and threaten its overthrow." This language approximates the bad tendency test. If Whitney could be convicted merely for being a member of a communist organization, so could Herndon.

An optimist might find hope in the concurring opinion in *Whitney* penned by Justice Brandeis (joined by Justice Holmes). Brandeis conceded Whitney's guilt in advocating the commission of crime but maintained the test ought to be the clear and present danger test with the further requirements of the probability of serious injury to the state and no time to avert the evil. Herndon's conviction could be vacated on that standard. It was also promising that only a month after the court's decision, California Governor Clement Calhoun Young pardoned Whitney. He believed that putting her in jail was "unthinkable," "abnormal conditions attending the trial" greatly influenced the jury, and under "ordinary circumstances" the case never would have been prosecuted.[31]

The same day the *Whitney* decision was handed down, the Supreme Court issued its opinion in *Burns v. United States*, 274 US 328 (1927). *Burns* upheld the "sabotage" conviction of an IWW organizer distributing copies of the preamble to the group's constitution in Yosemite National Park. The statute prohibited only willful destruction of physical property. Burns had advocated merely work slowdowns through slacking and misloading. Another precedent boding ill for Herndon.

Stromberg v. California, 283 US 359 (1931) provided a basis beyond due process for Herndon to win. For the first time in US history, *Stromberg* struck down a state law on its face as a violation of the free speech clause. In this 7–2 ruling, the Court held the clause in the California statute banning red flags (as a symbol of communism) violated the Due Process and Equal Protection Clauses of the Fourteenth Amendment because it was an unduly vague and overbroad restriction on speech that could be applied to the constitutionally protected peaceful advocacy of political or economic change. The next month the Court "incorporated" First Amendment protection for freedom of the press through the Due Process Clause in *Near v. Minnesota*, 283 US 697 (1931). Perhaps a new era of First Amendment protection was dawning? Chief Justice Charles Evans Hughes, only reappointed to the court the year before, wrote the majority opinions in both *Stromberg* and *Near*.

In January 1937, a month before it heard Herndon's case, the court decided a freedom of assembly case. In *De Jonge v. Oregon*, 299 US 353 (1937), the court unanimously reversed Dirk De Jonge's conviction under the Oregon criminal syndicalism statute. De Jonge was convicted solely on the basis of participating in a public meeting held under the auspices of the Communist Party. There was no evidence he (or anyone else in the meeting) advocated illegal actions. Thus, the court found (as in *Fiske*) that the state violated the defendant's Fourteenth Amendment due process rights insofar as citizens are entitled "to discuss the public issues of the day and thus in a lawful manner, without incitement to violence or crime, to seek redress of alleged grievances. That was of the essence of his guaranteed personal liberty."[32] The Court did not rule on the constitutionality of the Oregon criminal syndicalism statute, nor did it clarify the distinction between protected and unprotected speech.

In sum, the legal landscape for free speech was a morass. When Herndon's case was argued February 8 and decided April 26, 1937, only two state laws restricting speech, press, or assembly had been struck down on their face as unconstitutional (*Near* and *Stromberg*) and only two state convictions for speech, press, or assembly had been struck down in their application (*Fiske* and *De Jonge*). Aside from those cases, the Court had consistently upheld convictions of political dissidents whether it used the clear and present danger test or the bad tendency test. The Court had not yet protected expression advocating illegal activity or membership in an organization advocating illegal activity; it had only asserted that state laws needed to avoid undue vagueness or overbreadth, and what constituted undue vagueness or overbreadth was not clear. As a note in the *Yale Law Journal* observed at the time, "The handful of Supreme Court decisions dealing with the limits imposed by the due process clause of the Fourteenth Amendment upon the power of the states to restrain political expression vary sufficiently on their facts to make possible any number of distinctions and conflicting generalizations."[33]

Herndon's lawyers appealed to Court rulings on the Espionage Act of 1917 to argue that the proper test was the "clear and present danger" test and that Herndon's expression did not rise to that level. They argued that section 56 was unduly vague and thereby threatened protected speech. The state appealed to *Gitlow v. New York* to argue that the proper test was the bad tendency test and maintained Herndon's expression had a "dangerous tendency." They also urged judicial deference to state legislative authority.

The Supreme Court ruled 5–4 in favor of Herndon. Chief Justice Hughes and Justice Roberts changed sides from the 1935 decision. The court relied on two main rationales. First, the state failed to prove that Herndon's pamphlets or meetings constituted incitement to insurrection as defined in section 56. Swing voter Justice Roberts, writing for the majority, stated: "The only objectives appellant is proved to have urged are those having to do with unemployment and emergency relief which are devoid of criminality. His membership in the Communist Party and his solicitation of a few members wholly fails to establish an attempt to incite others to insurrection."[34] Like *Fiske* and *De Jonge*, it reversed a state conviction of radical speech when the state failed to prove the defendant advocated illegal activity to achieve political or economic change. Second, the Georgia statute was void for vagueness and a threat to protected speech because it failed to provide an ascertainable standard of guilt.[35] Roberts wrote,

> The statute, as construed and applied, amounts to merely a dragnet which may enmesh anyone who agitates for a change of government if a jury can be persuaded that he ought to have foreseen his words would have some effect in the future conduct of others. No reasonably

> ascertainable standard of guilt is prescribed. So vague and indeterminate are the boundaries this set to the freedom of speech and assembly that the law necessarily violates the guarantees of liberty embodied in the Fourteenth Amendment.[36]

Here the court followed its *Stromberg* decision, finding a state speech restriction unconstitutional for being overly broad on its face (*Near* was struck down as a prior restraint, not for overbreadth).

There was widespread support for the Supreme Court's decision insofar as it protected Herndon's speech and reversed "Southern justice," but other aspects of the case remained contentious. For example, the April 27, 1937, *Daily Worker* praised the decision while insisting that the Court was reluctant and moved to the decision only by mass pressure. The May 8 Pittsburgh *Courier* called the *Herndon* decision "a legal victory that brings the frontiers of freedom a little closer to the South," but also stressed that communism must be rejected. Mark Tushnet argues that the four dissenters agreed with the legal principles the majority employed and merely disagreed about what the evidence showed regarding the clear and present danger Herndon's speech posed.[37] If so, one might wonder: what makes *Herndon v. Lowry* a pivotal case?

Herndon AND THE FIRST AMENDMENT

One reason *Herndon* is a pivotal case is its role in the development of First Amendment protections. It was only the third decision (with *Fiske* and *De Jonge*) to reverse a state speech conviction on due process grounds and only the second (with *Stromberg*) to strike down a state speech restriction as unduly vague or overly broad. The facts of Herndon's case make it more significant. *Stromberg* struck down a red flag clause in a recently enacted California syndicalism statute; *Herndon* struck down an incitement to insurrection statute with roots going back eighty years to the Nat Turner slave rebellion and the Antebellum era. More important, Herndon's organizing activities and possession of pamphlets urging revolution and creation of an autonomous, communist Black Belt in a city with thousands of poverty-stricken, disenfranchised, angry black people posed a far greater threat to law and order than did Stromberg's display of a red flag at a youth camp for working-class children. The *Herndon* majority's rejection of the statute on its face and in its application were critical steps in the development of the void-for-vagueness and overbreadth doctrines that played a crucial role in supporting later civil rights movement protesters (chapter 3) and striking down broad legal restrictions on hate speech (chapter 4).

Herndon did not establish the clear and present danger test as the sole criterion for protected speech, and this test was eventually replaced, but *Herndon* is a pivotal First Amendment decision because it rejected the bad tendency test. As we saw earlier, the bad tendency test had a long history and had been used in *Gitlow* in 1925 and *Whitney* in 1927 to suppress socialist and communist speech. Hence Zechariah Chafee Jr. observes, "the most interesting point to me in the *Herndon* case is that Justice Roberts flatly repudiated [the dangerous tendency test]."[38] *Herndon* thus became the first case to apply the clear and present danger test since *Schenk* in 1919 and the first to use it to protect speech. Its precedent, setting forth a protective version of the clear and present danger test (which had been urged by Brandeis and Holmes in dissents in *Abrams* in 1917 through *Whitney* in 1927), was used over the next fifteen years to protect First Amendment rights in *Thornhill v. Alabama*, 310 US 88 (1940) (state cannot ban labor picketing), *West Virginia v. State Board of Ed. v. Barnette*, 319 US 624 (1943) (state cannot compel Jehovah's Witnesses to salute flag or say Pledge of Allegiance), *Taylor v. Mississippi*, 319 US 583 (1943) (state cannot punish Jehovah's Witnesses for antiwar expression), *Hartzell v. United States*, 322 US 680 (1944) (Hartzell's expression did not violate Espionage Act), *Thomas v. Collins*, 323 US 516 (1945) (state cannot require prior permit to recruit members to labor organizations), *Craig v. Harney*, 331 US 367 (1947) (protecting newspaper criticisms of Texas court), and perhaps most famously, *Terminiello v. Chicago*, 337 US 1 (1949) (protecting a suspended Catholic priest's racist and inflammatory speech).[39]

Herndon is also important in the development of First Amendment doctrine because its use of the void-for-vagueness doctrine signaled that the priorities of the Court were changing. This doctrine was relatively new. It was first invoked in *International Harvester Co. v. Kentucky*, 234 US 216 (1914), and had been used exclusively in its early years by the Taft Court and its conservative "Four Horsemen of Reaction" to strike down state and federal economic regulations.[40] Its application to *Herndon* reinforced the Court's shift from preferring economic rights and liberties to a preferred position for civil rights and liberties. After 1930 the Court used the void-for-vagueness doctrine "almost invariably for the creation of an insulating buffer zone of added protection at the peripheries of several of the Bill of Rights freedoms. With regard to one class of cases, those involving potential infringement of First Amendment privileges, this buffer zone has always been expressly avowed in the Court's opinions and recognized by commentators."[41]

In sum, *Herndon* was a key decision marking a change in the Supreme Court's understanding of the First Amendment. David Yassky writes, "First Amendment jurisprudence experienced a fundamental disjunction in the 1930s. The Court's entire approach to individual liberty changed, down to the basic aims animating its decisions. Common law rights to property lost their constitutional protection. Speech rights, previously unrecognized, became dominant."[42] This bifurcated judicial approach to constitutional issues reducing the weight of economic rights and liberties and increasing the weight of civil liberties did not have a consistent or coherent theory guiding it, nor a single explanation or cause for it, nor a linear and consistent path of expansion.[43] But G. Edward White notes

> the preferred position cases decided by the Supreme Court, beginning in 1937, reveal intuitions by several Justices . . . that First Amendment rights were in a different category from other constitutional rights and deserved greater constitutional protection than police power analysis afforded them. . . . [T]he reason for this enhanced protection for First Amendment rights lay not only in the close connection between free speech and democratic theory, but the enhanced significance of democratic theory itself as a defining aspirational feature of American civilization.[44]

Thus, the *Herndon* decision is commonly recognized in the roster of First Amendment victories. Unfortunately, it is rarely recognized in other significant ways.

Herndon, EQUALITY, AND MINORITY RIGHTS

One of the reasons Herndon's case deserves greater recognition concerns its role in the advancement of African American equality and minority rights. The law typically changes gradually, one decision narrowly expanding or limiting prior legal doctrine or application. For example, the US Supreme Court did not incorporate the entire Bill of Rights in a single decision: instead, it incorporated amendments and even individual clauses on a case-by-case basis over a period of many years.[45] Still, *Gitlow* has a special place in the history of incorporation of the Bill of Rights because it broke ground for later decisions. Similarly, the Supreme Court did not decide government could not restrict independent political spending by corporations in *Citizens United v. FEC*, 558 US 310 (2010) out of thin air. A long series of prior decisions involving corporate political speech rights led to it.[46] *First National Bank of Boston v. Bellotti*,

435 US 765 (1978), which challenged a Massachusetts law prohibiting corporate donations on ballot initiatives unless its interests were directly involved, was the first that explicitly affirmed a corporate right to political expression. *Herndon v. Lowry* played a similar, special role as the first in a series of First Amendment decisions advancing racial equality and minority rights over the next forty years (addressed in chapter 3).

Some might object to the claim that *Herndon* has a special role in the advancement of racial equality or minority rights since the Supreme Court majority was silent on these factors. Their silence has led nearly all legal accounts of *Herndon* to ignore his race or only mention it in passing.[47] Nan Hunter laments, "The majority . . . ignored the impact of the speaker's racial identity and the racial dynamics behind the case. As a consequence, the holding rendered it a pure speech case and also completely deraced it."[48] To think Herndon's case was not about race is to miss the forest for the trees. The fact that Herndon was black and his arrest and conviction were for his racial protest against the political and economic status quo is the crux of his ordeal, the Court's decisions, and their enduring significance.

First, Herndon's arrest and original trial were racially charged. He was hunted down and arrested because he was a black agitator trying to unify blacks and poor whites. An all-white jury for a black defendant was selected (yet again). The prosecutors and witnesses used racist epithets against Herndon. White jurors turned their backs on his black lawyers. Prosecutors focused on Herndon's race rather than his speech and inflamed the jury and audience with frequent references to violent sexual racism.

Second, Justice Van Devanter's dissent in *Herndon v. Lowry* (1937) claiming Herndon's expression was incitement to insurrection focused on Herndon being a black man recruiting blacks to the CPUSA to establish an autonomous Southern "Black Belt." Zechariah Chafee Jr., the leading free speech scholar of the era, makes two important points here. First, the white men involved in Herndon's prosecution

> were not worried in the slightest about any plotted insurrection or the possibility of a New Liberia between the Tennessee Valley Authority and the Gulf of Mexico. But they were worried . . . about . . . his demand for equal rights for Negroes. If he got going with that, there was a clear and present danger of racial friction and isolated acts of violence by individuals on both sides.[49]

Second, Chafee considered Herndon's case to be the only one of the many he reviews in which there was legitimate reason to think the expression might provoke violence: "given the unrest of Negroes, share croppers, mill-workers, his demands for equal racial rights, lavish relief, and the virtual abolition of debts might have produced some sort of disorder in the near future. Smoking is all right, but not in a powder magazine."[50] Here we see the crux of the case and the connection between inequality and illiberty: the denial of free speech to Herndon by the Georgia courts and the decisions by the white prosecution and judges deciding his fate lay precisely in black inequality. African Americans in the South could not hope for a solution through the ballot box because election rules disenfranchised them and the boldly racist Democratic Party had a stranglehold on the Southern vote.[51]

Furthermore, the Supreme Court was fully aware of Southern racial injustice and had taken steps to limit it in *Moore v. Dempsey*, 261 US 86 (1923), the Scottsboro Boys cases, the Texas voting rights cases *Nixon v. Herndon*, 273 US 536 (1927), and *Nixon v. Condon*, 286 US 73 (1932), and *Brown v. Mississippi*, 297 US 278 (1936) (reversed conviction of black man obtained by a forced confession through whipping). Chafee notes, "it was impossible [for the court] to ignore . . . the fact that if [Herndon] was validly imprisoned, then the next Negro Communist to enter Georgia could be validly put to death under the same statute without having done a bit more than Herndon."[52] For the first time the Supreme Court faced the prospect of a citizen, specifically, a black citizen in the Jim Crow South, being put to death for an objectionable idea or book. Since the Supreme Court had no say in the severity of the sentence, "it was a case of all or nothing, and the court chose nothing."[53]

Finally, the argument against a "tyranny of the majority" over racial, religious, or political minorities was gaining intellectual and doctrinal traction. The idea of a tyranny of the majority had been around for many years—the phrase "tyranny of the majority" was addressed by John Adams in *A Defence of the Constitutions of Government of the United States of America* (1788), Alexis De Tocqueville's *Democracy in America* (1835), and John Stuart Mill's *On Liberty* (1859)—but by the 1930s the focus was on nonpolitical minorities such as racial, ethnic, and religious minorities, especially those who were "discrete and insular." This concern for minority rights was international in scope. It is not an accident that the Court's decision protecting Herndon, a member of a "discrete and insular" minority, against a tyranny of the majority, coincided with developments in international law. Beginning in the nineteenth century and expanding after the peace treaty ending World War I, treaties and other international conventions called for international protection of racial, linguistic, or religious minorities from the domestic politics of certain nations.[54] International recognition of the need for judicial involvement in protecting minorities was evidenced in the jurisdiction of such cases being given to the Permanent Court of International Justice established by the League of Nations.[55] Indeed, the year after *Herndon v. Lowry*, the US Supreme Court explicitly identified heightened judicial inquiry of legislation prejudicially directed at a "discrete and insular" minority lacking recourse to ordinary political processes in its now famous footnote four in *United States v. Carolene Products*, 304 US 144 (1938).[56] Unless courts act to protect minorities in such cases, their only alternative is radical advocacy and violence. Robert Cover explains:

> Discrete and insular minorities are not simply losers in the political arena, they are perpetual losers. Indeed, to say that they lose in the majoritarian political process is seriously to distort the facts: they are scapegoats in the real political struggles between other groups. . . . It is therefore because of the discreteness and insularity of certain minorities (objects of prejudice) that we cannot trust the operation of those political processes "ordinarily to be relied upon to protect minorities."[57]

In the "easy" cases, the Court acts to protect noninsular minorities from a temporary legislative outbreak of hysteria or intolerance, but in the "hard" cases, as with racial apartheid, the protection must address ingrained, systematic injustice.[58]

Kendall Thomas hits the nail on the head in his 1991 article characterizing the Herndon case as "an important episode in the historical effort of African-Americans to find a political language with which to understand their past aspirations and to articulate their future aspirations."[59] The specific legal issue in question during Herndon's initial trial may have been incitement to insurrection, but for blacks and whites the trial

> opened up the whole history of the black experience in the American South: the exclusion of blacks from petit and grand juries in Georgia; the treatment of black prisoners in Georgia jails; the long-standing taboo against black lawyers arguing cases as politically charged as Herndon's; the ideology of southern law and order (laid bare when death threats were made against Herndon, his attorneys, and anyone else bold enough to publicly support or participate in the effort to build

> a defense movement around the case); the myth of white supremacy, which trumpeted the racial superiority of even the poorest, most illiterate white worker and demonized the class-color alliance of the Unemployed Council as an offense against God and nature; and the meaning of the Marxist theory of revolution generally and the theoretical platform of the CPUSA in particular.[60]

In the initial trial, the prosecution repeatedly focused the jury's attention on Herndon being black—more specifically, the alleged sexual threat Herndon posed as a black man to white women. This supposed threat was the basis for hundreds of lynchings in the South. Yet these factors were glossed over in the judicial consideration of the case and in the later dominant legal narrative, which focused on its incremental role in a line of constitutional cases.[61] Certainly it is important to recognize the role of *Herndon* in the development of First Amendment law, but stopping there ignores the fact that "questions of race, power and culture are not less central to Herndon's significance in our constitutional history."[62] Herndon's 1937 victory can only be understood and appreciated in its broader racialized context, but Thomas points out that the inclusion of *Herndon v. Lowry* (1937) in scores of books on constitutional law and political and civil rights, relegation of *Herndon v. Georgia* (1935) to some casebooks on federal court jurisdiction and procedure, and complete neglect of the Supreme Court's rejection of Herndon's petition for rehearing (1935) split up the cases and thereby marginalize one of the central themes—the intersection of race, culture, and politics in US law. In an interview with Lynne Tillman, Thomas noted, "Herndon really represents or contains, in a compressed form, all the old intractable themes of racial politics in the U.S."[63]

Indeed, Herndon's case is an anomaly in the Supreme Court's decisions involving Southern racial justice in that era. Thomas points out, "In each of [the other] cases, the Court placed the brute facts of racism and power in the forefront of its constitutional analysis. The opinions in *Brown*, *Norris*, *Powell*, and *Patterson* emphasize these realities of race and region even though on the face of it none of the cases required it."[64] So why did the Court view Herndon's case differently? Thomas argues it is because the other cases did not involve political dissent. The Court was prepared to address racial injustice in nonpolitical cases, but it was not ready to address race in the case of a black political radical:

> If Angelo Herndon was a political criminal, what of the white Southerners who, if the court upheld his conviction, stood ready to

> punish him? The Court had to face harsh historical and contemporary realities that it could neither ignore nor openly acknowledge. If it intervened, it would have to decisively condemn the racial and political culture that Herndon too had fought. This was a step that ideology and cultural experience did not yet allow the court to take.[65]

In other words, the Court could openly reject racist criminal enforcement (*Moore* and the Scottsboro Boys cases), state infringements of white communist/pro-labor dissent (*Fiske* and *Stromberg*), and even to a lesser extent state restrictions on black voting rights (the two Texas white primary cases), but it could not openly unite black equality and black liberty.

Yet uniting black equality and liberty is exactly what *Herndon v. Lowry* did. The millions of people supporting Herndon were responding to a black man's plea for free speech and racial justice, not a demand for an autonomous communist Southern Black Belt. Herndon's victory paved the way for further judicial decisions advancing minority rights during the civil rights era, some of which I examine in chapter 3. In an important sense, the case initiated a second Reconstruction advancing minority rights.

Herndon, RACE NEUTRALITY, AND RACE CONSCIOUSNESS

Angelo Herndon's ordeal was a significant step in the ongoing debate over race-neutral and race-conscious strategies. The struggle for racial equality requires advocates to make a principled or tactical decision whether to take a race-neutral approach or a race-based approach or, more broadly in the context of minorities, whether equal rights and liberties for a minority are more effectively advanced by emphasizing their differences from the majority or their uniqueness, or by emphasizing their similarities with the majority or a common interest. During the Antebellum era, this issue divided abolitionists who sought a gradual end to slavery from those who sought an immediate end; in the post–Civil War era, it divided supporters of Booker T. Washington from supporters of W. E. B. Du Bois. It arose in the US Supreme Court; for example, Harlan's dissent in *Plessy v. Ferguson* (1896) was an explicit argument for color-blind law in an era of color-conscious law. The argument for using race-neutral tactics in pursuing racial justice typically relies on two claims: (1) color-blindness is the ideal outcome and only race-neutrality is consistent with that ideal, and (2) emphasizing racial disparities, differences, or uniqueness is ineffective because it elicits white backlash. The argument for using race-conscious strategies turns both those claims around that (1) because we do not live in the ideal world, we must pay attention to racial disparities either because race-neutrality in practice merely perpetuates racial inequalities, or, more radically, race-neutrality is a myth; and (2) authorities should control backlash and transform public opinion rather than succumb to it. Herndon's case is a significant example intentionally and successfully using both strategies. The credit belongs largely to Herbert Wechsler (who had primary responsibility for the legal briefs) and the ILD (who coordinated the campaign for public support).[66] This section addresses Wechsler's race-neutral legal approach and the next section relates the ILD's race-conscious mass politics strategy.

Herbert Wechsler, a New York Jew, was ahead of his time in advocating a federal legislative reconstruction of the South to improve the conditions of African Americans. Anders Walker points out his support for antilynching legislation, eliminating obstacles to black voting, and school equalization requirements.[67] Impressed by the success of the ILD in the Scottsboro Boys cases, Wechsler eagerly agreed to assist in Angelo Herndon's case. Since he was not yet admitted to the Supreme Court bar, he wrote legal briefs providing the arguments that Whitney North Seymour urged at oral argument. His brief for *Herndon v. Georgia* (1935)—which Herndon lost—provided an extensive historical race-based context for the case. His brief for *Herndon v. Lowry* (1937)—which Herndon won—did not. Instead it emphasized (1) Herndon's speech was pro-labor (regardless of race) and (2) that tolerating labor agitation helped stabilize rather than destabilize democratic society by providing a peaceful avenue of expression to advocates of political and economic change.

Wechsler's move toward a race-neutral legal approach was tactical and principled. Tactically, a race-neutral approach made Herndon's plea more appealing to the liberal white public and more palatable to the two swing justices (Hughes and Roberts). As a result, the 1937 decision had a profound and lasting impact. Indeed, one of those swing votes, Justice Roberts, wrote the majority opinion that closely tracked Wechsler's brief.[68] The upshot of the decision was that even if blacks continued to face voting obstacles in the South, their freedom to agitate for change through speech, press, and assembly could result in change through ordinary political processes rather than riot or revolution. As we shall see in chapter 3, the ability to peacefully protest the legal status quo and expand the limits of peaceful protest was a crucial strategy in the civil rights movement. As Walker puts it, "Wechsler opened the door for more aggressive protest in Georgia, and arguably the rest of the South was well" and provided "a constitutional strategy for protecting the process through which blacks would ultimately achieve reform in the South in the 1960s."[69] Indeed, Wechsler viewed *Herndon v. Lowry* as nothing less than a "second revolution" in constitutional law and a "restoration" of the Fourteenth Amendment as a means to advance African American equality.[70] *Herndon*'s uniting equality and liberty was crucial to later racial progress.

Wechsler came to advocate race-neutrality as a matter of principle, that is, as a matter of doctrinal consistency and judicial legitimacy. He believed that politicizing race belonged to the legislative and executive branches of government, not the judiciary.[71] For Wechsler, like many other Jews living in an era of increased anti-Semitism, the commitment to a neutral strategy supporting black civil rights and liberties had personal dimensions[72] and was the basis for later cases he was involved in (such as *New York Times v. Sullivan* [1964]), as well as a precursor for the stand taken by later Jewish defenders of free speech, including anti-Semitic speech, most famously in *National Socialist Party of America v. City of Skokie*, 432 US 43 (1977).[73]

The success of the race-neutral legal approach in Herndon's 1937 decision does not mean a race-conscious approach cannot be tactically superior in another legal case. As we shall see in chapter 3, the education equalization victories after *Herndon*—most famously, *Brown v. Board of Education* (1954)—took a race-conscious legal approach. Nor does successful adoption of race neutrality as a legal strategy eliminate the potential success of a race-conscious strategy outside the courtroom. In fact, the ILD's "mass politics" strategy on behalf of Herndon was decidedly race-conscious.

Herndon AND MASS POLITICS

Herndon's case is not only a major First Amendment decision, a pivotal step in the defense of minority rights, the first case to unite black equality and liberty, and an important example of a successful race-neutral legal strategy, it was also a study in the successful employment of First Amendment values in mass politics and, more specifically, race-conscious mass politics. The credit goes to the ILD.

Founded in 1925, the ILD won a "vicious fight" with the NAACP in 1931 to provide legal counsel in the Scottsboro Boys cases. The ILD proposed an aggressive strategy pairing top-notch lawyers with mass politics, that is, organized publicity and protest. The NAACP proposed a more conservative approach, working within the legal profession and eschewing mass politics. The fight carried into the 1931 meeting of the National Bar Association—the black lawyers' professional group—which became nearly uncontrollable during discussion of a resolution to endorse the ILD's defense of black civil rights. The deadlocked resolution was abandoned for a watered-down compromise endorsing the legal efforts of all organizations and their lawyers to reverse the Scottsboro Boys verdicts. As the struggle for civil rights played out over the next two decades, the NAACP, the preeminent black organization in the civil rights movement, changed course to pair, as the ILD did, top-notch lawyers with mass politics.[74] *Herndon v. Lowry* played an important role in that transformation: the National Bar Association, which had been wracked with heated debate over the ILD in 1931, later expressed its "deep appreciation to the International Labor Defense for their unselfish and unstinting support of Angelo Herndon."[75] Mass politics were deployed at the local level in Herndon's initial trial and expanded as his case moved to the national stage, and these efforts contributed significantly to his ultimate success.

During the 1930s, the CPUSA aggressively advertised its support for racial equality (which they identified primarily with economic class justice) and actively sought black support and membership. Its legal arm, the ILD, energetically pursued legal cases involving oppression of African Americans.[76] The ILD quickly came to Herndon's defense, seeing the case as a political prosecution designed to divide the working class along racial lines. Because the ILD believed these prosecutions had both political and legal dimensions, they believed the defense also had to be political and legal and the political component was best addressed through mass publicity and protest. As Kenneth Mack puts it, "ILD lawyers and activists imagined into being a style of advocacy as theater—scripted performances that would generate direct action by potential supporters in the working class."[77] The NAACP objected to politicizing such cases, thinking the poisonous atmosphere such politics generated led to the conviction of innocent blacks and unfairly manipulated black defendants for ILD private gain.[78]

Benjamin Davis Jr., one of Herndon's trial lawyers, is a notable example of the radicalization of black activists. Davis had been part of the Harvard Law School cohort debating race and law strategies during the 1920s. The night before his closing arguments to the initial Herndon trial jury, he joined the CPUSA, the final move signaling his transformation from a liberal mentality of working within the legal establishment to fight racial injustice to a radical mentality viewing the legal establishment itself especially (but not exclusively)[79] in the South as an obstacle to racial justice. As Glenda Elizabeth Gilmore put it, Davis "walked into the packed courtroom a nominal Republican" and "strode out a card-carrying Communist."[80] After Davis defied the odds in successfully bringing a white policeman to trial for killing a blind black man, prosecutor John Hudson tried to have him sanctioned by the Atlanta Bar Association for his aggressive tactics pursuing racial justice.[81] Michael Belknap notes the law enforcement and judicial systems were entirely staffed by whites, black lawyers were restricted to minor cases involving black litigants, blacks were barred from jury duty, convicted blacks worked on chain gangs providing white employers a cheap and tractable labor supply, assertive blacks were jailed, and blacks received discriminatory sentences from judges and juries.[82] The radicalization of Davis was mirrored in the lives of many other blacks, though few joined the CPUSA as he and Herndon did. Leading black lawyers were recognizing the importance of the labor movement and mass politics to the black cause and agreeing to work with the ILD, which paid dividends in spawning further groups promoting first class citizenship for African Americans such as the National Negro Congress and its offshoot, the Southern Negro Youth Congress,[83] and contributing to the Supreme Court decision protecting black mass economic protest in *New Negro Alliance v. Sanitary Grocery*, 303 US 552 (1938), which is covered in chapter 3.[84]

To provide a sense of the extent of the ILD's use of mass publicity and protest, consider the following examples. At the local level, the month after Herndon's initial conviction they organized the provisional Committee for the Defense of Angelo Herndon, an interracial group identifying as a "united front from below" that recruited prominent Atlanta middle-class black leaders and white liberals.[85] The committee promoted awareness of Herndon's prosecution, solicited funds for his legal defense, and publicized the plight of blacks. When a white policeman shot and killed a blind forty-year-old black man in August 1933, the ILD handled the funeral arrangements, turning it into a mass protest closely watched over by fifty policemen. They sought to align Herndon's ordeal with the plight of the Scottsboro Boys case. Black support for Herndon solidified after a rally in December 1933 in which the Ku Klux Klan joined police in harassing the black protesters. Unfortunately, the Provisional Committee fell apart when ILD rivalry with the NAACP led it to mistakenly criticize the NAACP handling of an Atlanta murder trial.

Nationally, the ILD avoided such blunders.[86] In spring 1934 they launched a "Save Angelo Herndon" campaign, publicizing the poor conditions in jail, which resulted in improved physical conditions for Herndon. In July 1935 the ILD sponsored a delegation of northern liberals to visit Herndon and the Scottsboro Boys, which combined with other national publicity to increase public criticism of Georgia's legal system. When he was released on bail,

Herndon was greeted as a hero by a crowd of 6,000 well-wishers at Pennsylvania Station in New York City. By this time his case had attracted national and international media attention, and when the US Supreme Court rejected his plea, his case became a cause célèbre for blacks, liberals, and leftists. Periodicals such as the *Nation*, the *New Republic*, the *Christian Century*, and the New York *Post* derided the decision, as did black publications such as the Cleveland *Call and Post* and the NAACP magazine *Crisis*. That summer the ILD adopted a program of active cooperation with liberal groups, for example, getting the NAACP to file an amicus curiae (friend of the court) brief in support of Herndon's appeal for a rehearing at the Supreme Court. Herndon went on speaking tours across the country that included a life-size replica of the cage prisoners on a chain gang lived in. They created a petition calling for the repeal of Georgia's insurrection statute that was circulated by diverse groups such as the Socialist Party, the National Association of Colored Women, and the Southern Tenant Farmers Union. They created the Joint Committee to Aid the Herndon Defense to publicize the case, to which the ACLU (among many others) contributed. The powerful American Federation of Labor joined the Joint Committee in September 1936. Herndon ran a token campaign for a state assembly seat in New York and continued his speaking tours, including an audience with President Roosevelt.

Contrary to the dominant narrative putting the Scottsboro Boys cases ahead of Herndon in the public eye, Frederick Griffiths points out it was Herndon who became the national figurehead for the cases, often appearing with a Scottsboro mother.[87] Herndon wrote an autobiographical pamphlet, "You Cannot Kill the Working Class," that was rewritten and expanded into *Let Me Live*, a widely read book published by Random House shortly before his 1937 US Supreme Court trial.[88] In her review of Herndon's book in *Atlantic Monthly*, Dorothy Parker declared his trial "unbelievable; save that it happened." In her review for the *Journal of Negro History*, Martha Greuning described his story as "heroic, terrible and profoundly moving."[89] The *Daily Worker* ran pictures and stories on his plight on a regular basis. Two million people worldwide signed a petition calling for his release and his two national speaking tours went to more than fifty cities.[90]

To be sure, Herndon's cause was not the first to use mass politics or direct action, nor was it the first to do so in the struggle for racial justice in the United States. Mass protest has a long history in the United States going back to the mass protests by colonists against British rule.[91] The Abolitionist Movement used mass mailings to the South, mass petitions to Congress, mass speeches and rallies, and more in its push to end slavery. The Women's Suffrage Movement also used strategies of mass protest and eventually succeeded in amending the US Constitution. The National Organization for Women notes that "In 1914 and 1915, Black leftist Lucy Parsons led mass demonstrations of homeless and unemployed people in San Francisco and Chicago. In 1917, black women in white dresses were prominent in the front lines of a 15,000-person march in New York City protesting lynchings and racial discrimination."[92] The labor movement used mass protest to support worker rights and government regulatory legislation. African Americans boycotted segregated public transportation across the South in in the wake of the *Plessy v. Ferguson* (1896) decision. A grassroots campaign in Harlem produced a vibrant intellectual and activist black community and culture.[93] In the first two decades of the twentieth century black scholar and activist W. E. B. Du Bois and black nationalist Marcus Garvey provided popular intellectual and organizational structures for black mass action.[94] The National Negro Congress, founded during the Great Depression, sought to unite the working class in the struggle for workers' rights and racial justice.[95]

Previous racial justice movements largely failed to achieve their explicit and immediate goals, but they created a political and social context in which rapidly growing pro-labor, immigrant, and religious minority groups (especially Catholics and Jews) could unite with blacks to seek "a stronger right to free speech in order to protect their various self-interests."[96] Opponents of Roosevelt's New Deal had argued that its expansion of federal power would result in civil liberties violations, but the reverse happened:

> In the latter half of the 1930s, the labor movement's key strategic shift—seeking federal government involvement—helped bring free speech to the forefront of the American political agenda. Labor's new strategy resulted in an alliance with immigrant and religious minority groups as the election of 1936 approached. The interest in free speech shared by these overlapping groups exerted political pressure both at the state and federal level and led to some dramatic free speech reforms following the 1936 election.[97]

Roosevelt's 1936 election, winning 61 percent of the national vote and carrying all but two states, reflected support not only for the economic New Deal but a New Deal for free speech. After years of striking down New Deal legislation as unconstitutional infringements of individual economic rights, the Court upheld the Wagner Act in 1937. After years of upholding speech-based convictions for political dissidents (typically labor organizing immigrants), the Court reversed

Herndon's conviction in 1937. Georgia dropped all pending cases under the statute used to convict Herndon. The Justice Department began investigating complaints of official and vigilante suppression of labor organizing and established a special unit in its Criminal Division to address alleged violations of civil rights and liberties.

The ILD's mass politics strategy was crucial to Herndon's release. A black newspaper declared that if not for the ILD, "Herndon would have been wearing a number instead of civilian clothes"; Charles Martin observes, "The protest campaign built around the Herndon case, like that of Scottsboro, represented a growing awakening on the part of black America and its allies to the virtues of direct action and militant struggle, a discovery in which the ILD played an important, constructive, and hitherto underestimated role."[98] Dora Apel notes the ILD's mass protest "succeeded in widely publicizing the Scottsboro and Herndon cases and in gaining mass support for them, which ultimately influenced the political environment in which legal decisions were made and helped vindicate the black defendants in both cases."[99] Herndon himself wrote, "the Southern ruling class thought that they had just another 'nigger' case . . . but they discovered they had to take notice of millions of protests that came in from the masses all over the world."[100] His case stands out as the first in which mass politics achieved a major victory for black equality and black liberty.

CONCLUSION

Angelo Herndon's ordeal was one of the most famous legal sagas of the 1930s and had lasting effects.[101] It was the first case to unite racial equality and liberty and provide a precedent for future First Amendment decisions that continued to unite racial equality and liberty during the civil rights era. *Herndon v. Lowry* (1937) has been cited in more than 320 decisions by US courts,[102] but its legal significance might best be thought of not in terms of what new doctrines or arguments it added to the legal landscape but what a tragic reversal in racial equality and liberty it would have been if the Supreme Court had upheld his conviction. The death penalty would have been legally available in any state to execute black political dissidents whose speech had a "bad tendency." Moreover, its success using race neutrality in its legal arguments combined with race-conscious mass politics to provide models that were used successfully in future cases.

If I am right about the importance of Herndon's case, one might well wonder: why do the broader issues in his case get so little attention? Why have the legal, historical, social, and educational filters on racial justice focused on the Scottsboro Boys or later civil rights–era cases rather than Herndon's ordeal except to note its incremental role in First Amendment jurisprudence? I do not think Herndon's relegation to the margins was accidental.[103] He was an outspoken and targeted black dissident, which raises the issue of black political imprisonment, a far more complex and controversial issue than the false rape accusations and racist trials of the Scottsboro Boys or the antisegregation protests of the civil rights era. His being communist raises questions about the problems and crises of capitalism, especially for people of color. His opposition to the individualist, capitalist value system in favor of a more collectivist value system focusing on the disadvantaged and stressing solidarity in the struggle against racial and economic oppression posed a threat to US orthodoxy that the Scottsboro Boys and civil rights cases did not.

There have been attempts to revive Herndon's story beyond Charles Martin's excellent book and Kendall Thomas's insightful article. For example, new editions of *Let Me Live* with introductions by notable scholars were published in 1969 and 2007.[104] In 1991 a loose adaptation of Herndon's ordeal in jail was performed by a Working Theater production in New York.[105] But Herndon fell by the wayside after his case was won and done.[106] The ILD, ACLU, NAACP, and other supporters moved on to new cases and causes. Herndon married Joyce M. Chellis in 1938 and moved to Harlem to pursue a career, but he began to lose faith in the CPUSA in the wake of the 1939 Nazi–Soviet Pact and his literary aspirations fizzled. His coediting the *Negro Quarterly* with Ralph Ellison in 1943 lasted only for four issues, and his stint as editor-in-chief of *The People's Advocate*, published by the Negro Publication Society of America, ended in 1944. Herndon moved to the Midwest and disappeared from public notice. *Let Me Live* fell into obscurity. In 1997, Angelo Herndon died far from the limelight in Sweet Home, Arkansas, but his brave stand as a young man fighting for racial liberty and equality should not be forgotten.

CHAPTER 3

The Civil Rights Movement

Civil liberties and civil rights are not separable.
—Carey McWilliams[1]

Soon after the pivotal *Herndon* decision in 1937, the pursuit of racial equality became identified with civil rights, while the protection of First Amendment rights became identified with civil liberty. From the late 1930s to the early 1970s, civil rights and civil liberties expanded in dramatic and unprecedented ways that made evident their inseparability through a mutual commitment to greater inclusion and participation and opposition to orthodoxy. This chapter refers to this era and these developments as the civil rights era and civil rights movement.[2] Lawyers involved in the pursuit of racial equality and liberty during this time had to convince the US Supreme Court to abandon the "separate but equal" doctrine regarding civil rights and "learn and make an entirely new body of law dealing with freedom of expression."[3] The legal changes predominantly stemmed from Supreme Court decisions eroding or overturning precedents restricting liberty and equality. Although the legal changes were important, they did not cause substantial social change by themselves; rather, they combined with mass protests dwarfing the scale of the *Herndon* protests and political, economic, and social developments to advance racial equality and liberty.[4]

The civil rights era successes required tremendous effort and great sacrifice. Tom Watson observes, "There is a natural tendency to perfect our history—to purify its hard lessons and knock the edges off the stories. This makes it more easily digestible to be sure—but it also obscures the depth of the struggle."[5] It took a thousand US Army paratroopers, thousands of National Guardsmen, and a Supreme Court decision to integrate nine black students into Central High School in Little Rock, Arkansas, in 1957, and that was only the beginning of that saga.[6] White mobs and vigilantes murdered blacks and their supporters, bombed churches and homes, beat and terrorized people, and so on.[7] In many cases, white witnesses and government officials condoned the actions, turned a blind eye, or were intimidated into silence. A nearly unanimous Southern congressional bloc (101 of 104 elected representatives) signed the 1956 "Southern Manifesto" refusing to abide by the Supreme Court's order to integrate public schools in *Brown v. Board of Education*. Southern schools, state and local officials, and state judges defied federal court holdings. Civil rights lawyers had to conduct a protracted campaign state by state, county by county, city by city. Racial segregation in the South was instituted by law and custom, and violators were routinely arrested, convicted, and fined or imprisoned for trespass, breach of the peace, or whatever other charge was convenient.[8] Southern officials deployed a variety of legal tactics to combat the civil rights movement, requiring civil rights organizations to disclose members, barring lawyers from seeking civil rights clients, using school discipline rules to punish student protesters, regulating and arresting protesters, prosecuting civil rights advocates for tax evasion, and appealing to trespass and libel laws to prosecute and silence civil rights advocates.[9] Desegregation supporters were blacklisted, and guides were distributed to registrars explaining how to prevent blacks from voting. Many white Southerners agreed with the "bitter-end defiance" advocated by Mississippi newspapers opposing the admission of James Meredith to the University of Mississippi, thus integrating the college. This defiance led to a deadly firefight in Oxford in which hundreds of white supremacists attacked federal marshals with stones, bottles filled with acid or flaming gasoline, bricks, fists, guns, a bulldozer, a firetruck, and cars as state police watched. The battle subsided only when federal troops arrived seven hours later. Across the South, NAACP officials were assaulted and even murdered.[10] In Mississippi's racial violence during the summer of 1964, there were thirty-five shootings, sixty-five bombings, eighty beatings, and six murders.[11]

My study of this transformative and tumultuous era is organized in five sections. The first three sections examine civil rights and liberties from 1938 to 1959, covering civil rights and the judiciary, civil rights and the executive branch, and civil liberties. During this period, the federal judiciary increasingly protected civil rights in employment, education, travel accommodations, housing, marriage, voting, police procedure, and more; advancements in civil liberties came at a slower pace. The era began with a landmark Supreme Court decision in 1938 upholding the right of a black civil rights organization to conduct an economic boycott of a private business (continuing *Herndon*'s conjunction of equality and liberty), but from the early 1940s to the late 1950s, organizations pursuing racial justice retreated from active pursuit of civil liberties to avoid getting snagged in the communist witch hunt initiated by the Smith Act of 1940 and led by the House Un-American Activities Committee and Senator Joseph McCarthy.[12] As a result, the civil liberty legal victories in that time involved religious minorities and labor organizations rather than African Americans. The executive branch was slower than the judiciary to embrace civil rights, and to the extent it did so, it frequently did so only to further other domestic and foreign policy objectives. The fourth section explores the relationship between civil rights and liberties from 1960 to 1972, when courts delivered a series of stunning victories for African American equality and liberty. Indeed, some refer to this era as a Second Reconstruction or a civil rights revolution. [13] The victories were not limited to First Amendment cases or to African Americans, but the forms of protests used by African Americans and their supporters in pursuit of equality and the judicial decisions upholding and expanding the right to protest and dissent played critical roles in increasing equality and liberty during this celebrated era. First Amendment scholar Harry Kalven Jr. observed in his 1965 book *The Negro and the First Amendment* that the 1960s movement for racial equality won back First Amendment rights for all citizens that had been lost during the 1950s anticommunist hysteria, but the movement did more than win back rights, it expanded them. The final section addresses civil rights icon Thurgood Marshall's commitment to the inseparability of equality and liberty. An examination of the era further reveals how liberty and equality are mutually supportive in virtue of their commitment to greater inclusion and participation and opposition to orthodoxy.

CIVIL RIGHTS IN THE JUDICIARY, 1938–1959

Angelo Herndon's Supreme Court victory in 1937 uniting racial equality and liberty was followed the next year by another major ruling combining racial equality and liberty: *New Negro Alliance v. Sanitary Grocery*, 303 US 552 (1938). The case involved a Jobs-For-Negroes boycott.[14] Economic boycotts to promote political or social goals began in the colonial era[15] and were used to protest African American slavery, segregation, and second-class citizenship; organized labor used boycotts to demand better working conditions and pay.[16] The Jobs-For-Negroes movement began in St. Louis in 1929 when the Urban League organized a boycott against a white-owned chain store whose clientele was black but employed no blacks. The movement spread throughout the Midwest and North.

The New Negro Alliance (NNA) was formed in highly segregated Washington, DC, in 1933 to promote African American civic, educational, charitable, and economic interests after a grill manager fired three black workers and replaced them with whites. By picketing and boycotting the business, protesters succeeded in having the three black workers rehired with increased pay and reduced hours. The NNA's next targets included the A&P grocery chain, High Ice Cream Company, People's Drug Store, and Kaufman's Department Store. The NNA promoted its cause through slogans such as "Don't Buy Where You Can't Work" and "Jobs for Negroes" as well as a weekly newspaper. They devised a unique strategy: they conducted research to determine the percentage of black customers a store had, then lobbied the store to have the same percentage hired as employees; if the store refused, they escalated pressure.[17] When Sanitary Grocery (later Safeway) opened a store in a black neighborhood in 1936 but did not employ blacks or respond to requests to do so, the NNA began a peaceful boycott and picketed to pressure them into hiring blacks in managerial and sales positions in their 255 stores, especially those in black neighborhoods.

Sanitary Grocery immediately sought a court injunction to force the NNA to cease its protest. They claimed it was an "unlawful conspiracy in restraint of trade" and "danger to the life and health of the company's employees and customers." The trial judge granted the injunction on the basis that the relevant law (the Norris-LaGuardia Act[18]) did not protect the NNA's boycott because the dispute was not between an employer and employees; between a labor union, employee, and employer; or even between an employer and persons seeking employment. When the Court of Appeals agreed, the NNA sought relief from the US Supreme Court.

The Supreme Court voted 6–2 to overturn the lower court injunction. The NNA could legally boycott and picket because the Norris-LaGuardia Act applied to "any controversy concerning terms or conditions of employment . . . regardless of whether or not the disputants stand in proximate relation of employer and employee" and covers parties who have "a direct or indirect interest." According to Justice Roberts (writing the majority opinion just as he did for *Herndon*), "The desire for fair and equitable conditions of employment on the part of persons of any race, color or persuasion, and the removal of discrimination against them by reason of their race or religious beliefs is quite as important to those concerned as fairness and equity in terms of conditions of employment can be to trade or craft unions or any form of labor organization or association."[19] As long as the NNA did not engage in fraud, breach of the peace, or other illegal activity, its members were free to advertise and disseminate facts and information regarding Sanitary Grocery's employment practices and peacefully persuade others.

After winning the case, the NNA undertook boycotts targeting Safeway Grocery (Sanitary Grocery's new name) and People's Drug Store, but these boycotts failed and the organization eventually withered and disbanded. The NNA as an organization and the 1938 Supreme Court decision still had important impacts. The NNA estimated it secured more than 5,000 jobs for blacks in more than fifty businesses in Washington, DC, and numerous NNA officials or members went on to become influential civil rights advocates. Consider a few examples. Belford Lawson Jr. argued eight cases to the US Supreme Court. John Davis became a political scientist who headed the 200-member research team supporting the NAACP's *Brown v. Board* argument. Walter Washington was elected the first black mayor of Washington, DC. Eugene Davidson became head of the DC chapter of NAACP. William Hastie became the first black to be appointed to a US Court of Appeals and was governor of the US Virgin Islands. Moreover, the *New Negro Alliance* ruling greatly encouraged blacks by "declaring that the picketing of firms that refused to employ African Americans was a legal technique for securing relief."[20] "Buy black" campaigns became an integral part of the African American protest against employment discrimination in cities across the North for the next twenty years—protests that launched the careers of more civil rights advocates such as Adam Clayton Powell Jr., the first African American to be elected to Congress from New York.[21] The attention the *NNA* decision brought to racial discrimination in employment later helped A. Philip Randolph, head of the Brotherhood of Sleeping Car Porters, pressure President Franklin Roosevelt into signing Executive Order 8802 in 1941 establishing a Fair Employment Practices Committee to investigate racial discrimination in employment.[22]

The *NNA* decision also affected the law. By 1943 free speech was acknowledged to be the doctrinal protection for peaceful picketing.[23] *NNA*—cited in more than 270 cases—provided a precedent and stimulus for future African American economic boycotts in the cause of racial equality. Consider three major examples. The black boycott of segregated buses in Montgomery, Alabama, in 1955 led to a major legal victory for integration in *Browder v. Gayle*, 352 US 903 (1956). According to John Hope Franklin and Evelyn Brooks Higginbotham, the Montgomery boycott was "the first successful example of a mass nonviolent resistance in the United States" and played a major role in rejuvenating the struggle for black freedom.[24] The boycott of white businesses in

Tuskegee, Alabama, beginning in 1957 led to a major legal victory for African American voting rights by overturning racial gerrymandering in *Gomillion v. Lightfoot*, 364 US 339 (1960). In *NAACP v. Claiborne Hardware*, 458 US 886 (1982), the Court rejected the claim that protesters were economically liable for lost business during a seven-year boycott in a case that would have bankrupted the NAACP had it lost. This would have been disastrous for the advancement of civil rights because the NAACP "for most of [the twentieth] century . . . was the only civil rights organization that made a difference."[25] The *NNA* decision combined with other First Amendment decisions—such as the public forum protections announced in *Hague v. CIO*, 307 US 496 (1939)—to provide "growing legal protections for public political actions such as mass demonstrations."[26]

In sum, the NNA played a crucial role in establishing economic boycotts as expressive activities widely considered to "advance historically recognized First Amendment goals that are critical to our democracy" by providing information to voters, notifying the targeted person or organization that voters disagree with it, providing voters with a way to dissent when government is unresponsive, and enabling dissenters to participate in politics rather than go underground or resort to violence.[27]

As fear of socialists and communists led to legislative inquiries and criminal prosecutions of dissident political speech and membership in the 1940s and early 1950s, organizations devoted to racial justice began to focus on civil rights (equality) cases to avoid association with unpopular civil liberty (free speech) cases. The NAACP led the legal attack on American apartheid and focused on public education. The NAACP's initial strategy did not directly challenge the "separate but equal" doctrine but sought to indirectly undermine it through a series of cases forcing schools to integrate because they would not spend the money to provide the equal education required by law. The test case was *Murray v. Pearson*, 169 MD 478 (1936), in which the state court of appeals required the University of Maryland to integrate its law school. The US Supreme Court soon followed with its landmark decision *Missouri ex. rel. Gaines v. Canada*, 305 US 337 (1938), requiring the University of Missouri to integrate its law school. *Gaines* was followed by *Sipuel v. Oklahoma*, 332 US 631 (1948) (integrating University of Oklahoma law school); *Johnson v. Kentucky*, 83 F. Supp. 707 (E.D. KY 1949) (integrating University of Kentucky graduate program in history); *Sweatt v. Painter*, 339 US 629 (1950) (integrating University of Texas law school); and *McLaurin v. Oklahoma*, 339 US 637 (1950) (integrating University of Oklahoma education graduate program). After laying this legal groundwork,[28] the NAACP went after the separate but equal doctrine itself. *Brown v. Board of Education*, 347 US 483 (1954) (*Brown* I) was the most important civil rights decision of the era. *Brown* I unanimously struck down laws requiring racially segregated K–12 public schools. The next year the court held in *Brown v. Board of Education*, 349 US 294 (1955) (*Brown* II), that schools must integrate "with all deliberate speed."

Unfortunately, "all deliberate speed" turned out to be a lot of deliberation and not much speed. The number of black students attending K–12 schools with whites increased only by about 1 percent a year from 1955 to 1965.[29] Many states and communities as well as federal judges refused to integrate schools, so further judicial rulings were required. For example, *Cooper v. Aaron*, 358 US 1 (1958), reaffirmed federal law supremacy over state law in requiring Little Rock, Arkansas, integrate its public schools. School districts still doggedly sought alternatives to integration through discriminatory pupil assignment and freedom of choice schemes or closing public schools while providing vouchers for white students to attend segregated private schools. Some continued to refuse to integrate even after further courtroom victories for integration, the threat of segregated schools losing federal funds after passage of the Civil Right Act of 1964, and the Supreme Court holding in *Alexander v. Holmes County Board of Education*, 396 US 19 (1969), that school integration had to proceed forthwith without further argument or submissions. Another strategy was to open segregated private schools. In Louisiana there were sixteen all-white private schools prior to *Brown*; in the next ten years, the number increased to fifty-three.[30]

Similarly, continued resistance to integration in higher education required further judicial interventions, such as *Lucy v. Adams*, 350 US 1 (1955) (integrating University of Alabama); *Holmes v. Danner*, 191 F. Supp. 385 (M.D. GA 1961) (integrating University of Georgia), *Meredith v. Fair*, 313 F.2d 532 (5th Cir. 1962) (integrating University of Mississippi); *Gantt v. Clemson*, 320 F.2d 611 (4th Cir. 1963) (integrating Clemson Agricultural College of South Carolina); and *Parker v. Franklin*, 331 F.2d 841 (5th Cir. 1964) (integrating Auburn University).

Although public education was a primary focus, the attack on segregation and discrimination proceeded in many other areas. *Abbington v. Louisville*, Case No. 243 (W.D. KY 1941), and *Alston v. Norfolk*, 112 F.2d 992 (4th Cir. 1940), required schools to provide equal pay to black teachers. Courts continued to strike down police tactics to coerce confessions from black suspects in *Chambers v. Florida*, 309 US 227 (1940), and *Fikes v. Alabama*, 352 US 191

(1957). Courts began desegregating public transportation in *Mitchell v. United States*, 313 US 80 (1941) (integrating Arkansas interstate railcars); *Morgan v. Virginia*, 328 US 373 (1946) (integrating Virginia interstate buses), *Henderson v. United States*, 339 US 816 (1950) (integrating interstate railroad dining cars); and *Browder v. Gayle*, 352 US 903 (1956) (integrating Montgomery, Alabama, city buses). The Supreme Court banned racial exclusion in jury selection in *Patton v. Mississippi*, 332 US 463 (1947). It banned racial covenants in real estate in *Shelley v. Kraemer*, 334 US 1 (1948), and *Barrows v. Jackson*, 346 US 249 (1953). It struck down racially discriminatory state voting regulations in *Lane v. Wilson*, 307 US 268 (1939), and *Smith v. Allwright*, 321 US 649 (1944).[31] The Court unanimously held that the Railway Labor Act forbid labor unions from racial discrimination in *Steele v. Louisville and Nashville Railroad*, 323 US 192 (1944), and *Tunstall v. Brotherhood of Locomotive Firemen and Engineers*, 323 US 210 (1944).

CIVIL RIGHTS AND THE EXECUTIVE BRANCH, 1938–59

The executive branch played a role in advancing African American civil rights, although at a slower pace and to a lesser degree than the federal judiciary. In 1941, President Roosevelt established a "Black Cabinet" to advise him on racial matters and issued Executive Order 8802 establishing the Federal Employment Practices Committee (FEPC) and banning racial discrimination in employment in the national defense industry. In 1943, Roosevelt's Executive Order 9346 expanded the FEPC's ability to get business and industry to comply with desegregated employment. Although white men were the primary beneficiaries of Roosevelt's New Deal programs,[32] some programs benefited African Americans. For example, in 1933 there were 50,000 African Americans on the federal payroll; in 1946 there were approximately 200,000.[33] The Farm Security Administration, established in 1937, provided benefits to black sharecroppers and enabled many to own land for the first time.[34] As a result, African Americans began to abandon their traditional support for Lincoln's Republican Party. In the 1932 presidential election, blacks voted for Hoover over Roosevelt by about an eight-to-two margin. In 1936 blacks continued to vote predominantly for Republicans for state and local office but voted for incumbent Roosevelt over Republican Alf Landon by a seven-to-three margin. By 1940 blacks began to identify as Democrats and voted for Roosevelt by an eight-to-two margin.

President Harry Truman is considered to be the most sympathetic to racial equality of the presidents in this the era. He issued a series of Executive

Orders advancing civil rights. Executive Order 9808 in 1946 established the President's Committee on Civil Rights to make recommendations advancing civil rights and civil rights legislation. Executive Orders 9980 and 9981 in 1948 desegregated the federal workforce and armed forces. During the Korean War, integration of military units increased from 6 percent to 30 percent and a military report declared integration was an overall gain for the army.[35] Truman also appointed several committees to investigate racial issues. The Committee on Civil Rights 1947 report, *To Secure These Rights*, demanded an end to segregation across the board and had "unparalleled and historic impact" by setting the agenda for future civil rights reform.[36]

President Dwight Eisenhower is viewed by most historians as a president who took action on behalf of African Americans only when some larger political objective required it, rather than out of a sense of racial justice.[37] Whatever his motives, Eisenhower signed Executive Order 10590 in 1955 establishing the President's Committee on Government Employment Policy to strengthen the effort to desegregate the federal workforce, desegregated the District of Columbia and its schools, authorized military force to uphold judicial degrees requiring school integration, proposed and secured passage of the first civil rights legislation in eighty years in 1957, and appointed progressive judges at all federal levels (including five to the Supreme Court).

The civil rights and liberties agendas of Presidents Roosevelt, Truman, and Eisenhower were influenced by many domestic factors. For example, millions of blacks left their disenfranchised and impoverished status in the rural South to live in voting precincts and work better jobs in the urban, industrialized North and Midwest between 1940 and 1960. Blacks played a notable role in World War I and II. Black entertainers, athletes, and artists became popular. Technological advancements, increased mobility, and other factors contributed to a decline in local and regional identity, increased awareness of problems and issues across the country and the formation of a national culture.

International factors were also crucial to the advancement of civil rights. The federal government sought to lead the free world in the Cold War era but realized we could not plausibly claim to do so if African Americans (and others) were second-class citizens. In short, Jim Crow became a foreign policy liability after World War II. Michael Klarman notes,

> The war against Nazi fascism had impelled many Americans to reevaluate their racial preconceptions in an effort to clarify . . . how and why "Hitler's creed" was any different from "what the South believed." Furthermore, the ensuing Cold War required America to demonstrate

> to (mostly non-Caucasian) Third World nations that democratic capitalism was a superior system to communism, notwithstanding America's long history of racial oppression. This so-called "Cold War Imperative" for racial change played an enormous role in the civil rights calculations of the Truman, Eisenhower, and Kennedy administrations.[38]

Mary Dudziak writes, "As presidents and secretaries of state from 1946 to the mid-1960s worried about the impact of race discrimination on U.S. prestige abroad, civil rights reform came to be seen as crucial to U.S. foreign relations."[39] Racial progress—at least on paper and in the courtroom—became necessary to gain advantage in the Cold War and secure allies in Asia and Africa. Foreign governments and citizens watched closely as the civil rights movement unfolded. As the Herndon case demonstrated, international objections to US racist practices were not new to this era, but they gained greater importance as the United States competed with the Soviet Union for international power and influence. Consider some examples addressed by Dudziak in *Cold War Civil Rights*.

When black veterans of World War II returned home in 1946, they were met by a wave of violence in the South intended to "keep them in their place." The chief of police in Aiken, South Carolina, brutally beat veteran Isaac Woodard with his nightstick, permanently blinding him. The chief was acquitted by a white jury to the cheers of the white courtroom audience. Macio Snipes, a veteran and the only African American to vote in his district in Georgia, was murdered by four whites. Veteran George Dorsey and three other blacks were dragged from their car and executed by a mob near Monroe, Georgia. In response to the Dorsey murder, so many letters and telegrams protesting the murders came to the US Department of Justice that Attorney General Tom Clark held a press conference to demand rule of law and condemn mob violence. However, no white witnesses were willing to testify, so the investigation stalled. This led to demonstrations and critical headlines across the nation and world. California Republican Senator William Knowland called it a "blot on the entire United States of America." The world (except white South Africans) readily saw the hypocrisy of fighting a war to defeat the Nazi "master race" aggression and bring the "four freedoms" (freedom of expression, freedom of religion, freedom from want, and freedom from fear) to the world while upholding white supremacy at home.

The racist stain on the nation spread when the NAACP filed a petition titled "An Appeal to the World"—authored principally by W. E. B. Du Bois—with the United Nations the next year protesting the treatment of blacks in the

United States. The petition was an international sensation covered around the globe and exploited by the Soviets. In response, President Truman announced, "If we wish to inspire the people of the world whose freedom is in jeopardy, we must correct the remaining imperfections in our practice of democracy."[40] An information agency was created for a Cold War propaganda battle against the Soviets in which our nation's story was framed as steady progress against racism delivered by a democratic, capitalist government.[41]

International opinion, particularly in the postcolonial nations in South America, Africa, and Asia, improved in response to the Supreme Court's decision in *Brown v. Board* in 1954. It was a turning point in foreign skepticism toward US race policies and relations because it was perceived to be concrete evidence that America was making genuine racial progress. Two incidents in 1957 almost destroyed that perception. In one case, Jimmy Wilson, a black handyman who worked occasionally for an elderly white woman, was sentenced to death for stealing $1.95 from her. When the Alabama Supreme Court upheld the decision, his case quickly attracted national and international headlines and petitions and protests from governments, organizations, and individuals from such nations as Ethiopia, Ghana, Norway, Israel, Netherlands, Jamaica, Australia, Italy, Canada, and England. US embassies around the world sent a flood of dispatches about the case. Alabama Governor James "Big Jim" Folsom received about a thousand letters a day from around the world protesting Wilson's punishment. Pressure was relieved only when Folsom announced a reprieve for Wilson.

The second and more significant case was the struggle to integrate Little Rock's Central High School. A federal district court ordered the city's schools to integrate, but when nine black students came to attend, they were confronted by an angry mob and turned away by the Arkansas National Guard by order of Governor Orval Faubus. Coverage of the Little Rock crisis blanketed the international media as photos of troops in full battle dress with bayonetted rifles and tear gas denying the children access to the school circulated around the world.[42] The federal court ordered the state troops away from the school, but when eight black students came to school on September 23, city police had to shield them from the angry white mob. When violence and the threat of violence continued, officials secretly removed the students from school mid-day. Finally, President Eisenhower ordered 1,000 federal troops to carry out the federal court's orders. The integration of the school and the use of troops to ensure obedience to law and order was praised in countries such as the Netherlands, Indonesia, France, Uganda, Luxembourg, Egypt, Brazil, and Mozambique. However, international criticism lit up again when a new legal challenge to integration resulted in a decision to delay the process, and the governor and legislature contrived to enact laws allowing Little Rock to vote to close the public school and fund whites-only private schools. As a result, foreign opinion of the United States took a nosedive. Of Norwegians, 82 percent had a bad or very bad impression of the United States; this was also true for 66 percent in Great Britain, 65 percent in France, and 53 percent in West Germany. International opinion only improved after the Supreme Court unanimously held in *Cooper v. Aaron* that Arkansas had to comply with federal law, that desegregation was the law of the land, and *Brown v. Board* was the unanimous decision of twelve justices (nine in the original trial in 1953 and three more in 1954).

The role of international pressure in advancing racial equality declined by the mid-1960s. There were enough civil rights victories to appease many international critics and the escalating conflict in Vietnam began to draw the lion's share of international notice. Attention began to shift from civil rights to human rights.[43] Foreign interest declined as the civil rights coalition fragmented, "black power" advocates demanded more radical changes, divisions over tactics and objectives arose between activists, inner-city riots exploded across the country, and Richard Nixon devised his "Southern strategy" to win the White House and slow or reverse gains in racial equality.

CIVIL LIBERTIES, 1938–59

From the late 1930s to the mid-1940s, there were victories in some religious expression and labor cases, but civil liberties did not see gains equivalent to civil rights. *Lovell v. City of Griffin*, 303 US 444 (1938), and *Cantwell v. Connecticut*, 310 US 296 (1940), struck down laws requiring approval to distribute pamphlets. *West Virginia v. State Board of Ed. v. Barnette*, 319 US 624 (1943), ended compulsory flag salutes in schools. *Taylor v. Mississippi*, 319 US 583 (1943), held the state could not punish antiwar speech that lacked a sinister purpose, failed to incite subversion, or failed to create a clear and present danger. *Marsh v. Alabama*, 326 US 501 (1946), struck down trespass convictions of Jehovah's Witnesses proselytizing in Chickasaw, Alabama, a private company town. *Hague v. CIO*, 307 US 496 (1939), struck down a city ordinance banning organized labor speech. *Schneider v. New Jersey*, 308 US 147 (1939) (combining four cases), struck down city antilitter bans on distributing hand bills. *Thornhill v. Alabama*, 310 US 88 (1940), struck down a law banning only labor picketing. *Thomas v. Collins*, 323 US 516 (1945), struck down application of a state regulation restricting labor organizing speech. *Snyder v. Milwaukee*, 308 US 147 (1939) (combining four cases), provided protections for public distribution of pamphlets and handbills. The Supreme Court protected freedom of the press in *Pennekamp v. Florida*, 328 US 331 (1946), and *Craig v. Harney*, 331 US 367 (1947).

The *CIO* decision had special importance for blacks for three reasons.[44] First, the CIO was the only labor organization in that era to have a policy against racial discrimination. Second, the CIO organized unskilled labor, which included most black labor. Third, the CIO worked extensively with black civil rights groups.

The Supreme Court also accepted some speech restrictions. *Cox v. New Hampshire*, 312 US 569 (1941), upheld reasonable time, place, and manner restrictions. *Chaplinsky v. New Hampshire*, 315 US 568 (1944), created the "fighting words" category of unprotected speech. *Feiner v. New York*, 340 US 315 (1951), upheld an incitement conviction for a student labor organizer addressing a racially mixed crowd that officials claimed would lead to a riot. *Dennis v. United States*, 341 US 494 (1951), upheld convictions of communist officials for attempting to overthrow the government merely by being members of the party. The Smith Act of 1940—the basis for the *Dennis* convictions—aimed to undermine or destroy the communist and socialist movement in the United States and resulted in convictions of more than 200 people. The House Un-American Activities Committee became a standing committee in 1945 and used its authority to threaten, intimidate, blacklist, and otherwise punish private citizens, public employees, and organizations with suspected communist ties. Thus, in 1952 Robert Hutchins praised the great progress made in advancing "the rights of the Negro" but lamented the ground lost in the "freedom to differ and espouse unpopular causes."[45] By 1953, some scholars were announcing the First Amendment was in "hibernation,"[46] or even a "fiction."[47]

Congress's lack of interest in civil liberty was matched by its inability to improve civil rights. Due to the political clout of the Southern voting bloc, Congress did the least of the three branches of federal government to advance civil rights from the late 1930s to the late 1950s. Most notably, they failed to pass antilynching and integration legislation. Its first meaningful action was the Civil Rights Act of 1957, a watered-down bill focused on providing equal voting rights to African Americans. It was the first federal civil rights legislation since the 1870s and passed only after a record-setting twenty-four-hour, eighteen-minute filibuster by the outspoken and influential segregationist Senator Strom Thurmond of South Carolina.[48]

Christopher Schmidt convincingly argues that the major advocates of racial equality avoided most civil liberty cases in this rabid antiradical era to escape guilt by association.[49] The NAACP barred communists from membership and avoided any association with the CPUSA. This motivation led Thurgood Marshall to resign from the National Lawyers Guild. Indeed, the modern distinction between civil rights (legal claims involving the unequal treatment of different groups) and civil liberties (legal claims protecting persons from government restrictions or intrusion) arose for this reason. The phrases "civil rights" and "civil liberties" had been used interchangeably and with a variety of meanings from their coinage in the post–Civil War era to the early 1940s. They were distinguished in the 1940s because of the political need for advocates of racial equality to distance themselves from liberty claims by political radicals and the absence of mass protest supporting racial equality.

The attempt to separate civil rights from civil liberty faced significant criticism[50] and could not last. In *Watkins v. United States*, 354 US 178 (1957), the US Supreme Court ruled 6–1 that congressional committees did not have unlimited power to compel testimony. The case involved a United Auto Worker organizer's refusal to testify to the HUAC about whether past associates were communists. In another 6–1 decision, *Yates v. United States*, 354 US 298 (1957), overturned convictions of fourteen communist officials because their party membership and advocacy were not a clear and present danger.[51] *One, Inc. v. Oleson*, 355 US 371 (1958)—a landmark decision for LGBTQ rights[52]—unanimously struck down an obscenity conviction for a progay magazine.

Most important, the US Supreme Court reunited African American civil liberty and civil rights in *NAACP v. Alabama*, 357 US 449 (1958). The NAACP's many legal victories, growing membership, and increased media and social influence led Southern state officials to outlaw or undermine the group. Appealing to a state law requiring foreign corporations to qualify with the state, in 1956 the Alabama attorney general demanded that the NAACP submit qualifying information, including its membership list. The NAACP claimed it was exempt from the statute and refused to comply. The attorney general sought a state court injunction banning the NAACP from the state on the grounds that its refusal to comply would cause irreparable injury to the property and civil rights of Alabamans. The state court granted the injunction and the NAACP appealed. This led to a complicated series of legal maneuvers by the state and the NAACP as well as judicial proceedings in which the state continually attempted to overrule or subvert federal court rulings. Finally, the US Supreme Court took the case on its merits: the state demanded the NAACP disclose its members to qualify to do business, whereas the NAACP refused to do so based on the fear that its members, if disclosed, would suffer serious repercussions. In a landmark decision, the Supreme Court ruled that the state could not compel disclosure of members because that violates First Amendment freedom of association and the right to pursue lawful private interests.

The NAACP's legal ordeal in Alabama and its right to do business there was not finally settled until *NAACP v. Alabama*, 377 US 288 (1964), due to a related state contempt of court ruling, but the 1958 case served as precedent to overturn other attempts to outlaw or undermine the NAACP's lawful activities. *Bates v. Little Rock*, 361 US 516 (1960), struck down tax exemption regulation requiring membership disclosure. *Shelton v. Tucker*, 364 US 479 (1960), struck down a state law requiring teachers to annually disclose organization memberships. *Louisiana v. NAACP*, 366 US 293 (1961), struck down a state law requiring organizations to provide membership lists and officials to sign noncommunist affidavits. *NAACP v. Button*, 371 US 415 (1963), struck down state laws attempting to restrict the ability of the NAACP to file lawsuits. *Gibson v Florida Legislative Investigative Committee*, 372 US 539 (1963), held that legislative committees cannot compel a subpoenaed witness to disclose organizational members. Yet *NAACP v. Alabama* (1958) and its progeny are just the tip of the iceberg regarding the inseparability of equality (civil rights) and liberty (civil liberties) during the 1960s.

CIVIL RIGHTS AND LIBERTIES, 1960–72

Civil rights and liberties progressed in many ways during the 1960s. The Civil Rights Act of 1964 is the most prominent legislative example. It outlawed discrimination in education and employment based on race, color, religion, sex, or national origin; unequal application of voter registration requirements; and racial segregation in education, employment, and public accommodations. Courts played a crucial role in upholding and interpreting the act. For example, *Watson v. Memphis*, 373 US 526 (1963), struck down laws segregating public parks. *Willis v. Pickwick Restaurants*, 231 F. Supp. 396 (1964), required restaurants open to the public to desegregate. *Loving v. Virginia*, 388 US 1 (1967), struck down antimiscegenation laws. *Griggs v. Duke Power Company*, 401 US 424 (1971), struck down discriminatory employment and promotion tests. The advances in civil rights were fueled in significant measure by the exercise of, protection of, and expansion of civil liberties.[53] *Talley v. California*, 362 US 60 (1960), gave anonymous fliers constitutional protection in upholding a civil rights activist's liberty to distribute an anonymous handbill. *Organization for a Better Austin v. Keefe*, 402 US 415 (1971), upheld the right of an integrationist community group to protest a racist real estate "blockbuster" by distributing pamphlets in his neighborhood. *Street v. New York*, 394 US 576 (1969), struck down application of state flag desecration law to Sidney Street's burning an American flag to protest the attempted murder of James Meredith, the student who broke the University of Mississippi color barrier. *Gregory v. Chicago*, 394 US 111 (1969), upheld the right of entertainer Dick Gregory and others to protest school segregation via a march from the city hall to the mayor's residence. *Shuttlesworth v. City of Birmingham*, 394 US 147 (1969), protected civil rights marchers by striking down a city ordinance requiring a permit for parades or processions. *Gooding v. Wilson*, 405 US 518 (1972), overturned the breach of the peace conviction of a black Vietnam War protester. The tight bond between civil rights and civil liberties is illustrated in the turbulent Freedom Riders movement in 1961, in which black and white protesters rode together to oppose segregation in transportation,[54] and the University of California-Berkeley Free Speech movement in 1964, initiated by a campus crackdown on civil rights expression.[55] To give the inseparability thesis some depth to go with this breadth, this section focuses on three landmark Supreme Court decisions advancing liberty and equality: *Brown v. Louisiana* (1966), *Edwards v. South Carolina* (1963), and *New York Times v. Sullivan* (1964).

The African American struggle for equality reignited in 1960 when a new form of protest, the sit-in, inspired America's youth to take action.[56] The new generation of activists, dedicated to direct action, surprised the civil rights old guard—organizations such as the NAACP and Congress for Racial Equality—as well as social scientists and historians.[57] College and high school students were unwilling to wait for legislatures to pass laws or courts to issue decisions. They sought immediate change from the ground up, and their impact was immense. Jack Greenberg notes, "in 1960 the [sit-in] movement began a pervasive transformation of America with regard to race, not merely in constitutional law, but in the ways people treated each other, whether mandated by law or not. Black people, increasingly joined by whites, spoke up for racial equality in numbers so large and in protests so vigorous that they could not be ignored."[58]

The sit-in movement began on February 1, 1960, when four first-year students—David Richmond, Franklin McCain, Ezell Blair Jr., and Joseph McNeil—attending the historically black Agricultural and Technical College in Greensboro, North Carolina, sat at a whites-only lunch counter in a Woolworth's store and politely asked for cups of coffee.[59] By the end of the week, there were sit-ins in six other North Carolina cities. By the end of the month, there were sit-ins in more than thirty communities in seven states. By spring 1960, there were sit-ins in seventy-eight Southern communities. By the end of 1960, 70,000 people had participated in sit-ins, wade-ins, stand-ups, and sleep-ins to defy segregation in theaters, hotels, public parks, swimming pools, beaches, churches, courtrooms, libraries, art galleries, and more. Although the protesters were routinely nonviolent, many endured verbal and physical abuse from bystanders. Police arrested more than 2,000 protesters on trumped-up charges such as trespass, disturbing the peace, disorderly conduct, loitering, or even assault.[60] Greenberg, who succeeded Thurgood Marshall as chief counsel for the Legal Defense Fund (LDF) in 1961, said the sit-in cases had top priority.[61] Their courageous and nonviolent protest in the face of police and bystander abuse won many admirers and galvanized white student activism and support for civil rights.[62] Sit-ins posed a threat to the South's economy: John Wheeler, a black lawyer heading a Durham, North Carolina, bank, claimed, "the question was whether the South would grant the minority race full citizenship status or commit economic suicide by refusing to do so."[63]

Given the Supreme Court's desegregation decisions, Southern officials decided to arrest protesters on race-neutral charges, such as disturbing the peace, to avoid legal challenges to the segregation laws. Southern state courts routinely upheld the convictions, but the race-neutral strategy took a severe blow when the Supreme Court addressed sit-in protests. *Garner v. Louisiana*, 368 US 157 (1961), combined three cases with the same basic fact pattern. A small group of black students peaceably sat at a whites-only restaurant counter to protest segregation at the establishment. A store employee said they could be served at the Negro counter or they would not be served at all, but the students were not told to leave or that they were causing a disturbance. When they remained at the whites-only area, an employee phoned police. Police ordered the students to move; when they did not, police arrested them for disturbing the peace. However, the Court unanimously ruled that the state violated the Fourteenth Amendment right to due process of law because it failed to provide evidence that the accused engaged in disruptive conduct or that their peaceful and orderly behavior was likely to lead to a breach of the peace by others. Their "mere presence" at the counters got them arrested, and that is not sufficient to justify their arrest or conviction. *Garner* freed the protesters, but it left a key question open: does the First Amendment protect sit-in protests?

The Supreme Court took a monumental step in declaring that peaceful sit-in civil rights protests are constitutionally protected in its 5–4 decision *Brown v. Louisiana*, 383 US 131 (1966). This meant Louisiana had lost all five Supreme Court decisions regarding its convictions of blacks conducting peaceful protest! After *Garner* (1961), the Court overturned convictions for sit-in protesters in *Taylor v. Louisiana*, 370 US 154 (1962);[64] *Lombard v. Louisiana*, 373 US 267 (1963);[65] and *Cox v. Louisiana*, 379 US 536 (1965).[66] The Court also overturned sit-in convictions in other states in two 1963 decisions[67] and in eight 1964 cases.[68] *Brown* overturned the convictions of five students for breach of the peace and failure to obey a police order to disperse. Justice Abe Fortas, writing the lead opinion, held that the protesters could not be convicted merely for failing to obey a police order given (1) prior Court decisions and (2) the Louisiana statute required both a breach of the peace and failure to obey. Nor could they be convicted of breach of the peace because—like the prior sit-in cases—there was no evidence their protest disturbed the peace, was intended to disturb the peace, might have led to a disturbance of the peace, disrupted library activities, or violated any library regulations. However, this time the Court added,

> But there is another and sharper answer which is called for. We are here dealing with an aspect of a basic constitutional right—the right under the First and Fourteenth Amendments guaranteeing freedom of speech and assembly, and freedom to petition the Government for a redress of grievances. . . . [T]hese rights are not confined to verbal expression. They embrace appropriate types of action which certainly include the right in a peaceable and orderly manner to protest by silent and reproachful presence, in a place the protestant has every right to be, the unconstitutional segregation of public facilities.[69]

Thus, the court held that the Louisiana statute was unconstitutionally overbroad: peaceful sit-ins protesting segregation were symbolic speech protected by the First Amendment. *Brown* is cited in more than 290 judicial opinions and—like *Herndon*, *New Negro Alliance*, and *NAACP v. Alabama*—clearly exemplifies how judicial decisions protecting black civil rights protests protected and expanded First Amendment rights and how First Amendment values promoted racial equality.

The fundamental alliance of liberty and equality is demonstrated through the example of civil rights protest marches. African Americans and sympathizers had marched to protest racial inequalities many times before March 12, 1961, but that day should be remembered because it led to a landmark Supreme Court decision. One hundred eighty-seven African American high school and college students met at Zion Baptist Church in Columbia, South Carolina. They marched in groups of about fifteen to the State House grounds to protest racial segregation and discrimination and present a petition of their grievances. A police force of approximately thirty officers, forewarned of the protest, met them at the state capitol and informed them they could peacefully cross the grounds. For the next thirty to forty-five minutes, the students paraded peacefully and orderly around the grounds in single file or two abreast. Many carried placards. As they marched, a crowd of 200–300 onlookers gathered. There was no disturbance by marchers or onlookers, nor any obstruction of pedestrian or vehicular traffic. However, the city manager feared a disturbance was imminent and ordered the students to disperse within fifteen minutes or be arrested. The students stood their ground, singing patriotic and religious songs, clapping their hands, and stomping their feet. When the fifteen minutes passed, police arrested the petitioners for breaching the peace. They were convicted at trial and lost their appeal to the state supreme court. As the case proceeded through the courts, civil rights demonstrations across the country increased. So did related arrests and convictions: in just one week in 1963, 15,000 demonstrators were arrested.[70]

In *Edwards v. South Carolina* (1963) the Supreme Court voted 8–1 to affirm First Amendment protection for demonstrators peacefully protesting racial segregation and discrimination. In the majority opinion, Justice Potter Stewart maintained, "it is clear to us that in arresting, convicting, and punishing the petitioners under the circumstances disclosed by this record, South Carolina infringed the petitioners' constitutionally protected rights of free speech, free assembly, and freedom to petition for a redress of their grievances."[71] The statute under which they were convicted was unduly vague (the state admitted it could not sufficiently define "breach of the peace") and overbroad (because it banned the peaceful expression of disfavored views). Moreover, the Court pointed out *Terminiello v. Chicago*, 337 US 1 (1949), emphasizes First Amendment protection even for speech that stirs people to anger, invites public dispute, or brings about a condition of unrest. Why? At least since *Stromberg v. California* (1931), the Court has held that free political discussion is necessary to ensure government is responsive to the will of the people and to enable change through lawful means. The *Edwards* decision is cited in more than 650 subsequent judicial opinions and provided legal protection for the peaceful civil rights marches and demonstrations that were a major impetus for civil rights legislation and the national media coverage of them that further stimulated legislative and popular sympathy for the end of Jim Crow laws.[72]

A third major case evidencing the alliance of liberty and equality is *New York Times v. Sullivan*, 376 US 254 (1964). Southern officials and vigilantes despised national media coverage of the black struggle for equality and liberty in the South because it encouraged opposition to segregation and exposed violence against civil rights protesters. Journalists sometimes risked life, limb, and liberty when covering civil rights–related events. For example, three *Life* magazine staff observing the integration of Little Rock Central High School in 1957 were beaten by the mob and then convicted of inciting a riot. Unsurprisingly, Southern officials turned to libel laws to try to drive out the press.

In 1960, Montgomery's city commissioner, L. B. Sullivan, filed a lawsuit against the *New York Times* and four Alabama civil rights activists for a full-page ad titled "Heed Their Rising Voices" in the March 29 paper. Listing sixty-four signatories, the ad sought donations to fund the legal defense of black activists jailed in the South for protesting segregation, but some claims in the ad were erroneous. At that time, libel was generally presumed when publications critical of government authorities contained factual errors. As required by state law, Sullivan first sent a letter to the newspaper demanding a retraction. The newspaper refused because the ad did not name or implicate him. Sullivan demanded a retraction from the four Alabama activists, but until he contacted them, they did not know the ad even existed or that someone had included their names. When his demands for retraction were refused, Sullivan filed suit. The trial jury awarded him $500,000 in damages (over $4 million in 2017 dollars). After losing both state court appeals, the newspaper and the activists appealed to the US Supreme Court. As the case progressed, more Southern officials jumped on the libel bandwagon. Sympathetic state courts awarded $300 million in libel judgments against the press and civil rights advocates.[73]

In a landmark decision, the Court unanimously struck down the libel judgment as a violation of the First Amendment's Freedom of the Press Clause. William Brennan, writing for the Court, held that public debate must be "uninhibited, robust, and wide-open" and that public officials must accept that criticisms may be "vehement, caustic, and sometimes unpleasantly sharp." An impersonal attack on governmental operations can never be defamatory of a government official not named in the attack. More important, the Court held that erroneous facts are inevitable in debates over hotly contested issues, and thus public officials must prove the erroneous facts were motivated by actual malice to win a libel judgment. If the defendant in such a case had to be prepared to defend every detail as true, then fear of the expenses of going to court would chill "the vigor and limits the variety of public debate."

The *Times* decision, cited in more than 6,000 judicial opinions, is celebrated as a landmark. Widely read journalist Anthony Lewis notes the decision ended the systematic effort to drive the major media from the South.[74] Legal analysts portray it as the beginning of the modern constitutional law of freedom of the press.[75] It explicitly repudiated the Sedition Act of 1798, the first time in 166 years the Court had spoken to that issue. Although the decision focused on a First Amendment claim by the newspaper, Kermit Hall and Melvin Urofsky convincingly argue that the case would not have been taken by the Supreme Court, nor decided as it was, had it not been about civil rights.[76] It was a "major transformation of existing constitutional doctrine" intentionally adopted to protect the civil rights movement from the Southern strategy attempting to use race-neutral tactics to uphold the Jim Crow system.[77] Whether it is viewed primarily a civil rights case that involved the First Amendment or primarily a First Amendment case involving civil rights, it reaffirms the fundamental alliance between equality and liberty.

A caveat regarding the *Times* decision is appropriate.[78] Having held for the defendants on First Amendment grounds, the Supreme Court did not rule on the merits of the claim by the four black civil rights activists—Ralph Abernathy, S. S. Seay, Fred Shuttlesworth, and Joseph Lowery—that the racist aspects of their trial violated the Fourteenth Amendment's Due Process and Equal Protection clauses. The jury was all-white (which the court had ruled unconstitutional in several prior cases), the courtroom was forcibly segregated by the judge, and the judge allowed Sullivan's lawyers to use racially discriminatory language when addressing the black lawyers of the civil rights activists. Because the Supreme Court did not rule on their claim, the case is often remembered only as a great victory for freedom of the press. That is a mistake just as it is a mistake to view *Herndon v. Lowry* (1937) as merely a free speech case. The *Times* decision cannot be correctly or fully understood without knowing its racist dimensions and its place in the fight for racial equality.

The many victories combining the pursuit of racial equality with advances in civil liberties from the late 1930s to the early 1970s demonstrate why legal scholars widely agree the civil rights movement—intertwined with the labor movement—did the most to create the modern conception of free speech.[79] They also illustrate how and why numerous Supreme Court decisions expressed the belief that the First Amendment and the Equal Protection Clause were mutually supportive partners in advancing civil rights.[80] Indeed, in recognition of the symbiotic relationship between civil rights and civil liberty, Harvard Law School established a new journal in 1966: the *Harvard Civil Rights–Civil Liberties Law Review*. Some observers came to believe that the categories of civil rights and civil liberties were so inseparable that the distinction between them was largely dissolved.[81]

The advances in liberty and equality stimulated by civil rights activism in the 1960s contributed to major improvements in black voting, political leadership, and school integration.[82] In 1964, less than 7 percent of eligible black voters were registered; in 1970, 68 percent were registered. In 1964, there were 25 black elected officials in the South; in 1970, there were over 700. In 1966, there were 97 blacks serving in state legislatures across the country and 6 in Congress; in 1973 there were more than 200 blacks serving in thirty-seven state legislatures and 16 in Congress. In the 1965–66 school year, 6 percent of schools in the eleven former Confederate states were integrated; in 1970, 90 percent qualified as integrated. The movement also led to economic gains for Southern blacks and whites,[83] especially the black middle class.[84] Moreover, the civil rights movement is recognized as inspiring further social justice movements and benefiting other traditionally disadvantaged groups.[85]

THURGOOD MARSHALL

Thurgood Marshall was a colossal figure in the struggle for African American civil rights and liberties. Born and raised in strictly segregated Baltimore, grandson of a slave, Marshall made tremendous contributions to the advancement of civil rights and liberties as a lawyer with the NAACP and LDF (1934–61), judge on the Second Circuit Court of Appeals (1961–65), US Solicitor General (1965–67), and the first African American justice on the Supreme Court (1967–91). As chief counsel for the LDF, Marshall argued and won twenty-nine of thirty-two cases before the Supreme Court. His rise from a poor private practice lawyer in Depression-era Baltimore to the highest court in the land is too extensive to address here;[86] this section focuses specifically on his work on the Supreme Court protecting liberty and equality. Although Marshall is best known for his success advancing civil rights, he also was one of the most dedicated defenders of free speech because he recognized the inseparability of liberty and equality.[87]

Justice Marshall participated in 165 free speech decisions from 1967 to 1991 and consistently maintained "constitutional liberties contained a strong equality component and that liberty and equality, properly understood, complemented each other."[88] He knew from his long experience as an African American lawyer who fought for the rights of the disadvantaged and disfavored and often faced the imminent possibility that he could be jailed or lynched,[89] that "sweeping speech protection was necessary to ensure that the voice of the politically weak and despised was heard."[90] Free speech promotes self-realization and personal dignity by protecting a speaker's right of expression and a listener's right to hear other views, and promotes equality by protecting subordinate groups from suppression as well as their right to dissent, protest, and petition. As chief counsel for the LDF, Marshall had initially refused to defend sit-in protesters when they were convicted for trespassing because of his devotion to the rule of law. Later he promised to provide legal counsel to everyone arrested as a result of peaceful protest against segregation after his younger and more strident legal team convinced him that such convictions were racially motivated and such protests ought to be legal.[91] His realization that a facially neutral law such as trespass could be wielded in racist ways was a lesson he took to his service on the Supreme Court: J. Clay Smith Jr. and Scott Burrell explain that Marshall was a "realist" insofar as he considered the social and economic realities of a case and the actual effects a ruling would have on the parties and on society.[92] His realism did not preclude his judicial opinions from taking "formalist" aspects in other cases in which strict adherence to a legal rule was paramount. The unifying element to his realist-oriented and formalist--oriented opinions was his devotion to protecting speech, especially speech contributing to individual self-realization.[93] This is evident in his opinions for the majority and in his dissents.

Let's consider four of Marshall's free speech majority opinions. *Amalgamated Food Employees Union v. Logan Valley Plaza*, 391 US 496 (1968) upheld the right of labor to picket on private shopping mall property.[94] The owner of Logan Valley Plaza barred union members from peacefully picketing outside a shopping center store that employed only nonunion workers. The Court held that the shopping center served a public function and therefore the First Amendment applied. *Stanley v. Georgia*, 394 US 557 (1969), unanimously struck down an obscenity conviction for private possession of obscene materials. Stanley's home was searched on probable cause of bookmaking. Police found no evidence of bookmaking in the house but discovered three reels of pornographic films. Overturning *Roth v. United States*, 354 US 476 (1957), the Court expanded protected expression and helped establish a right to privacy since "A state has no business telling a man sitting alone in his own house, what books he may read or what films he may watch. Our whole constitutional heritage rebels at the thought of giving government the power to control men's minds." *Pickering v Board of Education*, 391 US 563 (1968), used a balancing test to uphold the right of a public school teacher to speak on issues of public concern, even if some claims were false, as long as they were not knowingly or recklessly made. Pickering had been fired for writing a letter to the editor of a local newspaper criticizing school board policies. *Rankin v. McPherson*, 483 US 378 (1987), found that a Texas constable had violated the free speech rights of a clerical worker fired for saying to a co-worker, "Shoot, if they go for him again, I hope they get him" after John Hinckley Jr. shot and wounded President Ronald Reagan. According to the majority, "Vigilance is necessary to ensure public employers do not use authority over employees to silence discourse . . . simply because superiors disagree with the content of employees' speech."

Marshall's dedication to individual liberty was more evident in his dissents. Here are four examples. In *Greer v. Spock*, 424 US 828 (1976), Marshall joined Justice William Brennan's argument that political candidates should have been allowed to enter and distribute campaign literature and hold a rally on public spaces at army base Fort Dix. Their political speech would not impair the government's ability to train recruits or to maintain a national defense, and the fact all types of political rallies were banned was no excuse: "An evenhanded exclusion of all public expression would no more pass muster than an evenhanded exclusion of all Roman Catholics." In their view, the only thing that could justify the suppression of free speech at Fort Dix was the threat of a clear and present danger. In *Clark v. Community for Creative Non-Violence*, 468 US 288 (1984), Marshall argued that protesters should have been allowed to create a sleeping camp in a national park to protest the plight of the homeless. Rather than accept the government's claim on its face that a ban on sleeping in the parks was necessary to keep them clean, Marshall argued the government had to—and failed to—produce evidence that the ban on sleeping was truly necessary. He continued to demand the government prove it had a legitimate interest in regulating speech and limit its reach to narrow regulation in *Bethel School District No. 403 v. Fraser*, 478 US 675 (1986), and *Ward v. Rock Against Racism*, 491 US 781 (1989). In *Fraser*, the court upheld the suspension of a student for making lewd double entendres at a school assembly. Marshall disagreed, pointing out the school had provided no evidence that the speech had disrupted school activities as required by *Tinker v. Des Moines School District*, 393 US 503 (1969). In *Ward*, the court upheld a New York City regulation requiring use of city-provided equipment and technicians to control volume levels at Central Park concerts. Marshall agreed with noise regulation but maintained that the ban on private amplification systems and technicians failed to be narrowly tailored to a legitimate government interest.

Marshall's ardent support for freedom of expression is perhaps most telling when tension with racial equality was involved in the case. In *Brandenburg v. Ohio*, 395 US 444 (1969), a Ku Klux Klan leader was convicted of violating

Ohio's criminal syndicalism statute banning the advocacy of violence. Clarence Brandenburg had given a racially inflammatory speech during a KKK rally threatening "revengeance" against blacks, Jews, and their supporters. An invited TV reporter filmed portions of the rally depicting men in robes and hoods, some bearing firearms and burning a cross. In a per curiam decision, the Court held that government cannot punish inflammatory speech unless that speech is "directed to inciting or producing imminent lawless action and is likely to incite or produce such action." The landmark decision overturned the less protective standards cited in earlier precedents such as *Schenck v. United States* (1919), *Abrams v. United States* (1919), *Gitlow v. New York* (1925), *Whitney v. California* (1927), and *Dennis v. United States* (1951). The Court applied the Brandenburg test four years later in *Hess v. Indiana*, 414 US 105 (1973), and it remains the standard used for evaluating government attempts to punish inflammatory speech.

In *Grayned v. Rockford*, 408 US 104 (1972), Marshall wrote the majority opinion upholding a city antinoise ordinance and striking down an antipicketing ordinance used to convict Richard Grayned, a black civil rights demonstrator protesting at a Rockford school on April 25, 1969. After school administrators rejected the grievances of black students, around 200 demonstrators marched with placards protesting discrimination at the school and clenched their fists in "power to the people" salutes on public sidewalks about 100 feet away. Government witnesses claimed the demonstration was disruptive to school operations, and police arrested forty demonstrators after they failed to obey the warning to disperse. The Court struck down the antipicketing ordinance because—citing another Marshall opinion, *Chicago Police Dept. v. Mosley*, 408 US 92 (1969)—it was impermissibly content-based because as it protected peaceful labor picketing but did not other peaceful picketing. The antinoise ordinance was upheld as a reasonable time, place, manner regulation because it served a legitimate and important government interest, was not content-based, and was narrowly drawn (neither overbroad nor unduly vague). Like *Tinker v. Des Moines* (1969), it was restricted to silencing disruptive expression. The disruptive nature of the demonstration in the proximity of the school is what made this case different from the peaceful civil rights sit-ins and marches the court protected in the 1960s.

In *Linmark Associates v. Willingboro*, 431 US 85 (1977), the Court addressed a city regulation intended to prevent or minimize white flight and thereby promote stable and orderly integration of the township. After its minority population increased from less than 1 percent to about 18 percent from the 1960s to 1973, Willingboro, New Jersey, enacted an ordinance prohibiting yard signs indicating a house was for sale or sold. The realty company Linmark Associates sued the township on the grounds the ordinance was a violation of its rights to commercial speech under the First Amendment. Marshall, writing another unanimous decision, acknowledged that the ordinance had a legitimate goal in seeking to promote a stable process for integration in the township, but held the ordinance was unconstitutional because that goal could be achieved by other means that did not restrict speech and the township cannot restrict the free flow of truthful commercial information.

Throughout his career, and especially during his time on the Supreme Court, Marshall acted on his belief that First Amendment values are inseparable from racial equality and that freedom of expression protections should apply even to the thought we hate as long as it does not produce imminent lawless action (*Brandenburg*); does not violate narrowly tailored time, place, and manner restrictions that serve a substantial government interest (*Ward* and others); materially and substantially disrupt the schoolhouse (*Tinker* and *Fraser*) or public space (*Grayned*); or otherwise violate narrowly tailored categories of illegal speech such as libel or obscenity. He offered strong protections for freedom of association, freedom of the press, and even commercial speech.[95]

CONCLUSION

The civil rights era, like developments during the earlier eras of American apartheid and the Herndon case, evidences the inseparability of First Amendment values and racial equality. Using innovative legal strategies[96] and methods of mass protest, civil rights activists used First Amendment values to overcome pernicious orthodoxies and tremendous legal, political, economic, and social obstacles to achieve greater inclusion and participation in US society. Eminent historian Eric Foner observes, "The court's emergence [during the civil rights era] as a vigorous protector of civil liberties had been foreshadowed in 1937, when the justices abandoned freedom of contract while arguing that the First Amendment right of free expression deserved enhanced protection."[97] The civil rights movement of the 1960s, epitomized by the 1963 March on Washington for Jobs and Freedom featuring the iconic "I Have a Dream" speech by Martin Luther King Jr. and subsequent passage of the monumental 1964 Civil Rights Act, was built on decades of earlier organizing and protesting. The use of traditional and innovative forms of civil liberty played an indispensable role in equality gains, and even expanded the range of protected expression. As

Gene Policinski from the First Amendment Center observes, "There is a good case to be made that the march toward civil rights for African-Americans in this nation is the best example of all five First Amendment freedoms fully at work"; he adds that those five core freedoms also nourished the push for women's suffrage, labor rights, and more.[98] The civil rights movement inspired a "rights revolution" in which other traditionally disadvantaged and oppressed groups pressed for and gained greater equality and liberty, including women, Chicanos, homosexuals, and Native Americans.[99] The leading black civil rights activists—such as Martin Luther King Jr., Fred Shuttlesworth, and Bob Moses—saw civil rights and civil liberties as indivisible.[100] By 1976, 85 percent of Americans agreed that the United States was meant to be made up of diverse races, religions, and nationalities.[101] Writing twenty years after the civil rights movement, activist and lawyer Margaret Burnham notes, "It is neither hyperbolic nor trite to say that no other historical event has so shifted the turf upon which constitutional issues are played out as did the Afro-American civil rights movement."[102]

We must never forget that these advances were "the fruit of struggles, tragic failures, tears, sacrifice, and sorrow."[103] Activists performing lawful actions were murdered, beaten, wrongfully imprisoned, and more. It took four years and at least thirty Supreme Court decisions between 1961 and 1965 before the Court finally protected sit-ins under the First Amendment. It took three years of legal battles and a Supreme Court decision to enroll Autherine Lucy at the University of Alabama, yet when she went to campus she faced hostile mobs and was expelled in three days by school officials because her presence caused "mob rule," an action that was upheld in court in 1957. Psychologically exhausted, Autherine gave up. It was thirty-two years before the university finally wrote her a letter saying she was no longer expelled. She enrolled with her daughter, and both graduated in 1992: 2 of about 1,800 blacks on a campus of more than 18,000 students in a state with 25 percent black population.

Some managed to flourish despite their trials and tribulations: Jack Greenberg reports seven of the Little Rock Nine attended a civil rights event hosted by the LDF in 1982: they had grown up to become successful company owners, managers, consultants, politicians, school counselors, and more. But the struggle for liberty and equality is far from over.

CHAPTER 4

Hate Speech

Civil liberties are no threat to civil rights.

—Henry Louis Gates Jr.[1]

From colonial days to the early 1930s, African Americans and their supporters in the United States employed speech, the press, assembly, petition, and religion to advocate for and gradually advance racial equality although these five values existed primarily as moral ideals rather than legally enforceable rights. Angelo Herndon's victory in *Herndon v. Lowry* (1937) signaled a new era in which First Amendment values were increasingly protected by law, and their vigorous exercise accelerated gains in racial equality and liberty that culminated in landmark legislation and judicial decisions in the 1960s. Liberty and equality were widely heralded as symbiotic allies.

However, two factors soon led to challenges to the belief that liberty and equality are fundamental allies. First, the formal recognition of legal equality did not produce the expected substantive gains for African Americans in education, economics, politics, business, social status, and so on.[2] Indeed, more than fifty years after the Civil Rights Act became law, race still matters a great deal.[3] Second, when African Americans pursued new opportunities in education and employment, they often endured verbal abuse as well as abusive conduct and even violence.[4] Since courts ruled that the verbal abuse—now commonly referred to as hate speech—could be banned or punished only under narrow conditions rather than broad ones, the alliance of civil liberties and civil rights began to unravel in the 1980s.[5] By 1993, eminent Harvard University scholar Henry Louis Gates Jr. could write,

> Today . . . [c]ivil liberties are regarded by many [African Americans] as a chief obstacle to civil rights. To be sure, blacks are still on the front lines of First Amendment jurisprudence—but this time we soldier on the other side. The byword among many black activists and black intellectuals is no longer the political imperative to protect free speech; it is the moral imperative to suppress "hate speech."[6]

Scholars argued that the United States was an international pariah with robust free speech protections out of step with hate speech bans adopted by the rest of the world. In short, civil liberty was perceived by many to fundamentally conflict with racial equality, and so much the worse for civil liberty.[7]

Attempts to ban hate speech from the late 1960s to the 1980s drew considerable scholarly and public attention and significant US Supreme Court decisions,[8] but starting in the late 1980s, campus hate speech codes became a focal point as hundreds of universities and colleges adopted student speech restrictions commonly referred to as speech codes. Such campus regulations had the noble aim of ensuring equal opportunity and equal protection for minority students, but critics argued they were the wrong method for achieving that goal because they constituted serious threats to free speech. When broad speech codes at public institutions were challenged in court, they were consistently struck down as unconstitutional. The inability to legally silence or punish hate speech broadly has led some to take matters into their own hands by silencing, disrupting, and even violently confronting speech they oppose. Recent years have seen an increasing number of disinvited and disrupted campus speakers and increasing censorship, quarantine, or vandalism of controversial historical art, names, or symbols. Fears that conservative speakers and ideas are disproportionately chilled or censored led more than twenty states with conservative legislative majorities to enact or propose new campus free speech laws.

At first glance, banning hate speech seems to be the right thing to do. Thirty years ago, I thought broadly worded bans on hate speech were a good idea. A closer look changed my mind. One of the main problems with broadly worded bans is that neither scholars nor legislators nor countries can agree on what hate speech is, what hate speech should be banned, or what makes it worthy of legal sanction.[9] US courts have neither defined hate speech nor identified it as unprotected speech; rather, they have defined it narrowly and banned expressive categories such as libel, threats, harassment, incitement to violence, fighting words, and obscenity.[10] Hate speech that meets the strict criteria for such a category may be banned; speech that does not fit them may not be banned. This fact was evidenced in the very first campus speech code decision, *Doe v. University of Michigan* (E.D. MI 1989). In ordinary usage, *hate speech* typically refers to a wide array of expression roughly equivalent to the Holmesian "thought we hate," and by the 1970s and 1980s most expression labeled hate speech was viewed by US courts as merely offensive and therefore protected.[11] For convenience, I refer to speech regulations that restrict hate speech only when that expression violates an existing narrowly defined category of unprotected speech (such as true threat, incitement to violence, or hostile environment harassment) as "narrow" speech codes and regulations that ban hate speech beyond existing narrowly defined categories of unprotected speech as "broad" speech codes.

Against those who reject the priority of free speech and view liberty and equality as fundamentally at odds, this chapter argues that robust free speech protections should remain a priority for advocates of racial justice and that First Amendment values (specifically free speech) and equality remain fundamental allies. In doing so, I defend a belief championed by a variety of eminent African American advocates of liberty and equality, such as abolitionist Frederick Douglass, activists Ida Wells and W. E. B. Du Bois, lawyer and newspaperman Robert Abbott, eminent lawyer and Supreme Court Justice Thurgood Marshall, comedian and activist Dick Gregory, Harvard scholar Henry Louis Gates Jr., and civil rights and liberty icon and Congresswoman Eleanor Holmes Norton.

My argument comes in four sections. The first addresses the origin and development of hate speech restrictions from the late 1880s to early 1980s.[12] Attempts to ban hate speech began when Irish, Jews, and African Americans sought to eliminate racial ridicule in the late 1880s. By the 1930s, these efforts waned and censors refocused on suppressing Jehovah's Witnesses and political dissidents such as communists and Nazis. These early attempts were plagued by difficulties in defining hate speech, arbitrary enforcement, shifting alliances and conflicting interests, and the double-edged nature of censorship. The result was a gradual trend toward greater protections for speech. In the second section, I examine the modern hate speech debate beginning in the 1980s premised on a fundamental conflict between liberty and equality that advocated broad campus speech codes. The codes attracted tremendous public attention and scholarly debate, resulting in a series of judicial decisions striking down broad campus hate speech restrictions. One of the most popular and important arguments for broad hate speech bans appeals to an international consensus, so the third section presents and evaluates the international argument. The final section brings us to the crux of the matter: are liberty and equality in fundamental conflict? Should robust free speech rights be curtailed to promote racial equality? The evidence shows that liberty and equality remain fundamental allies and robust free speech rights continue to be essential to protect the expression of advocates of racial equality.

HATE SPEECH IN THE UNITED STATES, 1880s–1980s

M. Alison Kibler provides a detailed account of the origins of hate speech as a public issue in the United States.[13] In the late 1800s and early 1900s, the Irish and Jews were considered by the dominant Protestant Anglo-Americans to be separate and inferior races, though not as inferior as African Americans.[14] The three groups sought to end racial ridicule directed at them in the theater, motion pictures, media, advertising, and elsewhere. Their efforts included legal strategies such as city ordinances, state laws, and lawsuits, as well as extralegal strategies like protests, lobbying, and educational campaigns. Organizations such as the Fenian Brotherhood (1858) and its offshoot Clan na Gael, the American Jewish Committee (1906) and American Jewish Congress (1916), the National Association for the Advancement of Colored People (NAACP, 1909), and Anti-Defamation League (1913) led the efforts. African Americans sought to end the practice of white actors using blackface, racist lies in the media, and racist stereotypes in theater and film productions such as *Birth of a Nation.* The Irish objected to theater and film depictions of them as drunken pugilists, apes, or sexually immoral. From the 1870s to the early 1900s, Irish protesters conducted "stage riots" with hissing, stink bombs, egg tossing, and fighting with actors to protest productions they objected to, and they lobbied hard against derogatory stereotypes in productions such as "McSwiggan's Parliament" and "McFadden's Row of Flats." Jews sought to end depictions of them as immoral, greedy, or criminal; suppress prejudicial films of Leo Frank's trial and lynching; and productions of plays and films such as *The King of Kings.*

These three groups had competing interests, so they were often at odds despite their common plight. For example, some Jewish entertainers made a living wearing blackface and some Jewish theater owners and film companies made money producing racially offensive plays and films—even plays and films negatively portraying Jews. The Irish often blamed Jews for their troubles and considered blacks racially inferior. At the expense of African Americans, both Jews and the Irish sought to advance their standing in US society in part by arguing they were "white."

Since the US Supreme Court did not incorporate the First Amendment until *Gitlow v. New York* in 1925, the legal status of racial ridicule prior to

1925 was entirely the jurisdiction of states and municipalities. Consider a few examples of legal prosecutions. In 1878, police arrested the actors in the Philadelphia production of "McSwiggan's Parliament." In 1905, police arrested actors performing in a racist production in Butte, Montana. Kentucky banned theater productions of "Uncle Tom's Cabin" in 1906, and Memphis banned film versions in 1914. Racist theatrical performances were banned in Des Moines in 1907 and Chicago in 1908. New Haven, Connecticut, and Portsmouth, Virginia, schools banned Shakespeare's "The Merchant of Venice." Numerous cities banned individual productions of plays such as "The Clansman," "Mrs. Warren's Profession," and "Birth of a Nation." New York's 1913 ban on ethnically offensive speech was followed by bans in Illinois, Colorado, New Hampshire, Connecticut, Pennsylvania, Maine, and Minnesota.[15] In *Bryant v. New York*, 278 US 63 (1928), the US Supreme Court upheld a New York law aimed at squelching the Ku Klux Klan by outlawing marching with a mask and requiring "oath-bound" organizations to register with the state and reveal their membership.

These legal efforts to ban racial ridicule were fraught with difficulties. Indeed, many Irish, Jews, and African Americans recognized that censorship was a problematic path to pursue. First, censorship is a double-edged sword: if New York can ban the Ku Klux Klan glorifying *Birth of a Nation* for its racial ridicule of blacks, then Kentucky can ban *Uncle Tom's Cabin* for its racial ridicule of whites. Second, there were significant disagreements on what counted as racial ridicule and on what legal basis it should be banned. Attempts were made to ban offensive speech on grounds of obscenity, nuisance, incitement to violence, libel, and racial ridicule. Finally, efforts to ban hate speech were plagued by selective and unprincipled enforcement, intragroup and intergroup conflicts, and the eventual adoption of various methods of self-censorship (especially in film).

The threat to free speech and free press posed by broad hate speech bans derailed attempts at federal legislation against racial ridicule in 1914, 1916, and 1926. Courts overturned convictions of entertainers on free speech grounds and rejected prior restraint injunctions on theater and film productions in cities such as Boston, Cleveland, Denver, Los Angeles, Pittsburgh, Providence, and New York. Federal judges struck down group libel laws in Cleveland, Detroit, Pittsburgh, Toledo, and Texas. After 1922, all forty-five state bills proposing prior restraint censorship on hate speech were rejected by legislatures because race-related themes came to be understood as protected political speech rather than incitements to racial violence. Preemptively banning racial ridicule became especially difficult after the US Supreme Court prohibited prior restraint of the press in *Near v. Minnesota* (1931).

There were further problems for the broad hate speech bans. Minority groups discovered that race-based censorship was highly arbitrary and often did not favor them. Moreover, their demands for censorship cast them in the unfavorable role of a "special interest" while putting defendants in the sympathetic role of free speech martyr. In some cases, the minority protest simply reinforced a negative stereotype. For example, critics of Irish attempts to censor offensive speech pointed out that violent disruptions of theatrical performances by the Irish reinforced their violent stereotype. Attempts to suppress objectionable expression often backfired: a targeted play or book or speaker became more popular. Eventually the organizations that had lobbied for racial ridicule laws decided that the legal defense of individual rights combined with moral persuasion and education were a stronger basis for achieving racial progress than censorship was.[16] By the 1930s and 1940s, the Irish, Jewish, and African American efforts to ban hate speech waned.

To be sure, the urge to censor did not wane: it merely shifted targets to religious and political extremists. In the 1930s, the previously docile Jehovah's Witnesses took a new direction as "God's chosen people" combatting what they believed was Satan's hand at work in other religions, especially Catholicism and Judaism.[17] This led to a tenfold increase in membership from 400,000 in the 1920s to 4,000,000 in the 1940s, but it also resulted in hundreds of legal prosecutions and vigilante violence against them. For about a decade, they were the most reviled group in the United States as they went door to door and face to face to spread their message of intolerance; they also refused to participate in school flag salutes and the Pledge of Allegiance. They were involved in more than fifty Supreme Court decisions (second only to the NAACP) and their fight for free speech helped establish individual rights to speech, assembly, and religion now enjoyed by all citizens. For example, *Lovell v. City of Griffin*, 303 US 444 (1938), struck down a city ordinance requiring a permit before distribution of any literature as a violation of freedom of the press. *Cantwell v. Connecticut*, 310 US 296 (1940), was the first case to apply the constitutional right to freedom of religion to state action. It upheld the right of religious speakers to disseminate their message even if listeners find it offensive. *Barnette v. West Virginia*, 319 US 624 (1943), protected the right of religious conscience by allowing public school students to be exempt from saluting the flag and saying the Pledge of Allegiance. It is important to note that *Barnette* directly reversed *Minersville v. Gobitis*, 310 US 586 (1940), largely because of the tsunami of legal prosecutions and mob violence directed at Jehovah's Witnesses in the wake of *Gobitis*. Samuel Walker notes, "The special contribution of the Witnesses to the hate speech issue was that the principle of inclusiveness, of toleration for small and offensive minorities, also meant tolerance of hate speech."[18]

Upholding only narrow free speech restrictions as a matter of principle meant white supremacists had the same protections as everyone else. The three most significant cases were *Terminiello v. Chicago*, 337 US 1 (1949); *Brandenburg v. Ohio*, 395 US 444 (1969); and *National Socialist Party v. City of Skokie*, 432 US 43 (1977). With a 5–4 vote, *Terminiello* struck down a city ordinance banning speech that "stirs the public to anger, invites dispute, brings about a condition of unrest, or creates a disturbance." The case involved the conviction of a suspended Catholic priest who had given a racist speech to an audience of 800 while 1,000 people protested outside, some violently. In an often quoted opinion, Justice William O. Douglas wrote,

> a function of free speech under our system of government is to invite dispute. It may indeed best serve its high purpose when it induces a condition of unrest, creates dissatisfaction with conditions as they are, or even stirs people to anger. Speech is often provocative and challenging. It may strike at prejudices and preconceptions and have profound unsettling effects as it presses for acceptance of an idea. That is why freedom of speech, though not absolute . . . is nevertheless protected against censorship or punishment, unless shown likely to produce a clear and present danger of a serious substantive evil that rises far above public inconvenience, annoyance, or unrest.[19]

Brandenburg unanimously struck down the Ohio syndicalism statute banning advocacy of violence as a violation of freedom of expression since it banned speech that did not constitute incitement to "imminent lawless action." The case involved a Ku Klux Klan leader who, among other hateful remarks, advocated violence against blacks and Jews at a rally filmed by a TV station. *Skokie* held 6–3 that the city, chosen by the Nazis for its large Jewish population, could not ban a planned Nazi march without proper procedural safeguards for freedom of expression.

There were two notable exceptions to the trend toward narrow free speech restrictions. *Chaplinsky v. New Hampshire*, 315 US 568 (1942), unanimously upheld a ban on fighting words, and *Beauharnais v. Illinois*, 343 US 250 (1952), upheld a ban on "group libel" in a 5–4 vote. While proselytizing in downtown Rochester, Jehovah's Witness Walter Chaplinsky attracted a hostile, even violent crowd and was taken by police to the station. There Chaplinsky was arrested for calling an officer a "God-damned racketeer" and "damned Fascist." *Chaplinsky* unanimously upheld the conviction for violating a state law prohibiting "any offensive, derisive or annoying word to anyone who is lawfully in any street or public place . . . or to call him by an offensive or derisive name." According to the Court, fighting words are not protected by the First Amendment because by their very utterance they inflict injury or incite an immediate breach of the peace. In Illinois, officers of the White Circle League were charged under the 1917 state group libel statute for distributing a leaflet urging the Chicago city government to stop Negro "encroachment, harassment and invasion of white people" and warned of the dire consequences of "rapes, robberies, knives, guns and marijuana of the negro" if no action were taken. *Beauharnais* upheld the state law banning published or exhibited material that "portrays depravity, criminality, unchastity, or lack of virtue of a class of citizens, of any race, color, creed or religion which said publication or exhibition exposes the citizens of any race, color, creed or religion to contempt, derisions, or obloquy or which is productive of the breach of the peace or riots." The majority held that the law was constitutional given its similarity to individual defamation law and racial tensions in Chicago.

The fighting words and group libel doctrines have been narrowed by subsequent judicial decisions to the point neither can justify broad hate speech regulations. *Cohen v. California*, 403 US 15 (1971), limited fighting words to direct, face-to-face insults. *Gooding v. Wilson*, 405 US 518 (1972), eliminated the first prong of the *Chaplinsky* formula so that only words inciting imminent violence constitute fighting words. *Rosenfeld v. New Jersey*, 408 US 901 (1972), held each challenged expression must be evaluated in its context so certain words (racist epithets, slurs, etc.) cannot be prohibited per se. Although some state courts have upheld some fighting words convictions in extreme circumstances,[20] the Supreme Court has rejected every fighting words conviction it has reviewed since *Chaplinsky*, including cases using the same epithets Chaplinsky used and worse.[21] Moreover, there is evidence that fighting words arrests have been used disproportionately to stifle minority criticism of authorities, usually police officers, rather than to protect minorities from verbal abuse.[22] Likewise, *Beauharnais* "has not fared well over time and would be cited at an advocate's peril."[23] Leading advocates of the group libel doctrine—David Reisman, Joseph Tanenhaus, and Gordon Allport—withdrew their support. Illinois repealed its law in 1961. *New York Times v. Sullivan* (1964) restricted libel to accusations "of and concerning" a specified individual. *Garrison v. Louisiana*, 379 US 64(1964), rejected the doctrine that protected speech is limited to speech with "good motives" and for "justifiable ends." A series of federal court decisions have stated that *Beauharnais* is no longer good law.[24]

In sum, a multitude of conceptual, legal, and practical problems have plagued attempts to ban or punish hate speech. From the 1930s to the 1980s, a national policy limiting hate speech sanctions to narrowly tailored legal categories developed through advocacy groups, legal scholars, the judiciary, and political bodies.[25] It is important to note that the move toward only narrow restrictions on hate speech developed during the same era that racial equality most progressed. This was not coincidental. As demonstrated in chapter 3, civil rights activists realized robust speech rights were essential to advocating and increasing racial equality.[26]

HATE SPEECH IN THE UNITED STATES, 1980S–PRESENT

The milestone 1964 Civil Rights Act combined with other factors led to gradual increases in employment and education for African Americans and other historically disadvantaged groups. When cases of racial discrimination arose in the 1970s, courts began to uphold sanctions against discriminatory speech and conduct in specific circumstances based on existing legal categories.[27] The problem of discrimination in higher education gained attention.

In an effort to protect minority students from discrimination and violence, many campuses adopted broad speech restrictions that became known as hate speech codes. These codes attracted extraordinary attention—thousands of books, articles, editorials, blogs, and so on—for two main reasons. First, the potential and actual threat to free speech they posed due to their overbreadth and undue vagueness drew criticism from across the scholarly and public spectrum. Second, the restrictions often arose after intense protests or lobbying by strident student groups and were intellectually spearheaded by controversial Marxists such as Herbert Marcuse[28] and Saul Alinsky,[29] as well as Charles Lawrence, Mari Matsuda, and Richard Delgado, who created the new field of critical race theory.[30] The movement was not limited to campuses, but the campus debate became the focal point. To many people, it was political correctness and leftist extremism run amok. To supporters it was "progressive" censorship.

In contrast to the civil rights–era belief that free speech and racial equality were inseparable, advocates of the broad campus hate speech codes framed the issue as two conflicting narratives or worldviews in which defenders of robust free speech rights privileged their own assumptions and failed to engage the egalitarian argument for limiting speech to protect the historically oppressed.[31] They perceived the individualistic basis of liberty law (particularly the Free Speech Clause in the First Amendment) to be incompatible with the immutable characteristic group basis of equality law (particularly the Equal Protection Clause in the Fourteenth Amendment) and thought so much the worse for free speech.[32] Given the perceived harmful effects—psychological and physical—of hate speech and its connection to hate crimes, some claimed that hate speech itself is violence no different from physical violence.[33] Thus, hate speech by members of the dominant group directed at the historically disadvantaged must be silenced, whereas hate speech directed at historically dominant persons by the historically subordinated was acceptable.[34] An "outsider jurisprudence" was necessary to champion a new speech regime grounded in an equality-based theory of free speech[35] in which racial respect and civility reigned.[36]

Campus speech codes initially invoked the fighting words and group libel doctrines to justify their restrictions, but these approaches were rejected by courts because those doctrines had been narrowed too much to sustain the overbroad and unduly vague codes. The pattern was set in the very first case, *Doe v. University of Michigan*, 721 F. Supp. 852 (E.D. MI 1989). Less than a year after the University of Michigan passed a hate speech code, a graduate student in biopsychology sued the university, fearing he would be prosecuted for discussing views about biologically based racial and sexual differences. The court struck down the policy because it was overbroad (banned expression protected by the First Amendment) on its face and in its application[37] and was unduly vague (its language was too ambiguous, which allowed officials to arbitrarily prosecute disfavored speech).[38] The court noted that the university is permitted to ban illegal behavior (such as discriminatory behavior, assault and battery, vandalism and property damage, and sexual harassment) and illegal expression (such as fighting words, obscenity, libel and slander, and credible threats of violence), but it cannot have a policy that "had the effect of prohibiting certain speech because it was found to be offensive, even gravely so, by large numbers of people."[39] Judge Avern Cohn acknowledged that this decision was "difficult" and "painful," but he cited a series of precedents authorizing only narrowly tailored speech restrictions. *Doe* was soon followed by courts striking down broad hate speech restrictions at the University of Wisconsin System (1991),[40] George Mason University (1991),[41] Central Michigan University (1993),[42] and Stanford University (1995).[43]

Universities appealed to the hostile environment harassment doctrine to justify broad hate speech restrictions. This approach also was rejected the first time it was litigated in *UWM Post, et. al. v. Board of Regents of the University of Wisconsin*, 774 F. Supp. 1163 (E.D. WI 1991). The university argued that student hostile environment harassment was a violation of the equal protection guarantee in Title VII of the Civil Rights Act. The court rejected this argument because (1) Title VII addresses employment contexts, not educational ones; (2) Title VII law is based in agency principles and students are not (normally) agents of the university; and (3) Title VII is a federal statute and cannot supersede the requirements of the First Amendment. Moreover, the policy was overbroad and unduly vague and could not be saved by any limiting construction. *Post* was followed by *Bair v. Shippensburg University*, 280 F. Supp. 2d 357 (M.D. PA 2003), and *DeJohn v. Temple University*, 537 F. 3d 301 (3rd Cir. 2008), striking down university speech codes using hostile environment harassment language as overbroad and unduly vague. Indeed, both policies were found to be so clearly unconstitutional that the courts granted preliminary injunctions against the universities.

Because the First Amendment sets a legal limit on government action, not private action, these judicial decisions applied to all public institutions of higher education but applied to private universities and colleges only in rare and special circumstances.[44] However, the proliferation of campus speech codes led conservative US Representative Henry Hyde (R-IL) to introduce the Collegiate Speech Protection Act of 1991. That bill directed federal courts to apply First Amendment free speech protections to public *and* private institutions (with some exceptions).[45] In an unlikely political alliance, the liberal-leaning ACLU supported Hyde's bill. National media mostly supported the bill as a necessary constraint on political correctness. Although the bill died in committee, as did a similar bill introduced in the Senate by Larry Summers (R-ID),[46] we shall see later that its spirit lives on.

Courts continued to strike down broad speech restrictions when new justifications or terminology were invoked. Consider three examples. *Roberts v. Haragan*, 346 F. Supp. 2d 853 (N.D. TX 2004) struck down Texas Tech University's "free speech zone" policy restricting free speech to a very small space and requiring a permit be acquired prior to the speech. *College Republicans v. Reed*, 523 F. Supp. 2d 1005 (N.D. CA 2007) struck down a San Francisco State University policy requiring "civility" and banning "intimidation" and "harassment." *McCauley v. University of the Virgin Islands*, 618 F.3d 232 (3rd Cir. 2010), struck down a university policy prohibiting "offensive" or "unauthorized" signs and conduct causing "emotional distress" and a policy banning speech causing "mental harm" or demeaning or disgracing any person.

Courts rejected broad hate speech restrictions on faculty as well. For example, *Silva v. University of New Hampshire*, 888 F. Supp. 293 (D.N.H. 1994) rejected the university's enforcement of its sexual harassment policy against a professor for using sexually themed metaphors in teaching a writing course. Similarly, *Cohen v. San Bernardino Community College*, 92 F.968 (1996), struck down the university's sexual harassment policy for undue vagueness in a case addressing a writing professor's assignment requiring students to define pornography.

The US Supreme Court continued to shape hate speech law as well. *Davis v. Monroe County Board of Education*, 526 US 629 (1999), defined student-to-student hostile environment harassment as expression that is both severe *and* pervasive (as opposed to severe *or* pervasive) and limited legal liability to cases where the school knew about the harassment and responded with "deliberate indifference." Its decision to strike down a St. Paul, Minnesota, ordinance punishing the expressive element of cross burning in *R.A.V. v. St. Paul*, 505 US 377 (1992), was widely interpreted as a stance against campus hate speech codes. The Court also struck down a state cross burning statute in *Virginia v. Black*, 583 US 343 (2003), that distinguished cross burning as political statement from cross burning as intimidation; a tort action against the Westboro Baptist Church for emotional distress caused by hateful speech in *Snyder v. Phelps*, 56 US 443 (2011); and a Pennsylvania state criminal conviction for hateful online threats in *Elonis v. United States*, 575 US — (2015).

THE INTERNATIONAL ARGUMENT

Given that the US legal precedents for only narrow speech restrictions have solidified in the past thirty years, one of the primary arguments supporting broad hate speech bans appealed to international law.[47] Our strong legal protections for hate speech are unusual among advanced democracies,[48] and many scholars began arguing that we should expand our legal restrictions to join the international consensus supporting broad hate speech restrictions.[49] In brief, the argument is that we should adopt broad hate speech restrictions because (1) there is an international consensus for such restrictions, (2) these restrictions are effective, and (3) the restrictions protect or even enhance overall freedom of speech.

Many countries allow prosecution for speech that may incite racial or ethnic hostility or social disharmony—for example, Austria, Belgium, Canada,

Cyprus, England, France, India, Italy, Netherlands, New Zealand, South Africa, and Switzerland.[50] Many advocates of broad bans appeal to Germany because article 5 of its constitution protects "worthless" and "dangerous" speech, yet its federal criminal code penalizes verbal and nonverbal expression that incites hatred or attacks human dignity (specifically Holocaust denials, lies, or approvals) as well as insults and defamation that attack a person's honor.[51] To illustrate the difference between hate speech protected in the United States but unprotected in Germany, Wilfried Brugger gives the example of a protester using a graphic and obscene poster to lambast the president, soldiers, and racial minorities and deny the Holocaust.[52] Advocates also claim international agreements such as article 10 of the European Convention for the Protection of Human Rights and Fundamental Freedoms and article 4 of the International Convention on the Elimination of All Forms of Racial Discrimination\ show an international consensus against broadly defined hate speech.

Advocates claim that broad hate speech restrictions will be effective. Alexander Tsesis argues these bans can decrease hate speech and hate crimes just as the Thirteenth, Fourteenth, and Fifteenth Amendments to the US Constitution have reduced unequal treatment in housing, employment, and voting rights. Legislation can change beliefs and behaviors and reduce the likelihood that "fringe groups will gain political ascendancy through sustained ideological dissemination."[53] Richard Delgado and Jean Stefancic claim that these laws "enable monitoring commissions to compile statistics, issue progress reports, and coordinate the work of different nations. They also provide the basis for occasional prosecution of notorious hatemongers, all of which presumably has some deterrent effect."[54]

Advocates maintain the restrictions ban only "low-value" or "worthless" speech and will enhance overall speech by increasing minority speech. Delgado claims free speech has not suffered in nations with broad hate speech bans,[55] and Canadian and European presses are "feistier," more "independent" of government influence, and "less beholden to corporate interests" than US media.[56] Hate speech bans enforced against the "in group" will empower members of "out groups" to exercise their right to free speech more fully and thereby enhance overall freedom of speech. Jeremy Waldron argues that hate speech is low-value speech that deprives its victims of a "public good," namely, the assurance that society regards them as people of equal dignity, and that is reason enough to enact European-style hate speech bans.[57]

We should reject the international argument for broad hate speech bans. Nadine Strossen's 2018 book *Hate: Why We Should Resist It with Free Speech, Not Censorship* provides the most up-to-date and thorough account of this approach's failures.[58] One problem is that there is little or no empirical evidence that they have been effective. Broad speech bans failed to prevent hate speech and hate crimes in the past. The German Weimar Republic had a law much like the one Tsesis proposes, but it did not prevent Nazi atrocities. The bad tendency speech test in the United States did not prevent the "misethnic" speech Tsesis believes contributed to slavery and the removal of Native peoples. There is no evidence provided showing the hate speech bans from the 1890s and early 1900s or the *Chaplinsky* and *Beauharnais* decisions deterred hate speech or hate crimes. Will broad bans have different results in the twenty-first century? There is little reason to think modern censors will apply the bans as supporters of broad hate speech codes desire or do so consistently because their overbreadth and undue vagueness invariably produce arbitrary enforcement. Finally, if the codes are effective as the international argument claims, then race relations and racial equality in countries with broad hate speech bans should be better than in the United States.[59] No evidence has been produced showing race relations or racial equality are better in those countries than the United States. Nor is there an established correlation between broad bans and the eradication of discriminatory views. Greece, for example, has broad hate speech laws, yet 69 percent of Greeks hold anti-Semitic views, whereas only 9 percent of Americans do.[60] Eric Heinze, professor of Law and Humanities at Queen Mary University of London, notes, "if defenders of bans were right about the dangers of hate speech, Western Europe would have progressed toward greater tolerance, and the US toward greater intolerance. The facts suggest otherwise, not least because intolerance breeds from many factors."[61] Broad bans do not get at the causes of hate, so hate groups simply go underground or rephrase their hate through coded expressions.

Second, broad hate speech bans are used to silence expression that should be protected. Consider some representative examples. In France, Roger Garaudy was convicted for referring to Nazi mass murders as "pogroms" or "massacres" rather than "genocide" or "Holocaust"; animal rights activist Brigitte Bardot was fined $23,000 for criticizing a Muslim ritual that involves the slaughter of sheep and was convicted for sending a letter to the Interior minister claiming that Muslims were ruining the country; a Basque cartoonist was convicted for a drawing of the attack on the World Trade Center with the words "We have all dreamed about it . . . Hamas did it." In Italy, journalist Oriana Fallaci was indicted for criticizing Islam and lamenting the Islamization of Europe. In Germany, punishment can apply to "giving the finger" or calling someone a "jerk"; yet women are not protected from even "spectacular" sexual insults or affronts, and anti-Turk speech is treated differently from anti-German Jewish speech. In Poland, a Catholic magazine was fined $11,000 for comparing abortion to Nazi medical experiments. In Sweden, protesters were convicted for distributing leaflets to high school students saying that homosexuality was "deviant," "morally destructive," and responsible for the development of HIV and AIDS. Dutch politician Geert Wilders was barred from Britain because he made a movie calling the Quran a "fascist" book and Islam a violent religion. In Belgium, a politician was convicted for distributing leaflets stating, "Stand up against the Islamification of Belgium," "Stop the sham integration policy," and "Send non-European job-seekers home." Henry Louis Gates Jr. asks,

> Does anyone believe that racism has subsided in Britain since the adoption of the 1965 Race Relations Act forbidding racial defamation? Or that the legal climate in that country is more conducive to searching political debate? Ask any British newspaperman about that. When Harry Evans, then editor of the London *Times*, famously proclaimed that the British press was, by comparison to ours, only "half-free," he was not exaggerating much. The result of Britain's judicial climate is to make the country a net importer of libel suits launched by tycoons who are displeased with their biographers. Everyone knows that a British libel suit is like a Reno divorce. It is rather a mordant irony that American progressives should propose Britain, and its underdeveloped protection of expression, as a model to emulate at a time when many progressives in Britain are agitating for a bill of rights and broad First Amendment-style protections.[62]

Canadian officials seized copies of Salman Rushdie's *Satanic Verses* after a complaint was made that it caused ill feelings toward white South Africans; confiscated copies of black feminist bell hooks' book *Black Looks*; and seized the Ayn Rand Institute newsletter "In Moral Defense of Israel" containing articles published in mainstream US newspapers.[63] When two popular media personalities faced charges of hate speech before a Canadian Human Rights Commission, Alan Borovoy, longtime general counsel for the Canadian Civil Liberties Association and a main contributor to the Canadian and Ontario Civil Human Rights Commissions, commented, "It never occurred to us that this instrument, which we intended to deal with discrimination in housing, employment and the provision of goods and services, would be used to muzzle the expression of opinion." Stephan Braun, also a Canadian, notes that hate speech law "tends to become whatever those with the power to threaten or enforce it think it is in the particular circumstances. In practice, it may be stretched, narrowed, even redefined, depending on the prevailing social times and changing political climates, without a single word [of the law] being changed."[64]

Broad hate speech bans proposed for the United States also go too far. Consider the proposals by Tsesis and Delgado and Stefancic. Tsesis argues "misethnic speech" must be banned to stop prejudice from leading to genocide.[65] He defines misethnic speech as expression that is an incitement to discriminate, persecute, or oppress members of an identifiable group where there is a substantial probability, based on the content and context of the message, that it will elicit such acts and where the speaker intended the message to promote such acts, except if the statement was uttered as an expression of opinion on a neutral scientific, academic, or religious subject and/or the statement was made to eliminate the incidence of hatred toward an identifiable group. His ban aims to "prevent disparaging stereotypes from ingraining themselves in the social conscience" and prohibit charismatic leaders from "harnessing racist, xenophobic, and anti-Semitic ideologies to further discrimination and achieve ruinous objectives." But these goals can be accomplished only by criminalizing a very broad spectrum of speech.[66] Tsesis notes that Wilhelm Marr, the man who popularized the term *anti-Semitic*, called on his fellow Germans to "elect no Jews" during the 1879 elections; Thomas Cooper of South Carolina College published a manuscript in 1826 arguing that slavery was justified because the Bible did not condemn it. Does this ban apply to them? If it does not, then the ban is too narrow to prevent misethnic speech from "paving the way" to genocide. If it does apply to these examples, then the statute is too broad. Misethnic speech may be a necessary condition for genocide, but so are other factors. Why ban misethnic speech but not the others? Tsesis also ignores institutions and practices that reduce misethnic speech and mitigate its harms. Most "publicized incidents of hate speech in the United States . . . produce an outpouring of opposition."[67] Richard Abel notes,

> it is important to recall how many forms of status degradation long taken for granted have been delegitimated. Racist, anti-Semitic, and sexist slurs that routinely infected daily discourse have been banished to the margins of deviance. . . . In most Western nations hegemonic religion has yielded to pluralistic tolerance. Public disapproval is curtailing sexual harassment. The differently abled, long forced to hide, beg or display

themselves as "freaks," have gained greater access to public life. Even homophobia is in retreat.[68]

The ban proposed by Delgado and Stefancic is equally problematic. They recommend universities ban "severe personal insults" in a content-neutral way (required by *R.A.V. v. St. Paul*) and enhance the penalty when motivated by hate (permitted by *Wisconsin v. Mitchell*).[69] "That way, the campus can end up punishing insults based on fatness or poor parking ('you idiot, why did you take up two spaces?') mildly, and ones based on race, gender, or sexual orientation ('you fag, you're going straight to hell') more severely."[70] They recommend two tiers because the latter attacks an immutable feature of the individual, which allegedly causes greater harm. The authors object to using the term "hate speech" loosely because it of its many variations. For example, it can be direct or indirect; veiled or overt; single or repeated; backed by authority and power or not; targeted at an individual, small group, or whole class of people; spoken or manifested in a symbol; accompanied by threats or assault; and it varies according to who is speaking.[71] However, their proposal does not consider these factors. Most significantly, they ignore the dozens of precedents rejecting broad hate speech bans. US law does not recognize a category of illegal insults, and their examples do not constitute fighting words, verbal harassment, incitement, libel, true threats, and so on.[72]

Third, there is no substantive international consensus on hate speech. Winfried Brugger observes, "On the whole, neither modern constitutional law nor international law consistently permits or consistently prohibits hate speech. In the world community, such speech is sometimes prohibited, and sometimes not."[73] For example, James Whitman notes that German personal honor law substantially discounts free speech, while French personal honor law is balanced against free speech.[74] Ronald Krotoszynski Jr. debunks the international consensus through an analysis of the legal context and national experiences of Canada, Germany, Japan, the United Kingdom, and the United States.[75] There are significant differences among them. They understand judicial review of legislation differently. They recognize different values as competing with free speech and weigh these values differently. They view government action to prevent private harms in contrasting ways. Their hate speech provisions and enforcement vary. This results in many contrasts. For example, Canada identifies free speech as one of four fundamental freedoms. Germany focuses on human dignity and personal honor. Japan uses Alexander Meicklejohn's theory of free speech grounded in democratic self-governance. The United Kingdom delegated its free speech protections to the European

Court of Human Rights. These and many other differences led Roger Alford to comment,

> If modern democracies disagree about the essentials of free speech theory and practice, there is little basis for shaming an outlier. Of course, one can try to play that game by analyzing a particular free speech variant—say, defamation or hate speech—comparing the United States' practice to a few select countries based on one or two contextual factors, and simplistically declaring the United States a "freedom of expression outlier." But [these] reductions ignore the reality that a careful examination of multiple free speech variants in multiple countries using multiple contextual factors suggests something quite different. Each country is different from the United States, but each country is also different from one another.[76]

In conclusion, the international argument fails. There is no international consensus because countries take dramatically different approaches to hate speech. Moreover, "in actual operation these laws have a terrible track record of being used by the politically powerful factions to suppress speech that criticizes them. It is hard to find a case anywhere in the world where speech in support of dominant ideologies is punished for the protection of the weak."[77] Both in theory and practice, the international argument fails to convince.

FUNDAMENTAL CONFLICT OR FUNDAMENTAL ALLIANCE?

We come to the bottom line: are liberty and equality fundamentally allied or fundamentally opposed? Is robust free speech the friend or foe of racial progress? Is progressive censorship necessary to advance equality for minorities and the historically disadvantaged? In her commencement speech at the 2018 Georgetown Law School graduation, former ACLU free speech lawyer, government civil and human rights officer, and current delegate to the House of Representatives Eleanor Holmes Norton focused on the importance of free speech.[78] Is this African American icon of civil liberty and civil rights substantially correct? The paradigm one thinks with and acts on makes a great deal of difference. This section argues that the fundamental conflict model is intellectually flawed and undermines progress in racial equality. Liberty and equality are fundamentally allies because both oppose orthodoxy and promote inclusion and participation. Robust free speech remains essential to protect the speech of advocates of racial equality.

We begin to see the problem with the fundamental conflict model when we ask what the conflict is thought to be. There are two ways liberty and equality could be in fundamental conflict: conceptually or empirically. Neither of these is tenable. The latter is clearly false. Liberty and equality conflict in specific individual cases, but they do not conflict in all or most cases. Our progressive history described in chapters 1 through 3 show that liberty and equality were closely intertwined and mutually supportive—indeed, inseparable.

What about a fundamental conceptual conflict between liberty and equality? Two concepts might be said to be in fundamental conflict if they are logically contradictory (for example, a man cannot be a bachelor and married at the same time) or conceptual opposites (for example, "up" is the conceptual opposite of "down," but "up" is not logically contradictory to "down"). However, liberty and equality are not logical contradictories because an expression can be consistent with free speech and equality at the same time. Nor are they conceptual opposites. The conceptual opposite of liberty (free speech) is illiberty (unfree speech), not racial equality; the conceptual opposite of racial equality is racial inequality, not liberty (free speech). Liberty and equality are not "two sides of the same coin" so that only one can land face up and win; rather, they are two stars within a constellation of values that constitute social and political justice.

In what sense are liberty and equality fundamentally allies? Consider Nan Hunter's exposition.[79] Hunter notes that modern free speech protections developed in the 1930s focused implicitly on the group identities and interests of labor organizers, immigrants, and disfavored religions, but the group aspect was neglected because defenders of free speech came from one of four strands of individualist thinking: (i) radical libertarians like the Wobblies; (ii) conservative libertarians, who linked freedom of contract and freedom of speech; (iii) Brandeisian progressives, who saw free speech as an individual right essential to the proper functioning of democracy; and (iv) the mainstream interpretative enterprise analyzing free speech in terms of a chain from the speaker's intention to the expression to the audience reaction. Stronger protections for free speech were won over the years by focusing on the expression rather than group identity or audience reaction. On the other hand, equality law developed through the twentieth century explicitly based on group identities and interests and predominantly on an immutable characteristic.[80] The resulting tension between individualistic liberty and immutable characteristic group equality may appear to be a fundamental conflict,[81] especially given the failure of courts in some cases to strengthen the liberty and equality connection.[82]

Hunter goes on to describe the fundamental liberty and equality alliance: both oppose orthodoxy and support inclusion. The "fault line in the expression/equality dichotomy is the proposition that one can fully separate the two principles in the first place."[83] Those who give expression the preferred position and those who give equality the preferred position use the expression/equality dichotomy as shorthand for disputes on a series of component issues. But those component issues exist independently of their framing as expression or dissent versus equality or difference. Hunter discusses three examples—socially constructed selves, assimilation and particularity, and orthodoxy and exclusion—to support her claim that the component issues are best addressed in terms of expression *and* equality. Violations of expression (censorship) and violations of equality (exclusion) perform the same ultimate function: "truncation of the richness of the public sphere."[84] To illustrate the shared function, Hunter explains how a narrowly drawn prohibition on hostile environment sexual harassment protects both equality and free expression through the shared objectives of reducing exclusion and subordination. In sum, the individualistic focus of free expression law and group focus of equality law have amplified their tensions and obscured their shared foundations to produce a perception that they are dichotomous/fundamentally conflicting when in truth, another model reflects the complexity and fluidity of these centrally important principles.

A different approach suggested by john a. powell leads to the same conclusion.[85] He explains how expression and equality are complex and contextual values—as opposed to generic or monolithic ones—that draw their substance from underlying values. Freedom of expression draws on the value of, for example, the pursuit of truth, the value of a stable but adaptive deliberative democracy, and the value of self-realization. Because these values will conflict in some cases, there is tension *within* freedom of expression itself, not merely tension with equality. Similarly, equality can be understood in terms of equal respect, equal opportunity, equal outcomes, and more. Because these values will conflict in some cases, equality—like expression—has internal tensions and external ones. The internal tensions within liberty and equality and the external tension between liberty and equality can distract us from a deeper and unifying value: participation. Appealing to the conditions of ideal communication defended by Jürgen Habermas (symmetry, reciprocity, and membership), powell shows how harms to participation undermine freedom of expression and substantive equality, and freedom of expression and substantive equality both promote participation. In practice, powell's appeal to participation is akin to Hunter's appeal to anti-orthodoxy and inclusion in demonstrating a fundamental alliance between liberty and equality.

In addition to the intellectual flaws in the fundamental conflict model, the mentality it produces undermines the quest for racial equality in practice. That mentality underpins the modern legal movement to enact broad hate speech codes and the modern vigilante movement to illegitimately silence, disrupt, and even violently oppose speech one finds hateful. Although the legal and vigilante movements can be said to have won some individual battles, they are Pyrrhic victories that undermine the overall struggle for racial equality.

One reason broad speech codes and the fundamental conflict ideology underpinning them are self-defeating is that broad codes can be, have been, and will be used to silence advocates of racial equality and justice. For example, in the year the University of Michigan's speech code lasted, more than twenty blacks were charged by whites with racist speech and not a single instance of white racist speech was punished.[86] The list of advocates of racial equality who would or could face punishment under a broad hate speech code includes (but is not limited to) academics whose scholarship, teaching, or public discourse offends;[87] Black Lives Matter protesters;[88] professional and student athletes;[89] artists, entertainers, and authors;[90] and critics of police actions.[91] Without legal defense on behalf of free speech and free assembly from the ACLU, racial protests in Ferguson, Missouri, would have been shut down and organizers of a peaceful Black Lives Matter protest at the Mall of America would have been prosecuted.[92] European-style broad hate speech bans, if applied consistently, would likely result in thousands of convictions of racial egalitarians or a significant lessening of advocacy for racial equality. Worse, since these laws are often enforced by the powers that be against their critics, during times anti-egalitarians are in power, racial egalitarians would face even greater persecution.[93] Gara LaMarche, president of the Democracy Alliance, notes that without robust free speech, "There could be no Movement for Black Lives, no Dreamers, no Fight for 15, no Occupy Wall Street—no vibrant resistance to the nearly hegemonic right-wing control of the federal government and more than 30 states."[94] Anthony Romero, executive director of the ACLU, summarizes: "Preventing the government from controlling speech is absolutely necessary to the promotion of equality."[95] This was true when the career of eminent black intellectual W. E. B. Du Bois was destroyed by government persecution in 1951 and he was rendered stateless ten years later for his attention to the racial roots of war, antiwar activism, and opposition to nuclear weapons,[96] and it's true in 2019. True in 1968 when the chancellor of the University of Tennessee tried to keep the "extreme racist" black comedian and civil rights activist Dick Gregory from speaking on campus because it "would tarnish the university's prestige" and anger the state legislature,[97] still true in 2019.

Second, censorship—even attempts at censorship—frequently transforms people into free speech martyrs while simultaneously reinforcing a stereotype of racial egalitarians as intolerant snowflakes or radical thought police enforcing extreme forms of political correctness. Consider just a few of the highly publicized examples concerning disinvited or disrupted speakers in spring 2017: Charles Murray at Middlebury College,[98] Heather MacDonald at Claremont McKenna College,[99] Milo Yiannopoulos and Ann Coulter at UC-Berkeley,[100] Ben Shapiro at UW-Madison,[101] Richard Spencer at Auburn University,[102] and Nobel Prize laureate James Watson at the University of Illinois at Urbana-Champaign,[103] as well as Bret Weinstein's persecution at Evergreen State[104] and Richard Dawkins's disinvitation to a Berkeley public radio station.[105] In the face of the assault on free speech by adherents of the fundamental conflict model, conservatives as well as fascists and white supremacists have used the "free speech martyr" and "political correctness" cards to significant rhetorical and political advantage. Offensive speech openly expressed can be opposed. Broad speech restrictions push offensive speech into the underground marketplace of ideas or are circumvented by coded or alternate expressions. Longtime gay rights advocate and free speech defender Jonathan Rauch observes, "As long as they remain bigoted, bigots will simply find other words."[107]

Third, and arising in part from the second, the prevalence of and widespread media attention to overbroad and unduly vague hate speech policies and arbitrary enforcements has contributed to a noticeable decline in the public's opinion of public colleges and universities, especially among conservatives. Conservatives have attacked free speech on campuses and criticized liberals and alleged liberal bias in higher education for many years,[107] but a 2017 Pew Research Center survey found that 58 percent of Republicans—compared with 32 percent in 2010—think higher education has a negative effect on the country.[108] An August 2017 Gallup poll found over half of those surveyed had only some or very little confidence in higher education (56% overall, with Republicans at 67% and Democrats at 43%).[109] Since higher education is an important platform for studying and promoting racial equality, a loss in higher education credibility and support directly undermines its ability to study and promote racial equality.

Finally, hate speech has value despite the harms it can cause. Historically, speech considered "hateful" in the United States has expanded the marketplace of ideas. The classic examples are abolitionism, women's suffrage, and civil rights protests. Modern examples include the field of sex research and the LGBTQ rights movement. Hate speech can serve as a safety valve to avoid or minimize violence. For example, abolitionist Carl Schurz, speaking to a hostile audience more than 150 years ago, observed,

> When a man is suppressed, the "inner life" is pent up in his breast; it longs for air which is forbidden it; it is pent up like the steam in an overcharged boiler, which, the more it is compressed, the more it approaches a violent and destructive explosion; and at last he cries out: "Let me speak, or I will fight!" Thus the peaceful devotee of an idea has become a rebel against the existing order. Bring demagogism to the test of free discussion, and it will soon unmask itself . . . when in the open light of day argument struggles with argument.[110]

Schurz's conviction that the truth will always win in an open contest is overly optimistic, but his point that speech can be cathartic remains. Finally, as Trevor Burrus notes, "Fostering self-expression and self-development is another important reason we have a strong and uncompromising First Amendment. As homosexuals who have 'come out' know all too well, expressing something publicly is crucial to defining oneself."[111]

In contrast to the fundamental conflict model, the fundamental ally model rejects broad speech bans and illicit silencing of speech while allowing, even encouraging, vigorous advocacy for equality. Expression that constitutes a true threat, hostile workplace or academic environment harassment, educational disruption, or other category of illegal speech can be prosecuted and punished. Beyond those narrow conditions, the fundamental ally model urges egalitarians to keep the moral and legal high ground by countering hate speech and discriminatory attitudes with their own speech, lawful protests, educational efforts, and other legal means. It is important to recognize a growing body of empirical evidence that noncensorial strategies for resisting constitutionally protected hate speech are more effective than punitive strategies, a fact that increasingly leads Europeans to call for US-style speech protections.[112]

Consider an example clarifying the difference between the two models. In 2013, a white female first-year university student sent a racist Facebook personal message to a friend during class.[113] Though she did not intend her message to go any further, it eventually came to the attention of two African American students who lived in the same dorm, and via their residence assistant to a university committee composed of administrators and faculty. The two African American students had a frank discussion with the message sender and were satisfied with the results of that conversation, but the committee dismissed the

African American students as naive and infected with internalized racism. Fully committed to the university's (unconstitutional) "zero tolerance" policy for hate speech,[114] they ordered the student to vacate her dormitory room within the week, write a formal letter of apology, take a class on racism and discrimination, and write a five-page essay—even though no formal or informal complaint was filed, no hearing was held, and no legal counsel or First Amendment expertise was sought. This is an example of the lack of due process afforded students at many universities and colleges.[115] Her crime? She allegedly violated the residence hall policies on harassment and disorderly conduct as well as the university's policies on computer use and discriminatory conduct.[116] At the time, all four policies were designated by the Foundation for Individual Rights in Education as "red light" policies that were overbroad and thus unconstitutional on their face. When some committee members later learned the multitude of constitutional problems with their approach and decision, some proclaimed they would do it again—until they learned that such an action could well forfeit their qualified immunity and expose them to personal legal liability.[117] The fundamental conflict model produces a close-minded mentality willing to go to any length to stamp out offensive speech. The two black students who exemplified the fundamental ally model by confronting and persuading the messaging student achieved a far more effective and constitutionally sound outcome.

This example leads to the second problem with the fundamental conflict model: it produces zealots who feel justified in opposing the speech they dislike by any means necessary, whether by illegitimately silencing, disrupting, or even violently responding to opponents. When a person is convinced there must be "zero tolerance" for hate speech, that speech itself is violence, that theft and vandalism in the name of antiracism is protected speech, and the law won't punish their opponents, an increasing number of people take matters into their own hands. To list a few examples: the "Irvine 11" who disrupted an invited Israeli speaker;[118] the students and community members who shouted down and assaulted Charles Murray and Allison Stanger at Middlebury College;[119] the antifas who violently disrupted Milo Yiannopoulos at UC-Berkeley,[120] the students who disrupted Bret Weinstein's class at Evergreen State University and led him to flee campus in fear of his safety;[121] the Black Lives Matter leader in Charleston, South Carolina, who stole and damaged a Confederate flag during a South Carolina Secessionist Party rally,[122] and the protesters at the University of North Carolina who toppled the confederate Silent Sam statue.[123] Conor Friedersdorf reports examples of students spitting on those they disagree with, using physical intimidation and bullying, and shredding newspapers.[124]

To be sure, rationales are offered to support such vigilante actions. Marcuse's argument for progressive censorship—banning repressive ideas and actions—is most frequently credited,[125] although other popular movements have also contributed to this mentality.[126] This is not the place for an extended evaluation of Marcuse's Marxist argument[127] or analysis of other popular movements; it will suffice to point out how these tactics are rationalizations that undermine the quest for racial equality in at least four ways. First, the vigilante movement reinforces the stereotype that racial equality advocates are intellectually or emotionally unwilling or unable to listen or respond to views they oppose. Like the Irish vigilantes who stormed stages, threw eggs, and silenced or disrupted or violently opposed speech they hated in the late 1880s and early 1900s, modern hate speech vigilantes merely reinforce the negative stereotypes. Second, the vigilante movement contradicts the role and value of civil and rational debate that underpins the egalitarian critique of hate speech and gives it the moral and legal high ground. If racist words are low value due to their metaphorical equivalence to physical violence, how much lower in value is antiracist expression that is actual physical disruption or violence? What began as a movement to improve civility, toleration, and respect for differences has become a movement that decreases civility, toleration, and respect for differences. Third, the vigilante movement invites opponents to respond in kind. The old saw "turnabout is fair play" comes to mind here. If antiracists silence and disrupt opponents and violently assert their opinions, racists will respond in kind and defend their actions on the same grounds. It is one thing to act in self-defense, it is another to be the aggressor. Moreover, as continuing police violence against innocent or vulnerable people of color and protesters indicate, one cannot assume that police who become involved in the mayhem will side with the oppressed or their supporters. Finally, the vigilante movement has triggered a nationwide legislative effort to enact new campus free speech protections that may endanger rather than protect free speech and academic freedom. The federal Hyde/Summers bill of 1991 failed to pass, but campus speech laws passed in Arizona, Colorado, Kentucky, Missouri, Tennessee, Utah, and Virginia and are under consideration at around a dozen more. In 2017, the US House and Senate both held hearings providing considerable testimony critical of campus censorship and political correctness, the first step toward potential legislation. A year after the University of Wisconsin Board of Regents passed a new policy on academic freedom and freedom of expression in October 2017 requiring mandatory punishments for "disruptive" student protests, no guidelines or clarification on what constitutes disruption have been provided by the university system.

In contrast to the fundamental conflict model, the fundamental ally model encourages counterspeech and education, lawful protest of opponents, civil and rational discussion, argument and debate, and other lawful strategies. These strategies do not guarantee advances in equality—*nothing* can guarantee advances in equality—but throughout US history these methods have proven more effective than censorship in promoting participation and inclusion and combating pernicious orthodoxies. A commitment to robust free speech remains essential to advocates of racial equality by providing a powerful moral and legal defense for race egalitarians who attack the status quo and demand a better future.

It bears repeating that robust free speech protection also applies to many hateful and offensive expressions by racists, sexists, homophobes, and others who deny fundamental human equality. African Americans and members of other historically oppressed and marginalized groups suffer a disproportionate amount of hate speech. However, if we pit liberty *against* equality rather than promote liberty *and* equality, those who strongly dissent against the status quo will certainly fall prey to the very restrictions they imagine will only be imposed on their opponents. Except in narrowly defined circumstances, counterspeech and other lawful methods, not government censors, are best suited to win the struggle against racism and other pernicious forms of discrimination. To those who object that verbal condemnations of racism are not sufficient, Henry Louis Gates Jr. replies,

> this skepticism about the power of "mere words" comports oddly with the attempt to regulate "mere words' that, since they are spoken by those not in a position of authority, would seem to have even less symbolic force. Why is it "mere words" when a university only condemns racist speech, but not "mere words" that the student utters in the first place? Whose words are "only words"? Why are racist words deeds, but anti-racist words just lip service? And is the verbal situation really as asymmetrical as it first appears? Surely the rebuke "racist" also has the power to wound.[128]

To be sure, the storm clouds of racism continue to hang over the nation. The increase in white supremacist and racist expression both on and off campuses coinciding with Donald Trump's campaign and election to the presidency is extremely disheartening.[129] But there is no reliable or convincing evidence that broad hate speech bans are effective methods for increasing equality. The best evidence is that over time and with great effort and sacrifice, the robust exercise of First Amendment values has and continues to be more effective. Limiting censorship to narrow categories may seem like two steps forward, one step back, but expanding censorship to broad categories would be one step forward and two steps back.

CONCLUSION

Richard Delgado observes that historically, "minorities have made the greatest progress when they acted in defiance of the First Amendment."[130] However, this observation conflates the old obnoxious "bad tendency" legal standard with more abiding First Amendment values. For too long, African Americans (and others) had to appeal to First Amendment values without the protection of law when exercising speech, press, assembly, petition, and religion to promote racial justice. It was only recently that First Amendment law caught up to those abiding values.

Now that First Amendment law has caught up to those values, we would do well to listen to the advice of Bennett Carpenter: "no one will save us but ourselves. Rather than relying on the state to censure hate speech, anti-racists can assume that task"[131] Conceptually, doctrinally, and empirically liberty and equality are fundamentally connected, rather than in fundamental conflict, due to their shared opposition to orthodoxy and commitment to inclusion and participation. To be sure, there are cases of conflict between liberty and equality. Robust speech rights sometimes result in real harms. However, the preponderance of historical and contemporary evidence shows that free speech as a value has been essential to progress in racial equality in the United States. To abandon that legacy, to accept a fundamental conflict between liberty and equality curtailing speech rights and illegally disrupting protected speech by opponents is intellectually flawed and detrimental to further progress in racial equality. We should punish hate speech that fits existing categories of illegal speech and resist hate speech that does not fit such categories with our own right to free speech since the preponderance of legal and empirical evidence (summarized most effectively by Strossen) shows that broad hate speech laws undermine free speech and equality, are invariably overbroad and unduly vague, are ineffective and even counterproductive at reducing hate speech, and are less effective than noncensorial methods.

In 1963, when Southern racist vigilantes had virtual carte blanche to racially discriminate and even physically attack antiracists, a student group invited Alabama governor and rabid segregationist George Wallace to speak at Yale University. Pauli Murray, a black lawyer and experienced civil rights activist, wrote a letter urging Yale President Kingman Brewster Jr. to allow Wallace to speak. Murray, who helped organize the historic March on Washington for Jobs and Freedom that same year and was serving on President Kennedy's Commission on the Status of Women, abhorred segregation and Wallace's message, but she recognized that the First Amendment "has been the principle behind the enforcement of the rights of the Little Rock Nine, James Meredith and others to attend desegregated schools in the face of a hostile community and threats of violence. It must operate equally in the case of Governor Wallace."[132] Her arguments to Brewster were repeated in the highly regarded Woodward Report in 1974.[133] Murray courageously devoted a lifetime to the promotion of civil rights and civil liberties and was honored by Yale in 2017 with a new residential college dedicated to her. Numerous surveys indicate that many Americans, especially younger generations, have little knowledge of or appreciation for the robust view of free speech that Murray defended.[134] Perhaps understanding and appreciating her embrace of liberty *and* equality—in fact, the centuries-long alliance of African Americans and First Amendment values—can help reverse the trend.

NOTES

PREFACE

1. *State v. Pierce*, 163 WI 615, 619 (1916).

2. *United States v. Schwimmer*, 279 US 644 (1929).

3. *Palko v. Connecticut*, 302 US 314, 327 (1937). Frank Palka (a clerk's error resulted in the name Palko) focused on whether the Fifth Amendment's protection against double jeopardy applied to states. The court determined that right was not "essential to a fundamental scheme of ordered liberty" and upheld Palka's conviction for murder. The court reversed itself and incorporated the ban on double jeopardy in *Benton v. Maryland*, 395 US 784 (1969).

4. Thomas Emerson, *Toward a General Theory of the First Amendment* (New York: Random House, 1966), 59.

5. David Hudson Jr., "Civil Rights & First Amendment," First Amendment Center, accessed 4-13-2016, http://www.firstamendmentcenter.org/civil-rights-first-amendment.

6. Owen Fiss, *The Irony of Free Speech*, 2nd ed. (Cambridge, MA: Harvard University Press, 1996), 12.

7. Richard Delgado and Jean Stefancic, *Understanding Words That Wound* (Boulder, CO: Westview Press, 2004), 114–18.

8. Alexander Tsesis, *Destructive Messages: How Hate Speech Paves the Way for Harmful Social Movements* (New York: New York University Press, 2002). See also George Anastaplo, *Campus Hate-Speech Codes, Natural Rights, and Twentieth Century Atrocities*, rev. ed. (Lewiston, NY: Edwin Mellen Press, 1999), and George Frederickson, *Racism: A Short History* (Princeton, NJ: Princeton University Press, 2002).

9. Catharine MacKinnon, *Only Words* (Cambridge, MA: Harvard University Press, 1993).

10. Mari Matsuda, "Public Response to Racist Speech: Considering the Victims Story," *Michigan Law Review* 87 (1989): 2320, 2358–59.

11. Even scholars who disagree with broad speech codes have acknowledged a fundamental conflict. For example, see Michael Kent Curtis, *Free Speech,*

The People's Darling Privilege (Durham, NC: Duke University Press, 2000), 64 (quoting E. F. Schumacher).

12. See, for example, Peter Moore, "Half of Democrats Support a Ban on Hate Speech," YouGov, May 20, 2015, accessed 9-19-2017, https://today.yougov.com/news/2015/05/20/hate-speech/; Jacob Poushter, "40% of Millennials OK with Limiting Speech Offensive to Minorities," Pew Research Center, November 20, 2015, accessed 10-12-2017, http://www.pewresearch.org/fact-tank/2015/11/20/40-of-millennials-ok-with-limiting-speech-offensive-to-minorities/; Jim McLaughlin and Rob Schmidt, "National Undergraduate Study," McLaughlin and Associates, October 26, 2015, accessed 11-12-2016, https://www.dropbox.com/s/sfmpoeytvqc3cl2/NATL%20College%2010-25-15%20Presentation.pdf?dl=0; Gallup, "Free Expression on Campus: A Survey of U.S. College students and U.S. Adults," Gallup, 2016, accessed 2-2-2017, https://www.knightfoundation.org/media/uploads/publication_pdfs/FreeSpeech_campus.pdf; John Villasenor, "Views among College Students Regarding the First Amendment: Results from a New Survey," Brookings Institution, September 18, 2017, accessed 9-19-2017, https://www.brookings.edu/blog/fixgov/2017/09/18/views-among-college-students-regarding-the-first-amendment-results-from-a-new-survey/.

13. See, for example, Yuya Kiuchi (ed.), *Race Still Matters: The Reality of African American Lives and the Myth of Postracial Society* (Albany: State University of New York Press, 2016).

14. See, for example, Laura Beth Nielsen, *License to Harass: Law, Hierarchy, and Offensive Public Speech* (Princeton, NJ: Princeton University Press, 2004), and "Subtle, Pervasive, Harmful: Racist and Sexist Remarks in Public as Hate Speech," *Journal of Social Issues* 58, no. 2 (2002): 265–80.

CHAPTER 1

1. Frederick Douglass, "West India Emancipation," August 3, 1857, speech in Canandaigua, New York, accessed 3-21-2016, http://www.blackpast.org/1857-frederick-douglass-if-there-no-struggle-there-no-progress.

2. Scholars use the phrase "American apartheid" variously. John Howard uses it to refer to housing segregation following *Plessy v. Ferguson* (1896). John Howard, *The Shifting Wind: The Supreme Court and Civil Rights from Reconstruction to* Brown (Albany: State University of New York Press, 1999). Douglas Massey and Nancy Denton use it to describe urban housing segregation and its relationship to the continuing poverty of African Americans in

American Apartheid: Segregation and the Making of the Underclass (Cambridge, MA: Harvard University Press, 1998).

3. John Hope Franklin and Elizabeth Brooks Higginbotham, *From Slavery to Freedom*, 9th ed. (New York: McGraw-Hill, 2009), 49.

4. Albert Blaustein and Robert Zangrando (eds.), *Civil Rights and the American Negro* (New York: Trident Press, 1968), 3.

5. William Loren Katz, *Black Indians: A Hidden Heritage* (New York: Atheneum, 1996), 109–25.

6. Mennonites in Germantown, Pennsylvania, offered the first protest to slavery in 1688. Blaustein and Zangrando (eds.), *Civil Rights*, 10. Judge Samuel Sewall of Massachusetts published the first abolitionist tract, *The Selling of Joseph*, in 1700. Blaustein and Zangrando (eds.), *Civil Rights*, 12–13. The last of the original thirteen colonies, Georgia initially prohibited slavery in 1732 but passed laws permitting slavery and prohibiting interracial marriage in 1750. Blaustein and Zangrando (eds.), *Civil Rights*, 26–27.

7. Blaustein and Zangrando (eds.), *Civil Rights*, 20–21.

8. Franklin and Higginbotham, *Slavery to Freedom*, 65.

9. For a summary of the racism and slavery debate, see Gao Chungchan, *African Americans in the Reconstruction Era* (New York: Routledge, 2000), chap. 1.

10. Louise Edward Inglehart, *Press and Speech Freedoms in America, 1619–1995* (Westport, CT: Greenwood Press, 1997), 6.

11. James Breig, "Early American Newspapering," *Colonial Williamsburg Journal* (spring 2003), accessed 3-24-2016, https://www.history.org/Foundation/journal/spring03/journalism.cfm.

12. Inglehart, *Press and Speech Freedoms*, 4–34.

13. Leonard Levy, *Legacy of Suppression* (Cambridge, MA: Harvard University Press, 1960), vi. Levy's more complete work was *Emergence of a Free Press* (New York: Oxford University Press, 1985).

14. The eminent English jurist William Blackstone summarized: "The liberty of the press is indeed essential to the nature of a free state: but this consists in laying no previous restraints upon publications, and not in freedom from censure for criminal matter when published. Every freeman has an undoubted right to lay what sentiments he pleases before the public: to forbid this, is to destroy the freedom of the press; but if he publishes what is improper, mischievous, or illegal, he must take the consequence of his own temerity." William Blackstone, *Commentaries on English Law*, book 4, chapter 11, section 13, para. 2 (Oxford: Clarendon Press, 1765–1769), available at http://avalon.law.yale.edu/subject_menus/blackstone.asp. For more on the bad tendency doctrine, see Michael

Kent Curtis, *Free Speech, The People's Darling Privilege: Struggles for Freedom of Expression in American History* (Durham, NC: Duke University Press, 2000), 10–12.

15. New York colonial governor William Crosby ordered John Peter Zenger arrested for criminal libel after Zenger published critical statements about him in the *New York Weekly Journal.* A grand jury refused to indict Zenger, but the attorney general put him on trial anyway. Zenger's lawyers, Alexander Hamilton and William Smith Jr., argued that truth was a defense against libel, and the jury acquitted Zenger after only ten minutes of deliberation. For details, see Richard Kluger, *Indelible Ink: The Trials of John Peter Zenger and the Birth of America's Free Press* (New York: Norton, 2016).

16. Harry Croswell was a Federalist convicted of criminal libel for statements made against various officials, including President Thomas Jefferson. Croswell appealed because the jury had been instructed only to determine if he made the statements, not whether the statements constituted libel. Despite Alexander Hamilton's argument that truth is a defense, the New York Supreme Court judges deadlocked. Croswell was not sentenced or retried, and the legislature made his conviction moot the next year when it passed a law protecting truthful statements from prosecution.

17. For example, Kenneth Davis writes: "The real story of religion in America's past is an often awkward, frequently embarrassing and occasionally bloody tale.... From the earliest arrival of Europeans on America's shores, religion has often been a cudgel, used to discriminate, suppress and even kill the foreign, the 'heretic' and the 'unbeliever'—including the 'heathen' natives already here." Davis, "America's True History of Religious Tolerance," *Smithsonian Magazine*, October 2010, accessed 3-4-2016, http://www.smithsonianmag.com/history/americas-true-history-of-religious-tolerance-61312684/. For details, see Peter Gottschalk, *American Heretics: Catholics, Jews, Muslims, and the History of Religious Intolerance* (New York: St. Martin's Press, 2013); and John Corrigan and Lynn Neal (eds.), *Religious Intolerance in America: A Documentary History* (Chapel Hill: University of North Carolina Press, 2010).

18. Warren Nord, *Religion and American Education: Rethinking a National Dilemma* (Chapel Hill: University of North Carolina Press, 1995), 64–69.

19. The United States played a comparatively small role in the transatlantic slave trade because the predominant use of slaves was in sugar production and the North American climate was not suited to sugar production. Less than 10 percent of the nearly 10 million Africans forced into slavery in the New World came to the United States, whereas 40 percent went to Brazil.

The slave population in 1800 in the United States was approximately 20 percent of the total; in the West Indies it was 90 percent. Moreover, the importation of slaves ended in the United States in 1807 but lasted into the 1860s in many other countries. David Mustard, *Racial Justice in America* (Santa Barbara, CA: ABC-CLIO, 2003), 2–5.

20. Fritz Hirschfeld, *George Washington and Slavery: A Documentary Portrayal* (Columbia: University of Missouri Press, 1997).

21. Katherine Hessler, "Early Efforts to Suppress Protest: Unwanted Abolitionist Speech," *Boston University Public Law Journal* 7 (spring 1998): 185, 197.

22. Blaustein and Zangrando (eds.), *Civil Rights*, 44.

23. See, for example, Gavin Wright, *Slavery and American Economic Development* (Baton Rouge: Louisiana State University Press, 2006).

24. Ruth Hawes, "Slavery in Mississippi," *Sewanee Review*, 21, no. 2 (April 1913): 231. Hawes, a Jim Crow–era apologist, concludes that much in slavery was "cruel, revolting and oppressive, [but] far more was humane, generous, loving and sympathetic." Hawes, "Slavery in Mississippi," 234.

25. Blake Touchstone, *Master and Slaves in the House of the Lord: Race and Religion in the American South 1740–1870* (Lexington: University Press of Kentucky, 1988), 99.

26. Touchstone, *Master and Slaves*, 105. Haven Perkins discusses white Christian attitudes and practices regarding religion for slaves in Southern states between 1830 and 1850, including Christian justifications for slavery and white ministry to the slaves. Haven Perkins, "Religion for Slaves: Difficulties and Methods," *Church History* 10, no. 3 (September 1941): 228–45.

27. Emily West, *Family or Freedom: People of Color in the Antebellum South* (Lexington: University Press of Kentucky, 2012), 22–23. See more generally Ira Berlin, *Slaves without Masters: The Free Negro in the Antebellum South* (New York: New Press, 2007).

28. Hawes, "Slavery in Mississippi," 223–34, 229.

29. S. Jonathan Bass, "Transportation Discrimination," in *Encyclopedia of Civil Rights in America*, vol. 3, ed. David Bradley and Shelly Fisher Fishkin (Armonk: Sharpe Reference, 1998), 851.

30. Laws disenfranchising black men passed in Virginia (1762), Georgia (1777), South Carolina (1790), Delaware (1792), Kentucky (1799), Maryland (1801), Ohio (1803), New Jersey (1807), Louisiana (1812), Indiana (1816), Mississippi (1817), Illinois and Connecticut (1817), Alabama (1819), Missouri and New York (1821), Rhode Island (1822), North Carolina (1835), Tennessee

(1834), Arkansas (1836), Michigan (1837), Pennsylvania (1838), Florida and Texas (1845), Iowa (1846), Wisconsin (1848), California (1850), Minnesota (1858), Oregon (1859), Kansas (1861), and West Virginia (1863). Christopher Malone, *Between Freedom and Bondage: Race, Party and Voting Rights in the Antebellum North* (New York: Routledge, 2008), 4–5.

31. Malone, *Between Freedom and Bondage*, 6.

32. Franklin and Higginbotham, *Slavery to Freedom*, 165.

33. For example, South Carolina banned slave education in 1740, and Virginia did so in 1819. See Heather Andrea Williams, *Self-Taught: African American Education in Slavery and Freedom* (Chapel Hill: University of North Carolina Press, 2005).

34. Franklin and Higginbotham, *Slavery to Freedom*, 175.

35. John Simpkin, "Education of Slaves," Spartacus Educational, updated January 2015, accessed 3-25-2016, http://spartacus-educational.com/USASeducation.htm.

36. In England, the doctrine of parliamentary sovereignty prevents courts from striking down primary legislation. In The Netherlands, the federal constitution prevents courts from ruling on the constitutionality of legislation.

37. Saikrishna Prakash and John Yoo, "The Origins of Judicial Review," *University of Chicago Law Review* 70 (2003): 887, and "Origins of Judicial Review: Questions for the Critics of Judicial Review," *George Washington Law Review* 72 (2003): 354.

38. *Marbury v. Madison* (1803) concerned one of the "midnight judges": fifty-eight Federalist judges and justices of the peace appointed by outgoing Federalist President John Adams prior to leaving office to weaken the incoming Democratic-Republican majority in Congress and administration of Thomas Jefferson. William Marbury was appointed justice of the peace in the District of Columbia, but the incoming secretary of State (James Madison) refused to deliver the appointing documents. Marbury petitioned the Supreme Court to require Madison to deliver the documents based on the Judicial Act of 1798.

39. *Marbury*, 180. Prakash and Yoo point out that state courts engaged in judicial review of state law prior to the Constitutional Convention and exercised judicial review even in the absence of any textual authority, including *Josiah Philip's Case* (VA 1778); *Holmes v. Walton* (NJ 1780); *Commonwealth v. Caton*, 8 VA (4 Call) 5, 20 (1782); *Rutgers v. Maddington* (NY City Mayor's Ct. 1784); *Symsbury Case*, 1 Kirby 444 (CT Super. Ct. 1785); *Trevett v. Weeden* (RI 1786); *Ten Pound Act Cases* (NH 1786); and *Bayard v. Singleton*, 1 NC (Mart.) 48 (1787). Moreover, leading constitutional framers such as James Madison,

Alexander Hamilton, Patrick Henry, and Samuel Adams and dozens of other public figures publicly endorsed judicial review.

40. Congressional Research Services, *The Constitution of the United States, Analysis and Interpretation*, 2013 Supplement (Washington, DC: Congressional Research Services, 2013), 49–50.

41. Tony Seybert, "Slavery and Native Americans in British North America and the United States: 1600 to 1865," Slavery in America, n.d., accessed 4-1-2016, https://web.archive.org/web/20040804001522/http:/www.slaveryinamerica.org/history/hs_es_indians_slavery.htm; Christina Snyder, *Slavery in Indian Country: The Changing Face of Captivity in Early America* (Cambridge, MA: Harvard University Press, 2010); Allan Gallay, *Indian Slavery in Colonial America* (Lincoln: University of Nebraska Press, 2009).

42. Almon Wheeler Lauber, *Indian Slavery in Colonial Times within the Present Limits of the United States (1913; reprint, Williamstown, MA: Corner House, 1970).*

43. Fay Yarbrough, *Race and the Cherokee Nation: Sovereignty in the Nineteenth Century* (Philadelphia: University of Pennsylvania Press, 2008), 112–23.

44. *Cherokee Nation v. Georgia* was the second of three Native American decisions by the Supreme Court known as the Marshall trilogy. The first case, *Johnson v. M'Intosh*, 21 US 543 (1823), held that Indians could not sell lands to individuals, and states do not have legal standing to settle aboriginal land claims. Years later, when gold seekers tried to purchase land from Athabascan people, the District of Alaska court held in *United States v. Berrigan*, 2 Alaska 442 (D. Alaska 1905), that only the federal government could negotiate with Indians over land rights.

45. *Cherokee Nation*, 15.

46. Laura Woliver, "Dissent Is Patriotic: Disobedient Founders, Narratives, and Street Battles," *Tulsa Law Review* 50 (winter 2015): 384.

47. Charles Warren, *The Supreme Court in United States History*, 2nd ed., vol. 1 (Boston: Little, Brown, 1926), 757.

48. Frederick Drake and Lynn Nelson (eds.), *States' Rights and American Federalism: A Documentary History* (Westport, CT: Greenwood Press, 1999); Kermit Hall (ed.), *A Nation of States: Federalism at the Bar of the Supreme Court* (New York: Garland, 2000).

49. *Worcester* served as beneficial precedent many years later. See, for example, *Iron Crow v. Ogalala Sioux Tribe*, 231 F.2d 89 (8th Cir. 1956) (Indian sovereignty authorized jurisdiction of tribal courts); *United States v. Washington*, 384 F. Supp.

312 (W.D.Wash. 1974) (tribal sovereignty protects Native American fishing rights); and *Merrion v. Jicarilla Apache Tribe*, 455 US 130 (1982) (tribal sovereignty enables tribes to impose taxes on non-Indians doing business on the reservation).

50. Amy Sturgis, *The Trail of Tears and Indian Removal* (Westport, CT: Greenwood, 2007); and Theda Perdue and Michael Green, *The Cherokee Nation and the Trail of Tears* (New York: Penguin, 2007).

51. Lewis Perry, *Civil Disobedience: An American Tradition* (New Haven, CT: Yale University Press, 2013), 60.

52. Ashland Kuersten, *Women and the Law: Leaders, Cases and Documents* (Santa Barbara, CA: ABC-CLIO, 2003); and Judith Baer and Leslie Friedman Goldstein, *The Constitutional and Legal Rights of Women: Cases in Law and Social Change* (Los Angeles: Roxbury, 2006).

53. Blackstone writes: "By marriage, the husband and wife are one person in law: that is, the very being or legal existence of the woman is suspended during the marriage, or at least is incorporated and consolidated into that of the husband: under whose wing, protection, and cover, she performs every thing." Blackstone, *Commentaries*, book 1, chapter 15, section 4, para. III.

54. Marylynn Salmon, "The Legal Status of Women 1776–1830," *History Now: The Journal of the Gilder Lehrman Institute of American History* 7 (spring 2006).

55. Melissa Homestead, *American Women Authors and Literary Property, 1822–1869* (New York: Cambridge University Press, 2005), 29.

56. Joyce Warren, *Women, Money, and the Law: Nineteenth-Century Fiction, Gender, and the Courts* (Iowa City: University of Iowa Press, 2005), 51–53.

57. "Frederick Douglass," in *101 Changemakers: Rebels and Radicals Who Changed American History*, ed. Michelle Bollinger and Dao Tran (Chicago: Haymarket Books, 2012), 20.

58. We must address both public and private suppression because liberty needs protection as an ethical ideal as well as legal norm. In 1857, Abraham Lincoln observed, "No law is stronger than is the public sentiment where it is to be enforced. Free speech and discussion, *and immunity from whip and tar and feather*, seem implied by the guarantee to each state of a 'republican form of government.'" In Inglehart, *Press and Speech Freedoms*, 84, emphasis added. More recently, David Yassky makes the same point in a critique of a Louisiana law setting a $500 maximum fine for battery but a $25 maximum fine if the battery was during a flag-burning incident, "Either I can burn a flag with impunity, or I do so at the risk of violent retaliation by the state or by 'private' onlookers. In

either case, my real rights—my actual day-to-day ability to do things—are very much the product of government (in)action." David Yassky, "Eras of the First Amendment," *Columbia Law Review* 91 (November 1991): 1699, 1751.

59. Yassky, "Eras of the First Amendment," 1711.

60. Nat Hentoff, *The First Freedom* (New York: Delacorte, 1980), 84.

61. John Barron and John Craig sued Baltimore for damages after the city had done street work diverting streams that made the water depth surrounding their wharf too shallow. Barron and Craig argued they deserved compensation under the Takings Clause, stating private property shall not be taken for public use without just compensation. They won at trial court but lost both appeals.

62. Congress did not punish another critic until 1916. Michael Gibson, "The Supreme Court and Freedom of Expression from 1791 to 1917," *Fordham Law Review* 55 (1986): 278. The Supreme Court ruled in that case, *Marshall v. Gordon*, 243 US 521 (1917), that Congress had a limited power to restrict criticism by members in out-of-chamber publications.

63. *People v. Croswell*, 3 Johns. Cas. 337 NY 1804.

64. *Commonwealth v. Morris*, 3 VA 176 (1811).

65. *Updegraph v. Commonwealth*, 11 Serg. & Rawle 394 PA (1824).

66. Inglehart, *Press and Speech Freedoms*, 84.

67. Gibson, "The Supreme Court," 263, 272.

68. Patrick Washburn, *The African American Press: Voice of Freedom* (Evanston, IL: Northwestern University Press, 2006), 25.

69. Washburn, *African American Press*, 36.

70. Hasan Crockett, "The Incendiary Pamphlet: David Walker's Appeal in Georgia," *Journal of Negro History* 86, no. 3 (2001): 1.

71. Howard Zinn, *A People's History of the American States: 1492 to the Present (New York: Harper Collins, 2003),* 180.

72. Nord, *Religion and American Education*, 64–69.

73. Michael deHaven Newsom, "Common School Religion: Judicial Narratives in a Protestant Empire," *Southern California Interdisciplinary Law Journal* 11 (spring 2002): 219–337; Neil G. McCluskey, S.J., *Catholic Viewpoint on Education* (Garden City, NY: Image Books, 1962); Tracy Fessenden, "The Nineteenth-Century Bible Wars and the Separation of Church and State," *Church History* 74 (December 2005): 788; and Robert H. Lord, John E. Sexton, and Edward Harrington, *History of the Archdiocese of Boston in the Various Stages of Its Development, 1604–1943*, vol. 2 (New York: Sheed and Ward, 1944), 673. For example, the Massachusetts constitution (1780) called for "public Protestant teachers" to foster "piety, education, and morality" through the KJB. In 1838,

KJB-centered public schools were developed in Cincinnati, Ohio, to "control Catholic and other unruly crowds." A Maine school committee member vowed in 1853, "We are determined to protestantize the Catholic children; they shall read the Protestant Bible or be dismissed from the schools."

74. Newsom, "Common School Religion," 238–39; and Fessenden, "Nineteenth-Century Bible Wars," 790.

75. *State ex rel Finger v. Weedman*, 55 SD 343 (1929).

76. Consider three examples. In 1834, a Protestant mob in Boston burned down a Catholic convent after Catholics protested KJB reading in public schools. In 1844, Protestant mobs invaded and burned Catholic neighborhoods in the murderous Philadelphia Bible riots after Catholics protested Protestant bias in public schools. In 1854, after Catholics opposed Bible reading in Ellsworth, Maine, Protestant mobs bombed the chapel housing the Catholic school and tarred and feathered the Jesuit priest.

77. Joan Delfattore, *The Fourth R: Conflicts over Religion in America's Public Schools* (New Haven, CT: Yale University Press, 2004), 46–51. *Donahoe v. Richards*, 38 ME 379 (1854) held school authorities could force Catholic pupils to read the KJB because it contained the true morality. The Boston Police Court upheld the beating of a Catholic student's hands with a rattan stick by his teacher until the pupil agreed to recite from the KJB. *Spiller v. Inhabitants of Woburn*, 94 MA 127 (1866), held that devotional reading of the KJB did not violate a Catholic student's right of conscience or interfere in any way with their religion. *McCormick v. Burt*, 95 IL 263 (1880) upheld the suspension of a Catholic student for refusing to discontinue his studies during class reading of the KJB. *Moore v. Monroe*, 64 IA 367 (1884) rejected the Catholic argument that devotional KJB reading made the public school a place of worship.

78. *Permoli*, 609. The decision meant that New Orleans could legally ban corpses from Catholic (but not Protestant) churches and require Catholics (but not Protestants) to use state-established mortuaries.

79. Hessler, "Early Efforts to Suppress" 193.

80. Patrick Rael, *Black Identity and Black Protest in the Antebellum North* (Chapel Hill: University of North Carolina Press, 2002).

81. Hessler, "Early Efforts to Suppress," 185.

82. Virginia, Georgia, and Louisiana authorized the death penalty for abolitionist speech. Yassky, "Eras of the First Amendment," 1713; and Hessler, "Early Efforts to Suppress," 190.

83. Curtis, *Free Speech*, chap. 8.

84. In 1835, Postmaster Amos Kendall authorized postmaster confiscation of antislavery materials. Hessler, "Early Efforts to Suppress," 206.

85. For example, the congressional gag rule prohibiting discussion of slavery was eliminated in 1844 by a vote of 108–80.

86. Stewart Jay notes, "Until the late 1830s, abolitionists were effectively shut out of the regular press, sometimes denied access to public and private halls to hold meetings, often condemned and at times violently attacked by mobs." Stewart Jay, "The Creation of the First Amendment Right to Free Expression: From the Eighteenth Century to the Mid-Twentieth Century," *William Mitchell Law Review* 34 (2008): 773. See also Curtis, *Free Speech*, chap. 10.

87. Hessler, "Early Efforts to Suppress," 203–4.

88. Bernard Schwartz, *A Book of Legal Lists: A List of the Best and Worst Law* (New York: Oxford University Press, 1997); and Paul Finkelman, "*Scott v. Sandford*: The Court's Most Dreadful Case and How It Changed History," *Chicago-Kent Law Review* 82 (2007): 3.

89. The five prior cases rejecting a slave's petition for freedom were *Scott v. Negro London*, 7 US 324 (1806); *Scott v. Negro Ben*, 10 US 3 (1810); *Wood v. Davis*, 11 US 271 (1812); *Queen v. Hepburn*, 11 US 290 (1813); and *M'Cutchen v. Marshall*, 33 US 220 (1834).

90. *Dred Scott*, 416–17.

91. Freedom of the press fared better in the wartime Confederacy than in the Union. See Debra Reddin Van Tuyll, "Freedom of the Press in a Slave Society at War," in *An Indispensable Liberty: The Fight for Free Speech in Nineteenth-Century America*, ed. Mary Cronin (Carbondale: Southern Illinois Press, 2016), 61–89.

92. Michael Linfield, *Freedom under Fire: U.S. Civil Liberties in Times of War* (Boston: South End Press, 1991), 25.

93. Curtis, *Free Speech*, 281.

94. Thomas Carroll, "Freedom of Speech and Press during the Civil War," *Virginia Law Review* 9 (1923): 516. See also Inglehart, *Speech and Press Freedoms*, 85–88.

95. Frank Klement, *The Copperheads in the Middle West* (Gloucester, MA: Peter Smith, 1972). Klement discusses examples from across the Union in "President Lincoln, The Civil War, and the Bill of Rights," *Lincoln Herald* 94, no. 1 (1992): 10–23.

96. Carroll, "Freedom of Speech and Press," 551. Historians place most of the blame on Lincoln's military commanders; however, US Supreme Court Justice William Brennan later condemned Lincoln's "use of military arrests and trials throughout the war, relying on the insidious principle that if military detentions are constitutional in places of rebellion, they are constitutional as well in places where they may prevent the rebellion extending." Linfield, *Freedom under Fire*, 28.

97. Alexis Anderson, "The Formative Period of the First Amendment," *American Journal of Legal History* 24 (January 1980): 56, 56.

98. For example, David Yassky writes, "When the Civil War dramatically re-shaped the federal-state relationship, the structural purpose of the Bill of Rights changed in response.... No longer were the Constitution's protections of individual rights aimed exclusively at the federal government. Indeed, over the seventy years following the Civil War, imposing restrictions of state government became a central constitutional concern. But this concern found expression not through the. . .First Amendment but through the property-focused guarantees of the Fifth and Fourteenth Amendments. Free speech was relegated to the periphery." Yassky, "Eras of the First Amendment," 1702–3.

99. For details, see Howard, *Shifting Wind*.

100. *Acts of the General Assembly of the State of South Carolina, 1864–1865*, 291–304.

101. History.com Staff, "Black Leaders during Reconstruction," accessed 3-21-2016, http://www.history.com/topics/american-civil-war/black-leaders-during-reconstruction. For details, see Matthew Lynch (ed.), *Before Obama: A Reappraisal of Black Reconstruction Era Politicians* (Santa Barbara, CA: Praeger, 2012).

102. Nia-Malika Henderson, "The New Lynching Memorial Rewrites American History," CNN Travel, April 26, 2018, accessed 5-12-2018, https://www.cnn.com/travel/article/lynching-memorial-montgomery-alabama/index.html.

103. Richard Perloff, "The Press and Lynchings of African Americans," *Journal of Black Studies* 30, no. 3 (January 2000): 315.

104. Rayford Logan, *The Betrayal of the Negro: From Rutherford B. Hayes to Woodrow Wilson* (Boston: Da Capo Press, 1965), 261.

105. Perloff, "Press and Lynchings," 322.

106. After the US Supreme Court decision, Blyew and Kennard were tried in state court with black testimony allowed because the state law banning it had been repealed. Kennard was convicted and sentenced to life in prison, but was pardoned by the governor in 1885. Blyew's trial ended in a hung jury, and he escaped before he could be retried in federal court. He was recaptured in 1890 and sentenced to life in prison, but was pardoned by the governor in 1896. "The Family of Jack and Sallie Foster," University of Kentucky Libraries Notable Kentucky African American Database, accessed 4-29-2016, http://nkaa.uky.edu/record.php?note_id=2045.

107. Steven Andre, "The Transformation of Freedom of Speech: Unsnarling the Twisted Roots of *Citizens United v. FEC*," *John Marshall Law Review* 44, no. 1 (2010): 78.

108. Andre, "Transformation of Freedom of Speech," 79.

109. Andre, "Transformation of Freedom of Speech," 78.

110. For example, *United States v. Morrison*, 529 US 598 (2000), upheld its narrow interpretation of the Enforcement Clause to strike down parts of the Violence Against Women Act.

111. The first Civil Rights Act (March and April 1866) overturned *Dred Scott* but became moot when the Fourteenth Amendment was ratified. The next two acts (May 1866 and March 1867) outlawed kidnapping with the intent to deliver the victim as a slave domestically or abroad and prohibited "peonage" in New Mexico and "other parts" of the United States. The Enforcement Act of 1870 criminalized interference with the right of former slaves to vote. The 1871 Ku Klux Klan Act prohibited "those who go in disguise upon the public highway" to violate civil rights. Like the Civil Rights Act of 1875, many of these laws or provisions therein were ruled unconstitutional. Blaustein and Zangrando (eds.), *Civil Rights*, 227–29.

112. Frank Latham, *The Rise and Fall of Jim Crow, 1865–1964* (Danbury, CT: Franklin Watts, 1969), 56–57.

113. George de Huszar, *Equality in America* (New York: H.W. Wilson, 1949), 8.

114. See, for example, Leon Friedman, *Southern Justice* (New York: Pantheon Books, 1965), vi.

115. Latham, *Rise and Fall of Jim Crow*, 59.

116. Franklin and Higginbotham, *Slavery to Freedom*, 268.

117. Huszar, *Equality in America*, 9.

118. Comer Vann Woodward, *The Strange Career of Jim Crow*, 3rd rev. ed. (New York: Oxford University Press, 1974), chap. 1–3.

119. Peggy Pascoe, "Miscegenation Law, Court Cases, and Ideologies of 'Race' in Twentieth Century America," *Journal of American History* 83, no. 1 (June 1996): 49.

120. James Browning, "Anti-Miscegenation Laws in the United States," *Duke Bar Journal* 1 (1951): 33.

121. *Scott v. State*, 39 GA 321, 324 (1869); *Ford v. State*, 53 AL 150 (1875); *Hoover v. State*, 59 AL 57 (1877); *Kennedy v. State*, 76 NC 251 (1877); and *State v. Thrasher*, 3 TX App. 262 (1877).

122. For details see Pascoe, "Miscegenation Law."

123. Bass, "Transportation Discrimination," 852.

124. *Plessy*, 559.

125. Washburn, *African American Press*, 42–44.

126. *Berea College v. Kentucky*, 211 US 45 (1908), upheld a state law prohibiting private educational institutions chartered as corporations from admitting both black and white students. *McCabe v. Atchison, Topeka & Santa Fe Railway Co.*, 235 US 151 (1914), upheld a state law requiring separate but equal railway accommodations.

127. Blair Kelley, *Right to Ride: Streetcar Boycotts and African American Citizenship in the Era of Plessy v. Ferguson* (Chapel Hill: University of North Carolina Press, 2010).

128. Bass, "Transportation Discrimination," 852–53.

129. Vann Woodward, *Strange Career of Jim Crow*, 7.

130. Vann Woodward, *Strange Career of Jim Crow*, 68.

131. Franklin and Higginbotham, *Slavery to Freedom*, 286.

132. Chauncey DeVega, "White America's Racial Amnesia: The Sobering Truth about our Country's 'Race Riots,'" *Salon*, May 1, 2015, accessed 9-2192017, http://www.salon.com/2015/05/01/white_americas_racial_amnesia_the_sobering_truth_about_our_countrys_race_riots_partner. For details, see Howard, *Shifting Wind*, 159, 183–84, 196–98; Kimberley Harper, *White Man's Heaven: The Lynching and Expulsion of Blacks in the Ozarks 1894–1909* (Fayetteville: University of Arkansas Press, 2010); Steven Ash, *A Massacre in Memphis: The Race Riot that Shook the Nation One Year after the Civil War* (New York: Hill and Wang, 2013); and Ann Collins, *All Hell Broke Loose: American Race Riots from the Progressive Era through WWII* (Santa Barbara, CA: ABC-CLIO, 2012).

133. Janell Byrd-Chichester, "The Federal Courts and Claims of Discrimination in Higher Education," *Journal of Negro Education* 69, no. 1/2 (winter–spring 2000): 11–12.

134. Franklin and Higginbotham, *Slavery to Freedom*, 292–93.

135. Albert Kirwan, *Revolt of the Rednecks: Mississippi Politics, 1876–1925* (Lexington: University of Kentucky Press, 1951), 145–46.

136. Gil Kujovich, "Equal Opportunity in Higher Education and the Black Public College: The Era of Separate but Equal," *Minnesota Law Review* 72(1987): 26, 66.

137. Byrd-Chichester, "Federal Courts," 17.

138. Erika Lee, *At America's Gates: Chinese Immigration during the Exclusion Era, 1882–1943* (Chapel Hill: University of North Carolina Press,

2003); Joyce Kuo, "Excluded, Segregated and Forgotten: A Historical View of the Discrimination of Chinese Americans in Public Schools," *Asian American Law Journal* 5 (1998): 181–212; and James Gordon, "Was the First Justice Harlan Anti-Chinese?," *Western New England Law Review* 36 (2014): 291.

139. William Carrigan and Clive Web estimate that 597 Mexicans were lynched between 1848 and 1928, "The Lynching of Persons of Mexican Origin or Descent in the United States, 1848–1928," *Journal of Social History* 37, no. 2 (winter 2003): 413.

140. Rosemary Radford Ruether, *Christianity and Social Systems: Historical Constructions and Ethical Challenges* (Lanham, MD: Rowman and Littlefield, 2008), 84.

141. Ruether, *Christianity and Social Systems*, 81–82.

142. The court struck down the "grandfather" exemptions to literacy voting requirements of Oklahoma and Maryland in *Guinn and Beal v. United States*, 238 US 347 (1915), but upheld other intentionally discriminatory voting tests. *Blake v. McClung*, 172 US 239 (1898) (upheld residence requirements), *Pope v. Williams*, 193 US 621 (1904) (upheld residence requirements and registration system), *Myers v. Anderson*, 238 US 368 (1915) (upheld property qualifications), *Breedlove v. Suttles*, 302 US 277 (1937) (upheld poll taxes).

143. Robert Cover, "The Origins of Judicial Activism in the Protection of Minorities," *Yale Law Journal* 91 (June 1982): 1305.

144. Blacks were excluded from the jury, and black witnesses were whipped until they agreed to testify against the defendants. The court-appointed defense counsel called no witnesses, did not request a change of venue despite the white threats of violence, and called no defendants to the witness stand. The trial lasted less than an hour, and the jury returned guilty verdicts for all seventy-nine defendants within five minutes. Twelve defendants were sentenced to death for murder, and the rest were sentenced to long prison terms.

145. Ron Avery, "Late 1800s Bad for Blacks only in Vice Was There Equal Job Opportunity," Philly.com, Feburary 16, 1998, accessed 3-30-2016, http://articles.philly.com/1998-02-16/news/25752508_1_black-customers-philadelphia-blacks-black-lawyer.

146. Juliet Walker, *The History of Black Business in America: Capitalism, Race, Entrepreneurship*, 2nd ed., vol. 2 (Chapel Hill: University of North Carolina Press, 2009), 183.

147. Cecilia Conrad, John Whitehead, Patrick Mason, and James Stewart (eds.), *African Americans in the U.S. Economy* (Lanham, MD: Rowman and Littlefield, 2005).

148. James Stewart, "The Critical Role of African-Americans in the Development of the Pre–Civil War U.S. Economy," in *African Americans and the U.S. Economy*, ed. Cecilia Conrad, John Whitehead, Patrick Mason, and James Stewart (Lanham, MD: Rowman and Littlefield, 2005), 26.

149. Daniel Fusfeld and Timothy Bates, "The Black Sharecropping System and Its Decline," in *African Americans and the U.S. Economy*, ed. Cecilia Conrad, John Whitehead, Patrick Mason, and James Stewart (Lanham, MD: Rowman and Littlefield, 2005), 32–37.

150. Philip Foner, "The Rise of the Black Industrial Working Class, 1915–1918," in *African Americans and the U.S. Economy*, ed. Cecilia Conrad, John Whitehead, Patrick Mason, and James Stewart (Lanham, MD: Rowman and Littlefield, 2005), 38–43.

151. The most famous liberty of contract decision, *Lochner v. New York*, 198 US 45 (1905), overturned a state law limiting the hours bakers could work to ten a day and sixty a week. For further discussion, see Joseph William Singer, "No Right to Exclude: Public Accommodations and Private Property," *Northwestern University Law Review* 90 (summer 1996): 1283.

152. Singer, "No Right to Exclude," 1389.

153. Derrick Bell, *Race, Racism, and American Law*, 3rd ed. (Boston: Little, Brown, 1992), 43–50.

154. Leland Ware, "Brown at 50: School Desegregation from Reconstruction to Resegregation," *University of Florida Journal of Law and Public Policy* 16 (August 2005): 267–68.

155. David Rabban, *Free Speech in Its Forgotten Years, 1870–1920* (New York: Cambridge University Press, 1997), 145–46.

156. See, for example, Thomas Cooley, *A Treatise on Constitutional Limitations* (Boston: Little, Brown, 1868), particularly the chapter on free speech and press. Cooley still advocated restrictions and punishments for false, malicious, scandalous, blasphemous, or obscene speech.

157. Anderson, "Formative Period of the First Amendment," 58, 65–66; Paul Murphy, *The Meaning of Free Speech: First Amendment Freedom from Wilson to FDR* (Santa Barbara, CA: Praeger, 1972), 100.

158. Samuel Walker explains, "Freedom of speech . . . was enshrined in the First Amendment in 1791. Until the middle of the twentieth century,however, it had little practical meaning for most Americans. It certainly had no force in protecting ideas advanced by radical political groups, labor union organizers, dissenting religious sects, or advocates of alternative life-styles (birth control, plural marriage, whatever): in short, those who needed it most." Walker, *Hate Speech: The History of an American*

Controversy (Lincoln: University of Nebraska Press, 1994), 14. See also Rabban, *Free Speech*, 13.

159. Hentoff, *First Freedom*, 98.

160. William Carter Jr., "The Thirteenth Amendment and Pro-Equality Speech," *Columbia Law Review* 112 (2012): 1856.

161. Carter, "Thirteenth Amendment," 1857.

162. Washburn, *African American Press*, 5.

163. When asked why there was a "black press," T. Thomas Fortune answered, "A sufficient answer to all those who do not understand why we have colored newspapers, would seem to be the fact that white men have newspapers; that they are published by white men for white men; given the main news about white men, and pitch their editorial opinions entirely in the interest of white men." Inglehart, *Press and Speech Freedoms*, 95.

164. Washburn, *African American Press*, 67–69.

165. Washburn, *African American Press*, 96–97.

166. Inglehart, *Press and Speech Freedoms*, 116.

167. Washburn, *African American Press*, 102.

168. Inglehart, *Press and Speech Freedoms*, 113.

169. Washburn, *African American Press*, 101–2.

170. William Jordan, "African-American Accommodation and Protest during World War I," *Journal of American History* 81, no. 4 (March 1995): 1562–83.

171. Philip Taft, "Workers of a New Century," US Department of Labor, accessed 3-8-2016, http://www.dol.gov/general/aboutdol/history/chapter4.

172. Inglehart, *Press and Speech Freedoms*, 105.

173. Taft, "Workers of a New Century."

174. Anderson, "Formative Period of the First Amendment," 70–73.

175. Rabban, *Free Speech*, 72.

176. Inglehart, *Press and Speech Freedoms*, 92.

177. Inglehart, *Press and Speech Freedoms*, 99. For details, see Edwin Hoyt, *The Palmer Raids 1919–1920: An Attempt to Suppress Dissent* (New York: Tor Books, 1993).

178. Inglehart, *Press and Speech Freedoms*, 101.

179. Rabban, *Free Speech*, 77–128.

180. Taft, "Workers of a New Century." Nat Hentoff notes Wobblies were subjected to mass arrests, torture in police custody, vigilante beatings, and murder. Hentoff, *First Freedom*, 102–7.

181. Nan Hunter, "Escaping the Expression-Equality Conundrum: Toward Anti-Orthodoxy and Inclusion," *Ohio State Law Journal* 61 (2000): 1677–78.

182. See, for example, Robert Michael Smith, *From Blackjacks to Briefcases—A History of Commercialized Strikebreaking and Unionbusting in the United States* (Athens: Ohio University Press, 2003); and Robert Hunter, *Violence and the Labor Movement* (New York: Macmillan, 1919), 317.

183. Inglehart, *Press and Speech Freedoms*, 110.

184. For details, see Doris Stevens, *Jailed for Freedom: American Women Win the Vote* (Troutdale, OR: New Sage Press, 1995).

185. America's Story from America's Library, Library of Congress, http://www.americaslibrary.gov/jb/jazz/jb_jazz_sufarrst_2.html.

186. *People v. Malone*, 29 NY Crim. Rpts. 325 (NY S.Ct. 1913).

187. Rabban, *Free Speech*, 67–68.

188. Rabban, *Free Speech*, 67.

189. Rabban, *Free Speech*, 27–44.

190. Rabban, *Free Speech*, 66.

191. Anderson, "Formative Period of the First Amendment," 67.

192. Inglehart, *Press and Speech Freedoms*, 94.

193. Inglehart, *Press and Speech Freedoms*, 102.

194. Inglehart, *Press and Speech Freedoms*, 103.

195. Yassky, "Eras of the First Amendment," 1706.

196. Yassky, "Eras of the First Amendment," 1718.

197. Inglehart, *Press and Speech Freedoms*, 100.

198. Inglehart, *Press and Speech Freedoms*, 95.

199. Ingelhart, *Press and Speech Freedoms*, 124.

200. Gibson, "Supreme Court and Freedom of Expression," 267.

201. Gibson, "Supreme Court and Freedom of Expression," 268–69.

202. Geoffrey Stone describes the World War I era as "one of the most fiercely repressive periods in American history" and "palpably" worse than the Civil War. Stone, *Perilous Times: Free Speech during Wartime* (New York: Norton, 2004), 153, 184. Paul Murphy writes, "Americans . . . stood by on the domestic scene and saw liberty and justice prostituted in ways more extreme and extensive than at any other time in American history." Murphy, *World War I and the Origin of Civil Liberties in America* (New York: Norton, 1979), 15.

203. Inglehart, *Press and Speech Freedoms*, 106.

204. Examples of World War I–era lower court decisions protecting speech include *United States v. Hall*, 248 Fed. 150 (D MT 1918); *United States v. Schutte*, 252 F 212 (D ND 1918); *Masses Publishing Co. v. Patten*, 244 F 535 (SD NY 1917) but reversed, 246 F 24 (2d Cir 1917); *Grubl v. United States*, 264 F 44 (8th Cir. 1920); *Fontana v. United States*, 262 F. 283 (8th Cir. 1919); *Harshfield v. United States*, 260 F 659 (8th Cir. 1919); *Kampmann v. United States*, 259 F. 192

(7th Cir. 1919); *Shilter v. United States*, 257 F 724 (9th Cir. 1919); and *Sandberg v. United States*, 257 F. 643 (9th Cir. 1919).

205. Huszar, *Equality in America*, 24.

206. Huszar, *Equality in America*, 25.

207. Hasia Diner, *The Jews of the United States: 1654–2000* (Berkeley: University of California Press, 2004), 165.

208. John Corrigan and Lynn Neal (eds.), *Religious Intolerance in America* (Chapel Hill: University of North Carolina Press, 2010), 148.

209. Corrigan and Neal (eds.), *Religious Intolerance*, chap. 6, "Anti-Semitism."

210. For example, David Rabban writes, "Throughout the period from the Civil War to World War I, the overwhelming majority of decisions in all jurisdictions rejected free speech claims, often by ignoring their existence.... No court was more unsympathetic to freedom of expression than the Supreme Court, which rarely produced even a dissenting opinion." Rabban, *Free Speech*, 131. David Yassky observes, the "logical extension of the [Ex parte Jackson, 96 US 727 (1878)] decision was federal authority to engage in the same sort of political censorship that the states had always perpetrated." Yassky, "Eras of the First Amendment,"1720. *Ex parte Jackson*, 96 US 727 (1878), held the US Postal Service had authority to determine what was included in or excluded from the mail.

211. Andre, "Transformation of Freedom of Speech," 73.

212. Anderson, "Formative Period of the First Amendment," 58.

213. Rabban, *Free Speech*, 50–54.

214. Roscoe Pound, "Interests of Personality and Honor," *Harvard Law Review* 28 (1915): 455.

215. Ernst Freund, *The Police Power, Public Policy and Constitutional Rights* (Chicago: University of Chicago Press, 1904), 513.

216. Franklin and Higginbotham, *Slavery to Freedom*, 352–53.

217. For example, a 1939 *Harvard Law Review* Note observed, "It is impossible in reviewing decisions to avoid the conclusion that the Supreme Court, until recently at least, has been no great friend to the black man." "Note: The Negro Citizen in the Supreme Court," *Harvard Law Review* 52 (March 1939): 831.

218. Howard, *Shifting Wind*, 195.

219. See, for example, Richard W. Steele, "Fear of the Mob and Faith in Government in Free Speech Discourse, 1919–1941," *American Journal of Legal History* 38 (January 1994): 55.

220. For abolitionist usage of these strategies, see Hessler, "Early Efforts to Suppress," 188–89.

221. Grif Stockley, *Blood in Their Eyes: The Elaine Massacres of 1919* (Fayetteville: University of Arkansas Press, 2001).

222. Alexis de Tocqueville, *Democracy in America*, trans. George Lawrence, ed. J. P. Mayer (New York: Harper, 1969), 342.

CHAPTER 2

1. For more details, see Joe Trotter, "Impact of the Great Depression on African Americans," in *Encyclopedia of the Great Depression*, vol. 1, ed. Robert McElvaine (New York: Macmillan, 2004).

2. Paul Finkelman, *The Supreme Court: Cases, Controversies, and Character from John Jay to John Roberts* (Santa Barbara, CA: ABC-CLIO, 2014), 724.

3. Frederick Griffiths, "Ralph Ellison, Richard Wright and The Angelo Herndon Case," *African American Review* 35 (winter 2001): 622.

4. Angelo Herndon, *Let Me Live* (New York: Random House, 1937), 110–13.

5. John Hammond Moore, "The Angelo Herndon Case, 1932–1937," *Phylon* 32, no. 1 (1971): 62.

6. Moore, "Herndon Case," 64.

7. Michael Belknap, *American Political Trials*, rev. ed. (Westport, CT: Greenwood, 1994), 162–63.

8. Belknap, *American Political Trials*, 162.

9. Griffiths, "Ellison, Wright and Herndon," 623.

10. Benjamin Davis, *Communist Councilman from Harlem: Autobiographical Notes Written in a Federal Penitentiary* (New York: International, 1991), 62–63.

11. Bennett Parten, "Communism and Race in the 1930s Deep South," *History Is Now Magazine*, July 15, 2015, accessed 9-2-2016, http://www.historyisnowmagazine.com/blog/2015/7/5/communism-and-race-in-the-1930s-deep-south#.V8i9cpgrLIU.

12. Angelo Herndon, "You Cannot Kill the Working Class" (New York: International Labor Defense and League of Struggle for Negro Rights, 1937), 26.

13. Charles Martin, *The Angelo Herndon Case and Southern Justice* (Baton Rouge: Louisiana State University Press, 1976), 60.

14. Anne Emmanuel, *Elbert Parr Tuttle: Chief Jurist of the Civil Rights Revolution* (Athens: University of Georgia Press, 2011), 119.

15. John Spivak, "Foreword," in Angelo Herndon, *You Cannot Kill the Working Class* (New York: International Labor Defense and League of Struggle for Negro Rights, 1937), 3.

16. Moore, "Herndon Case," 66, quoting January 20, 1934, issue: "Undoubtedly there was about it an element of 'teaching a Negro a lesson,' as the attorneys for Herndon charged. A statute that was 62 years old was raked out of the dusty law books as the basis for the grand jury indictment. The law itself represented a time when it was necessary to suppress Negroes by violence. We in this day ought to know the best way to keep any people, Negroes or whites, in good relations with one another is to deal fairly and live justly toward each other. It is not necessary to resort to repressive measures. It is something of which all of us ought to be ashamed: that the dignity of our court could be used for such a farcical purpose as to protect us from a red army that would march in to destroy our civilization.

"After all, those who stupidly use our courts for such purposes ought to keep in mind the ultimate purpose of the Communism is to provide food and clothes and shelter for oppressed people and that danger of over-throw, if there is any danger, is not from outside propaganda, but from fathers who look at the faces of pinched and hungry children and mothers who are not able to protect their children against the most intense of all sufferings, the suffering of cold.

"The *Telegraph* hopes the Supreme Court of this state will substitute common sense for the Bourbonism of the jury which tried Herndon."

17. *Herndon v. Georgia*, 178 GA 832, 869 (1934), quoting *People v. Lloyd*, 304 IL 23, 34 (1922).

18. Mark Tushnet, "The Hughes Court and Radical Political Dissent: The Case of Dirk De Jongc and Angelo Herndon," *Georgia State University Law Review* 28 (winter 2012): 364.

19. Police evidence of the suspects' communist plot included issues of *New Republic*, *Nation*, *Redbook Magazine*, "Einstein's Space Theory," and "Are Petting Parties Dangerous." Moore, "Herndon Case," 67.

20. Such threats were taken seriously. One of the worst murders became a race riot in October 1934. Claude Neal, arrested for the rape and murder of a white woman, was taken from Florida to Alabama by the sheriff for safekeeping but was tracked down by vigilantes and taken back to Florida. There he was stabbed, burned with hot irons, castrated, forced to eat his genitalia, had his toes and fingers cut off, and strangled until he died. His body was dragged back to the home of the victim, where a mob stabbed, kicked, and cut pieces to keep as souvenirs. The rampage finished with a white race riot attacking blacks and driving them from their homes, which required the National Guard to put a stop to it. See James McGovern, *Anatomy of a Lynching: The Killing of Claude Neal* (Baton Rouge: Louisiana State University Press, 1982).

21. Charles Martin, "Communists and Blacks: The ILD and the Angelo Herndon Case," *Journal of Negro History* 64, no. 2 (spring 1979), 132.

22. "Comer Vann Woodward, 1908–1999," *Encyclopedia of Arkansas History and Culture*, n.d., http://www.historyisnowmagazine.com/blog/2015/7/5/communism-and-race-in-the-1930s-deep-south#.V8i9cpgrLIU.

23. Kendall Thomas, "Rouge et Noir Reread: A Popular Constitutional History of the Angelo Herndon Case," *Southern California Law Review* 65 (September 1992): 2687.

24. There was widespread confusion in the nation's courts between Schenk-type statutes allowing punishment for words that pose a clear and present danger and Gitlow-type ones allowing punishment for words with a bad tendency. Justice Brandeis had rejected that distinction in his *Whitney* dissent. The Georgia Supreme Court had failed to draw the distinction. The US Supreme Court rhetorically invoked the clear and present danger test in Whitney but applied a version of the bad tendency test. See, for example, Tushnet, "Hughes Court," 370.

25. Martin, *Angelo Herndon Case*, 150.

26. Belknap, *American Political Trials*, 171.

27. "Note: Recent Cases," *University of Pennsylvania Law Review* 84 (1935–1936): 257.

28. Moore, "Herndon Case," 68.

29. For more on the Leo Frank case, see Leonard Dinnerstein, *The Leo Frank Case*, rev. ed. (Athens: University of Georgia Press, 2008).

30. Zechariah Chafee Jr., *Free Speech in the United States* (New York: Atheneum, 1941), 396.

31. "Unthinkable," *Time*, July 4, 1927.

32. *De Jonge*, 365–66.

33. "Note: Supreme Court as Protector of Political Minorities," *Yale Law Journal* 46 (1937): 862.

34. *Herndon v. Lowry*, 260.

35. As Lewis Sargentich pointed out in his groundbreaking 1970 analysis of overbreadth, "The Court often uses the idioms of due process vagueness and first amendment overbreadth interchangeably. Both doctrines are responsive to the fact that precision and predictability of governmental intervention are vital to persons planning the exercise of fundamental rights. Both vague and overbroad statutes covering first amendment activities tend to deter privileged conduct." Sargentich, "The First Amendment Overbreadth Doctrine," *Harvard Law Review* 83 (1970): 874.

36. *Herndon v. Lowry*, 263–64.

37. Tushnet, "Hughes Court," 375.

38. Chafee, *Free Speech*, 393. See also Rabban, *Free Speech*, 375–76.

39. Rabban, *Free Speech*, 377–78.

40. "Note: The Void-for-Vagueness Doctrine in the Supreme Court," *University of Pennsylvania Law Review* 109 (November 1960): 74n38.

41. "Note: Void-for-Vagueness," 75.

42. Yassky, "Eras of the First Amendment," 1732.

43. Geoffrey Berman points out four possible explanations for the changes in the judicial understanding of the Constitution, namely, changes in legal doctrine isolated from larger social or political events, intrapersonal judicial psychology, principled social enlightenment, and the political force of the labor movement. G. Berman, "A New Deal for Free Speech: Free Speech and the Labor Movement in the 1930s," *Virginia Law Review* 80 (February 1994): 291.

44. G. Edward White, "The First Amendment Comes of Age: The Emergence of Free Speech in Twentieth-Century America," *Michigan Law Review* 95 (November 1996): 330.

45. Consider some examples. *Gitlow v. New York* (1925) incorporated the free speech clause. *Near v. Minnesota* (1931) incorporated the free press clause. *De Jonge v. Oregon* (1937) incorporated the freedom of assembly clause. *Cantwell v. Connecticut*, 310 US 296 (1940), incorporated the free exercise of religion clause. *Everson v. Board of Education*, 330 US 1 (1947), incorporated the establishment clause. *Edwards v. South Carolina*, 377 US 229 (1963), incorporated the Petition Clause, and *Mapp v. Ohio*, 367 US 643 (1963), incorporated the Fourth Amendment's clause banning unreasonable searches and seizures.

46. See, for example, Andre, "Transformation of Freedom of Speech," 69.

47. See, for example, "Note: Supreme Court as Protector."

48. Hunter, "Escaping the Expression-Equality Conundrum," 1703.

49. Chafee, *Free Speech*, 392.

50. Chafee, *Free Speech*, 397.

51. Chafee, *Free Speech*, 397.

52. Chafee, *Free Speech*, 396.

53. Chafee, *Free Speech*, 397.

54. Cover, "Origins," 1297.

55. Cover, "Origins," 1298.

56. *United States v. Carolene Products, Co.* (1938), 152–53.

57. Cover, "Origins," 1296.

58. Cover, "Origins," 1300.

59. Thomas, "Rouge et Noir Reread," 2625.

60. Thomas, "Rouge et Noir Reread," 2637.

61. Thomas delves into four major legal analysts' treatment of the *Herndon* case: Wallace Mendelson, Paul Murphy, David Currie, and Felix Frankfurter, and Henry Hart Jr.

62. Thomas, "Rouge et Noir Reread," 2665.

63. Lynne Tillman, "Kendall Thomas by Lynne Tillman," *BOMB—Artists in Conversation* 59 (spring 1997), accessed 4-26-2016, http://bombmagazine.org/article/2059/kendall-thomas.

64. Thomas, "Rouge et Noir Reread," 2701.

65. Thomas, "Rouge et Noir Reread," 2702–3.

66. Anders Walker, "'Neutral' Principles: Rethinking the Legal History of Civil Rights, 1934–1964," *Loyola University Chicago Law Journal* 40 (2009): 385.

67. Walker, "Neutral Principles," 391–94.

68. Walker, "Neutral Principles," 402–3.

69. Walker, "Neutral Principles," 398.

70. Walker, "Neutral Principles," 404.

71. Walker, "Neutral Principles," 387n14.

72. See Walker, "Neutral Principles." For a broader discussion of Jewish support for black civil rights and complications in the Jew–black relationship, see Hasia Diner, *In the Almost Promised Land* (Baltimore, MD: Johns Hopkins University Press, 1995).

73. See, for example, David Dalin, "Jews, Nazis and Civil Liberties," in *American Jewish Yearbook 1980* (New York: American Jewish Committee and Jewish Publication Society of America, 1980), 3–28.

74. Kenneth Mack, "Law and Mass Politics in the Making of the Civil Rights Lawyer, 1931–1941," *The Journal of American History* (June 2006): 37–62.

75. Mack, "Law and Mass Politics," 59.

76. Martin, "Communists and Blacks," 132. The ILD also defended whites such as Dirk De Jonge.

77. Mack, "Law and Mass Politics," 39.

78. Martin, "Communists and Blacks," 133.

79. See, for example, *Commonwealth v. Brown*, 309 PA 515 (1933), reversing a black man's conviction on the grounds the trial was unfairly conducted in a racially prejudicial manner.

80. Glenda Elizabeth Gilmore, *Defying Dixie: The Radical Roots of Civil Rights, 1919–1950* (New York: Norton, 2008), 114.

81. James Lorence, *The Unemployed People's Movement* (Athens: University of Georgia Press, 2011) 84. The white policeman was acquitted by an all-white jury.

82. Belknap, *American Political Trials*, 161.

83. For a study of the National Negro Congress and Southern Negro Youth Congress, see Erik Gellman, *Death Blow to Jim Crow: The National Negro Congress and the Rise of Militant Civil Rights* (Chapel Hill: University of North Carolina Press, 2014).

84. Mack, "Law and Mass Politics," 54.

85. Martin, "Communists and Blacks," 133–35.

86. Martin, "Communists and Blacks," 135.

87. Griffiths, "Ellison, Wright, and Herndon," 616.

88. Griffiths notes there are some fabrications and exaggerations in *Let Me Live*, but the overall story is accurate. See Griffiths, "Ellison, Wright, and Herndon," 617.

89. Martha Greuning, Review of *Let Me Live*, *Journal of Negro History* 22, no. 3 (July 1937): 348–50.

90. Angelo Herndon Papers, New York City Public Library, Schomberg Center for Research in Black Culture, accessed 4-27-2016, http://www.nypl.org/sites/default/files/archivalcollections/pdf/scmmg124.pdf.

91. Mark Kesselman, Joel Krieger, and William Joseph, *An Introduction to Comparative Politics: Political Challenges and Changing Agendas* (Boston: Cengage Learning, 2015), 348.

92. "History of Marches and Mass Actions," National Organization for Women, accessed 9-4-2016, http://now.org/about/history/history-of-marc hes-and-mass-actions.

93. Shannon King, *Whose Harlem Is This Anyway?: Community Politics and Grassroots Activism in the New Negro Era* (New York: New York University Press, 2015).

94. See, for example, Elliott Rudwick, "W.E. B. DuBois: Protagonist of the African-American Protest," in *Black Leaders of the Twentieth Century*, ed. John Hope Franklin and August Meier (Urbana-Champaign: University of Illinois Press, 1982); and Robert Hill, "Marcus Garvey, 'The Negro Moses,'" Schomberg Center for Research in Black Culture, accessed 9-4-2016, http://exhibitions.nypl.org/africanaage/essay-garvey.html.

95. Gellman, *Death Blow to Jim Crow*.

96. Berman, "New Deal for Free Speech," 294.

97. Berman, "New Deal for Free Speech," 304.

98. Martin, "Communists and Blacks," 139.

99. Dora Apel, *Imagery of Lynching: Black Men, White Women, and the Mob* (New Brunswick, NJ: Rutgers University Press, 2004), 80–81.

100. Gilmore, *Defying Dixie*, 182n108.

101. Karen Ferguson, *Black Politics in New Deal Atlanta* (Chapel Hill: University of North Carolina Press, 2002), 55.

102. Shepard's Citation Service, April 26, 2016.

103. See, for example, "'History' as Ideology: the Case of Angelo Herndon," Writings from the Barricades, March 21, 2016, accessed 9-2-2016, https://daretostruggle.wordpress.com/2010/03/21/%E2%80%9Chistory%E2%80%9D-as-ideology-the-case-of-angelo-herndon.

104. Angelo Herndon, *Let Me Live* (New York: Arno Press, 1969); Angelo Herndon, with an introduction by Marlon Ross, *Let Me Live* (Ann Arbor: University of Michigan Press, 2007).

105. Mel Gussow, "Review/Theater; Black Leftist's Jail Ordeal in the South in the 1930's," *New York Times*, January 17, 1991, accessed 9-4-2016, http://www.nytimes.com/1991/01/17/theater/review-theater-black-leftist-s-jail-ordeal-in-the-south-in-the-1930-s.html.

106. Griffiths, "Ellison, Wright, and Herndon," 625.

CHAPTER 3

1. Carey McWilliams, "The Witch Hunt and Civil Rights," *Nation*, June 28, 1952, 651.

2. Studies of civil rights during other time periods include Harvard Sitkoff, *A New Deal for Blacks: The Emergence of Civil Rights as a National Issue: The Depression Decade* (New York: Oxford University Press, 1978); Ai-min Zhang, *Origins of the African American Civil Rights Movement, 1865–1956* (New York: Routledge, 2014); Gilmore, *Defying Dixie*; and Howard, *Shifting Wind.*

3. Mark Tushnet, *Making Civil Rights Law: Thurgood Marshall and the Supreme Court, 1936–1961* (New York: Oxford University Press, 1994), 313. See also Margaret Burnham, "Reflections on the Civil Rights Movement and the First Amendment," in A Less Than Perfect Union: Alternative Perspectives on the U.S. Constitution, ed. Jules Lobel (New York: Monthly Review Press, 1988), 340.

4. Gerald Rosenberg, *The Hollow Hope: Can Courts Bring About Social Change?* 2nd ed. (Chicago: Chicago University Press, 2008); and Anne Braden, "The Constitution and the Civil Rights Movement: The First Amendment and the Fourteenth," in *A Less Than Perfect Union: Alternative Perspectives on the U.S. Constitution*, ed. Jules Lobel (New York: Monthly Review Press, 1988), 176, 178.

5. Tom Watson, "This Is What a Movement Looks Like: Civil Rights, Civil Liberties, and Feet on the Ground," *Forbes*, August 24, 2013, accessed

9-21-2016, http://www.forbes.com/sites/tomwatson/2013/08/24/this-is-what-a-movement-looks-like-civil-rights-civil-liberties-and-feet-on-the-ground/#3a652bae4109.

6. For details on the Little Rock desegregation case, see Elizabeth Jacoway, *Turn Away Thy Son: Little Rock, The Crisis That Shocked the Nation* (New York: Simon and Schuster, 2007); and Karen Anderson, *Little Rock: Race and Resistance at Central High School* (Princeton, NJ: Princeton University Press, 2013).

7. See, for example, Michael Belknap, *Federal Law and Southern Order: Racial Violence and Constitutional Conflict in the Post-*Brown *South* (Athens: University of Georgia Press, 1987).

8. Jack Greenberg, *Crusaders in the Courts: Legal Battles of the Civil Rights Movement*, anniversary ed. (New York: Twelve Tables Press, 2004), 289.

9. Christopher Schmidt, "*New York Times v. Sullivan* and the Legal Attack on the Civil Rights Movement," *Alabama Law Review* 66 (2014): 293.

10. Harry Moore and his wife were killed in a Christmas Day 1951 bombing in Mims, Florida. Lamar Smith was shot to death on the Lincoln County Courthouse lawn in Brookhaven, Mississippi, in 1955. George Washington Lee was shot to death driving his car near Midnight, Mississippi, in 1955. The home of Arthur Shores, Alabama's "drum major for justice," was firebombed in 1963. Police stood by and watched as a white mob beat NAACP lawyer Henry Aronson in Grenada, Mississippi, in 1966.

11. Rosenberg, *Hollow Hope*, 82.

12. The Smith Act of 1940, the first peacetime sedition act since the Sedition Act of 1798, criminalized the advocacy of violent sedition, conspiring to commit these offense, or being a member of an organization advocating violent overthrow of government. It passed with only the ACLU, CIO Maritime Union, and AFL testifying against it. Legislative witch hunts for disloyal citizens or communists or communist sympathizers were led by the House Un-American Activities Committee (HUAC), founded in 1938 and made a permanent committee in 1945. Although Joseph McCarthy of Wisconsin is remembered as the "most ferocious and reckless of the Communist-hunters," he was never a member of the HUAC because he was a senator, not a representative. Hentoff, *The First Freedom*, 137–38.

13. See, for example, Vann Woodward, *Strange Career of Jim Crow*, 139.

14. A boycott is an organized set of activities using economic pressure to achieve an economic, political, or mixed result. See, for example, Kay Kindred, "When First Amendment Values and Competition Policy Collide: Resolving

the Dilemma of the Mixed-Motive Boycott," *Arizona Law Review* 34 (1992): 710–11.

15. For example, American colonists refused to buy stamps required by the English Stamp Act of 1765 to protest taxation without representation, and merchants in Boston and New York in 1768 and Philadelphia in 1769 refused to buy British-made goods for the same reason. In the 1790s, English abolitionists—such as William Fox in *An Address to the People of Great Britain, on the Utility of Refraining from the Use of West India Sugar and Rum* (1791)—encouraged people to stop buying slave-produced sugar. Although the tactic dates to the 1700s, the term *boycott* is derived from an 1880s case in Ireland involving the English land agent Charles Boycott.

16. See, for example, Harry Wellington Laidler, *Boycotts and the Labor Struggle: Economic and Legal Aspects* (New York: Columbia University Press, 1914); and Daniel Jacoby, *Laboring for Freedom: A New Look at the History of Labor in America* (New York: Routledge, 2015).

17. Portia James, "New Negro Opinion Newspaper," Smithsonian Collections blog, May 20, 2011, accessed 9-27-2017, http://si-siris.blogspot.com/2011/05/new-negro-opinion-newspaper.html.

18. The Morris-La Guardia Act, named for its Republican sponsors George Norris of Nebraska and Fiorello La Guardia of New York, passed in 1932. It banned "yellow-dog" contracts that prohibited an employee from joining a union, barred federal courts from issuing injunctions against peaceful labor protests, barred employers from interfering with employees joining a union, and protected collective bargaining.

19. *New Negro Alliance v. Sanitary Grocery*, 561.

20. Franklin and Higginbotham, *From Slavery to Freedom*, 421.

21. Howard, *Shifting Wind*, 254. Adam Clayton Powell Jr. was a well-educated Baptist minister from a successful mixed-race family. He represented Harlem in the House of Representatives from 1945 to 1971. Before entering politics, Powell was chairman of the Coordinating Committee for Employment and organized mass meetings, rent strikes, picketing, and other campaigns to force companies to hire black workers and at higher levels of skill and responsibility. For example, a picket of the 1939 World's Fair in New York increased the number of black employees from about 200 to over 700; a bus boycott in 1941 led the Transit Authority to hire 200 black workers.

22. Disappointed with federal efforts to integrate blacks, A. Philip Randolph called for an all-black march on Washington protest that foreshadowed the direct action in the 1960s. Richard Dalfiume, "The 'Forgotten Years' of the Negro Revolution," *Journal of American History* 55, no. 1 (June 1968): 98–99.

23. See, for example, "Note: Recent Cases," *University of Pennsylvania Law Review and American Law Register* 91 (January 1943): 477.

24. Franklin and Higginbotham, *Slavery to Freedom*, 513.

25. Greenberg, *Crusaders in the Courts*, 14.

26. Lucy Barber, *Marching on Washington: The Forging of an American Political Tradition* (Berkeley: University of California Press, 2004), 115.

27. Elian Dashev, "Economic Boycotts as Harassment: The Threat to First Amendment Protected Speech in the Aftermath of *Doe v. Reed*," *Loyola of Los Angeles Law Review* 45 (2011): 213 and 238–47.

28. See, for example, Ware, "*Brown* at 50," 268.

29. Greenberg, *Crusaders in the Courts*, 409.

30. Rosenberg, *Hollow Hope*, 83–84.

31. John Howard notes that the Texas primary decisions merely prevented further decline in black political power. They did not result in more African American registered voters or greater black political power. Howard, *The Shifting Wind*, 219–20.

32. Eric Foner, *The Story of American Freedom* (New York: Norton, 1998), 206.

33. Franklin and Higginbotham, *Slavery to Freedom*, 428

34. Franklin and Higginbotham, *Slavery to Freedom*, 430.

35. Franklin and Higginbotham, *Slavery to Freedom*, 538.

36. Franklin and Higginbotham, *Slavery to Freedom*, 500.

37. Contrary to most historians, David Nichols admits that Eisenhower was no "civil rights saint" but argues his role in advancing civil rights has been underappreciated. Nichols, *A Matter of Justice: Eisenhower and the Beginning of the Civil Rights Revolution* (New York: Simon and Schuster, 2007).

38. Michael Klarman, "Rethinking the Civil Rights and Liberties Revolution," *Virginia Law Review* 82 (February 1996):34 .

39. Mary Dudziak, *Cold War Civil Rights: Race and the Image of American Democracy* (Princeton, NJ: Princeton University Press, 2000), 6.

40. Franklin and Higginbotham, *Slavery to Freedom*, 537.

41. The federal government was insistent on the message that the United States was making good and steady progress on racial issues. Even prominent blacks such as Josephine Baker and Louis Armstrong, who were deemed too critical of US racial relations, were penalized for failing to relay the government-approved message. Dudziak, *Cold War Civil Rights*, chapter 2.

42. Dudziak, *Cold War Civil Rights*, 119.

43. Christopher Schmidt, "Civil Rights–Civil Liberties Divide," *Stanford Civil Rights and Civil Liberties* 12 (February 2016): 32–34.

44. Franklin and Higginbotham, *Slavery to Freedom*, 492–94.

45. Robert Hutchins, "Foreword," in *Political and Civil Rights in the United States*, ed. Thomas Emerson and David Haber (Buffalo: Dennis, 1952), iv.

46. John Frank, one of the great legal scholar-practitioners of the era, quoted in Foner, *American Freedom*, 256.

47. Richard Sklar, "The Fiction of the First Amendment," *Western Political Quarterly* 6, no. 2 (June 1953): 302–19.

48. Strom Thurmond was a South Carolina senator from 1954 to 2003. Initially a Dixiecrat (Southern Democrat), he became a Republican in 1964 because he opposed the 1964 Civil Rights Act. He never renounced his segregationist and pro–states' rights positions.

49. Schmidt, "The Civil Rights–Civil Liberties Divide." See, for example, Arthur Schlesinger, *The Vital Center: The Politics of Freedom* (Boston: Houghton-Mifflin, 1949), 189–91; and Will Maslow and Joseph Robison, "Civil Rights Legislation and the Fight for Equality, 1862–1952," *University of Chicago Law Review* 20 (1953): 362n1. Despite attempts to distance themselves, civil rights organizations were often labeled "red" anyway, especially in the South. Braden, "Constitution and the Civil Rights Movement," 181. The accusation successfully intimidated many white sympathizers from taking action. Braden, "Constitution and the Civil Rights Movement," 182.

50. See, for example, Thomas Eliot, Book Reviews, *Harvard Law Review* 61 (1948): 899; and Robert Jackson, "Messages on the Launching of the 'Bill of Rights Review,'" *Bill of Rights Review* 1 (1940): 35.

51. First Amendment scholar Thomas Emerson, along with Justices Black and Douglas, thought the *Yates* decision did not go far enough. The decision distinguished advocacy of ideas (protected by the *Yates* decision) from advocacy of action (unprotected by the earlier *Dennis* decision), but critics point out advocacy—whether advocacy of ideas or action—is speech, not action. Until speech becomes "intertwined" with action, it should be protected. Nat Hentoff, *First Freedom*, 145–48.

52. See, for example, Jonathan Rauch, "The Unknown Supreme Court Decision that Changed Everything for Gays," *Washington Post*, February 5, 2014, accessed 10-20-2016, https://www.washingtonpost.com/news/volokh-conspiracy/wp/2014/02/05/the-unknown-supreme-court-decision-that-changed-everything-for-gays/?utm_term=.8d744be0c80b.

53. Political and economic factors also played roles, along with the media and entertainment. National press coverage of the 1960s civil rights struggles in the South led many to oppose Jim Crow laws. See, for example, Nat

Hentoff, "How Jazz Helped Hasten the Civil Rights Movement," *Wall Street Journal*, January 15, 2009, accessed 10-22-2016, http://www.wsj.com/articles/SB123197292128083217. Emilie Raymond describes the role major entertainers played in promoting racial progress in *Stars for Freedom: Hollywood, Black Celebrities, and the Civil Rights Movement* (Seattle: University of Washington Press, 2015). Jules Tygiel explores the impact of Jackie Robinson as the first black man to play Major League Baseball in *Baseball's Great Experiment: Jackie Robinson and His Legacy*, expanded ed. (New York: Oxford University Press, 1997).

54. In 1955, the Interstate Commerce Commission (ICC) ruled against segregated interstate bus and train accommodations but did not enforce the ruling. In 1960, to protest racial segregation, Bruce Boynton refused to leave a whites-only dining area in a bus depot. He was charged and convicted for trespassing. Boynton argued that his conviction violated the Interstate Commerce Act and the Constitution's Equal Protection Clause, Due Process Clause, and Commerce Clause. He lost his appeal to the state supreme court, but the US Supreme Court held 7–2 in *Boynton v. Virginia*, 364 US 454 (1960) that racially segregated interstate public transportation violated the Interstate Commerce Act. The *Boynton* decision, coinciding with the explosion of sit-ins in 1960, led the Congress of Racial Equality (CORE) and the Student Non-Violent Coordinating Committee to organize the Freedom Riders, groups of blacks and whites riding together in defiance of segregated public transportation, in 1961. The original Freedom Ride, starting in Washington, DC, and scheduled to end at a civil rights rally in New Orleans, ended in mob violence in Alabama abetted by "Bull" Connor, the Birmingham commissioner of Public Safety. Riders had to be rescued by armed local civil rights activists. Yet the Freedom Rides continued. The next riders were arrested by Connor, but when he could no longer stand their protest songs, he dropped them off at the Tennessee border. When original riders and sympathizers attempted to renew the Freedom Ride, their police escort (only provided because of federal political pressure) left them to a mob wielding baseball bats and iron pipes in Montgomery, Alabama. White hospitals refused to treat the victims, and they had to be rescued by local blacks. The following Sunday, a mob of 3,000 whites attacked a civil rights rally held in a church to support the Freedom Riders. The mob overwhelmed the few federal marshals protecting the rally and did not disperse until the governor sent the National Guard the next morning after the threat of US military intervention. More Freedom Riders arrived in Montgomery to continue the protest; to avoid further mob violence, the Kennedy administration made a deal with the

governors of Alabama and Mississippi to allow them to arrest Freedom Riders for violating local segregation ordinances if they also provided the riders with police and National Guard protection. The riders were duly arrested at their first stop. As scores of more Freedom Riders arrived, they were also arrested; when they filled local jails, they were taken to a maximum-security prison and endured terrible treatment and conditions. President Kennedy called for a cooling-off period after earning considerable unfavorable international attention, but James Farmer from CORE responded, "We have been cooling off for 350 years, and if we cooled off any more, we'd be in a deep freeze." More than sixty Freedom Rides, with most riders arrested, continued throughout the summer of 1961. In August, violence broke out when police ignored a white mob attack on a Freedom Ride in Monroe, North Carolina. The attack led to a shootout between armed blacks and whites that ended in a standoff and the arrests of the Freedom Riders and their defenders. Finally, in November 1961, the Kennedy administration and the ICC agreed to enforce the transportation desegregation orders. See Raymond Arsenault, *Freedom Riders: 1961 and the Struggle for Racial Justice* (New York: Oxford University Press, 2006).

Many people at the time criticized the Freedom Riders for "provoking' the violence and increasing racial tensions, but others admired their courage and were inspired to support civil rights. Eventually the bogus convictions of Freedom Riders—328 just in Mississippi—were squashed in *Abernathy v. Alabama*, 380 US 447 (1965), and *Thomas v. Mississippi*, 380 US 524 (1965), both of which merely announced, "The judgments are reversed."

55. Mario Savio, an Italian American student at the University of California, Berkeley, was arrested in March 1964 with 167 others protesting the San Francisco Hotel Association exclusion of blacks from nonmenial jobs. A jailhouse conversation led him to participate in the Freedom Summer project registering black voters in Mississippi. Upon his return to Berkeley, he found the campus had banned all political activity and fundraising. When campus police arrested Jack Weinberg on October 1 for manning a table for CORE, Savio emerged as a leader of a crowd of up to 3,000 that conducted a thirty-two-hour sit-in protest that ended with Weinberg's release. In a subsequent December protest, Savio delivered a fiery speech to a crowd of up to 4,000 that was popularized and immortalized as "The Operation of the Machine." That protest ended with the arrest of more than 800 students. When the organizers of the student protest were charged by the university a month later, an even larger protest was held that essentially shut down the university. The movement dissipated when the administration granted some concessions, but the Berkeley student protests

demanding recognition of their right to freedom of speech inspired similar movements on campuses across the country. For details, see Robert Cohen and Reginald Zelnik (eds.), *The Free Speech Movement: Reflections on Berkeley in the 1960s* (Berkeley: University of California Press, 2002).

56. Vann Woodward, *Strange Career of Jim Crow*, 169.

57. Dalfiume, "'Forgotten Years' of the Negro Revolution," 90–106.

58. Greenberg, *Crusaders in the Courts*, 287.

59. Sit-ins go back at least to 1942 when James Farmer led a CORE sit-in at a Jack Spratt coffeehouse in Chicago. In 1943 Howard University students conducted sit-ins at Washington, DC, restaurants. Black students in Wichita, Kansas, and Oklahoma City conducted in sit-ins in 1958, and so did Washington University students in St. Louis in 1959, but being outside the Deep South, these sit-ins were local sensations, failing to attract national attention or inspire a national movement.

60. Greenberg, *Crusaders in the Courts*, 290; Alan Gartner and Christopher Ferreira, "A State of Action," *New York Law School Law Review* 59 (2014–2015): 99.

61. Greenberg, *Crusaders in the Courts*, 326.

62. Foner, *American Freedom*, 288.

63. Gartner and Ferreira, "State of Action," 101n26.

64. Blacks conducting a sit-in protest in the whites-only waiting room in a bus depot made white onlookers "restless."

65. *Lombard v. Louisiana* overturned the criminal mischief conviction of three blacks and one white protesting the segregated lunch counter at McCrory's dime store in New Orleans. For discussion of the case, see Gartner and Ferreira, "State of Action."

66. *Cox v. Louisiana* overturned the breach of the peace conviction despite the restlessness of white onlookers because there was no violence until the police initiated it; moreover, the Court held the Louisiana statute was overbroad and unduly vague.

67. *Peterson v. Greenville*, 373 US 244 (1963); *Gober v. Birmingham*, 373 US 374 (1963).

68. *Bell v. Maryland*, 378 US 226 (1964); *Green v. Virginia*, 378 US 550 (1964); *Harris v. Virginia*, 378 US 552 (1964); *Williams v. North Carolina*, 378 US 548 (1964); *Fox v. North Carolina*, 378 US 587 (1964); *Mitchell v. Charleston*, 378 US 551 (1964); and *Drews v. Maryland*, 378 US 547 (1964). *Hamm v. Rock Hill*, 379 US 306 (1964), erased about 3,000 convictions by holding that new civil rights laws desegregating public accommodations "abated" the convictions

of sit-in protesters. In one of life's ironies, Robert Bell, the named defendant in *Bell v. Maryland* (1963) later became chief judge of the Maryland Court of Appeals, the court that had upheld his conviction prior to its reversal by the US Supreme Court.

69. *Brown v. Louisiana*, 141–42.

70. Foner, *American Freedom*, 280.

71. *Edwards v. South Carolina*, 235.

72. Rosenberg, *Hollow Hope*, 130–33. President Kennedy, for example, did not support the strong version of the Civil Rights Act until the racial violence in the spring of 1963, and the 1965 Voting Rights Act was motivated by the racial violence in Selma, Alabama. See also Braden, "Constitution and Civil Rights Movement," 179.

73. Christopher Schmidt argues the libel threat to the civil rights movement was real but has been exaggerated. Schmidt, "*New York Times v. Sullivan*," 326–32.

74. Anthony Lewis, *Make No Law: The Sullivan Case and the First Amendment* (New York: Random House, 1991).

75. Alexander Meiklejohn, one of the leading framers of modern free speech theory, said the *Times v. Sullivan* decision was "an occasion for dancing in the streets." Anthony Lewis, the famous Supreme Court reporter and author, believed the decision "gave [the First Amendment] bold words their full meaning." Geoffrey Stone, a leading contemporary First Amendment scholar, says it "remains one of the great Supreme Court decisions in American history." See also Klarman, "Rethinking the Civil Rights and Liberties Revolutions," 42; Samuel Walker, *In Defense of American Liberties: A History of the ACLU* (New York: Oxford University Press, 1990), 217, 240–41; Adam Fairclough, *Race and Democracy: The Civil Rights Struggle in Louisiana* (Athens: University of Georgia Press, 1995), 324–25; and Garret Epps, "The Civil Rights Heroes the Court Ignored in *New York Times v. Sullivan*," *Atlantic*, March 20, 2014, accessed 9-27-2016, http://www.theatlantic.com/national/archive/2014/03/the-civil-rights-heroes-the-court-ignored-in-em-new-york-times-v-sullivan-em/284550.

76. Kermit Hall and Melvin Urofsky, *New York Times v. Sullivan: Civil Rights, Libel Law and the Free Press* (Lawrence: University Press of Kansas, 2011).

77. Schmidt, "*New York Times v. Sullivan*," 308.

78. Epps, "Civil Rights Heroes the Court Ignored."

79. Klarman, "Civil Rights and Liberties Revolutions," 39–43.

80. Schmidt, "Civil Rights–Civil Liberties," 29.

81. Schmidt, "Civil Rights–Civil Liberties," 29.

82. Franklin and Higginbotham, *Slavery to Freedom*, 547.

83. See, for example, Gavin Wright, *Sharing the Prize* (Cambridge, MA: Harvard University Press, 2013).

84. See, for example, Jack Bloom, *Class, Race and the Civil Rights Movement* (Bloomington: Indiana University Press, 1987), 171.

85. See, for example, "Tensions among Minority Groups," Symposium with S. M. Miller, Wade Henderson, Don T. Nakanishi, john a. powell, Maria Blanco, and Howard Winant in Chester Hartman, (ed.), *America's Growing Inequality: The Impact of Race and Poverty* (Lanham, MD: Lexington Books, 2014), 32–35.

86. For details, see Tushnet, *Making Civil Rights Law.*

87. N. Douglas Wells, "Thurgood Marshall and 'Individual Self-Realization' in First Amendment Jurisprudence," *Tennessee Law Review* 61 (fall 1993): 238; J. Clay Smith and Scott Burrell, "Justice Thurgood Marshall and the First Amendment," *Arizona State Law Journal* 26 (summer 1994): 477; and Lynn Adelman, "The Glorious Jurisprudence of Thurgood Marshall," *Harvard Law and Policy Review* 7 (winter 2013): 129.

88. Adelman, "Glorious Jurisprudence of Marshall," 129.

89. For example, when dealing with a case in Tennessee in 1946, Marshall was falsely stopped by police for drunk driving and saved from a waiting lynch mob only by the brave intervention of armed black citizens. The local lawyers Marshall worked with faced even more challenging circumstances since after a case was won they had to "take the heat from an enraged redneck population." Greenberg, *Crusaders in the Courts*, 39.

90. Smith and Burrell, "Justice Thurgood Marshall," 462.

91. Tushnet, *Making Civil Rights Law*, 309–10.

92. Smith and Burrell, "Justice Thurgood Marshall," 461, 471–73.

93. Wells, "Thurgood Marshall and Self-Realization."

94. *Amalgamated Foods* was soon overturned by *Hudgens v. NLRB*, 424 US 507 (1976).

95. Wells, "Thurgood Marshall and Self-Realization," 261-280.

96. Burnham, "Reflections," 338. Burnham notes that the NAACP used at least four new legal strategies: class-action litigation, strategic long-term employment of the judicial system to achieve a social-political goal, strategically selecting cases that forced courts to put flesh on the First and Fourteenth Amendment bones, and winning cases that forced attention to the issues in legislative and other forums.

97. Foner, *American Freedom*, 301.

98. Gene Policinski, "Civil Rights Movement Rode Assembly, Petition to Greater Freedom," First Amendment Center, January 31, 2013, accessed

9-9-2016, http://www.firstamendmentcenter.org/civil-rights-movement-rode-asse
mbly-petition-to-greater-freedom. See also Burnham, "Reflections," 341 and 344.

99. Foner, *American Freedom*, 298–303; Braden, "Constitution and Civil Rights Movement," 180.

100. Braden, "Constitution and Civil Rights Movement," 185.

101. Foner, *American Freedom*, 282.

102. Burnham, "Reflections," 337.

103. Samuel DuBois Cook, quoted in Martin Luther King Jr., *The Papers of Martin Luther King, Jr.*, vol. 3, ed. Clayborne Carson et al. (Berkeley: University of California Press, 1997), 204.

CHAPTER 4

1. Henry Louis Gates Jr., "Let Them Talk," *New Republic* (September 20, 1993): 37–48.

2. For example, school integration took a severe blow when whites began to flee the inner city for the suburbs, and the US Supreme Court held in *Milliken v. Bradley*, 418 US 717 (1974), that suburbs were exempt from desegregation plans. Economic disparities increased: white average income rose from $34,500 in 1970 to $37,000 in 1990 whereas black average income $21,151 in 1970 was almost completely stagnant at $21,453 in 1990. In 1982 black unemployment was about 19 percent, whereas white unemployment was about 8 percent.

3. See, for example, the essays collected in Yuya Kiuchi (ed.), *Race Still Matters*.

4. Prior to World War II, only a few blacks, and only at Northern colleges, attained college degrees from non–historically black colleges; by 1970, 378,000 black students attended non–historically black colleges, and nearly twice that number (727,000) did so in 1984. The result? The National Institute Against Prejudice and Violence reported that between 1986 and 1989 more than 250 college campuses had experienced ethnoviolence, between 800,000 and 1,000,000 students were involved each year, about 20 percent of minority students were victimized each year, and about 5 percent were victimized more than once. Howard Ehrlich, *Campus Ethnoviolence and the Policy Options*, Report no. 4, National Institute Against Prejudice and Violence (1990).

5. Charles Lawrence III, one of the first proponents of new campus hate

speech regulations, noted in a debate at Duke University with then–ACLU Executive Director Nadine Strossen, "this issue has divided old allies and revealed unrecognized or unacknowledged differences in the experience, perceptions, and values of members of longstanding alliances." Lawrence, "If He Hollers Let Him Go: Regulating Racist Speech on Campus," *Duke Law Journal* 1990 (1990): 431–83.

6. Gates, "Let Them Talk," 37.

7. For example, Jon Gould argues that campus hate speech codes lost the legal battles but won the campus culture war and political correctness infiltrated other institutions. Gould, *Speak No Evil: The Triumph of Hate Speech Regulation* (Chicago: University of Chicago Press, 2005).

8. Two significant scholarly works from the era include Thomas Emerson, *The System of Free Expression* (New York: Random House, 1970), and Lee Bollinger, *The Tolerant Society* (New York: Barnes & Noble, 1986). Three significant judicial decisions include *Carroll v. Princess Anne* 393 US 175 (1968) (preemptive attempt by city to prevent public meeting of the National States Rights Party, a white supremacy group, was unconstitutional); *Brandenburg v. Ohio*, 395 US 444 (1969) (upheld the right of a Ku Klux Klan member to advocate the violent overthrow of government); and *National Socialist Party of America v. City of Skokie* (a.k.a. *Smith v. Collin*), 432 US 43 (1977) (upheld the right of Nazis to march in a predominantly Jewish community, including many Holocaust survivors).

9. For some of the competing definitions of hate speech in the United States, see J. Angelo Corlett and Robert Francescotti, "Foundations of a Theory of Hate Speech," *Wayne State Law Review* 48 (fall 2002): 1071. For discussions of different national interpretations and justifications, see note 49 in this chapter.

10. To understand what "narrow" means, consider *United States v. Alkhabaz*, 104 F.3d 1492 (6th Cir. 1997), and *United States v. Machado*, 195 F.3d 454 (9th Cir. 1999). In *Alkhabaz*, a student indicated a sexual interest in violence against women and girls through fictitious stories he posted to an online group and wrote in emails to another individual. One of the stories used the name of a classmate. Alkhabaz did not communicate any of the stories to the named classmate. Although a threat does not have to be directly communicated to the intended target—it can be communicated through a third party or website—the court held there was no true threat, since a true threat involves an attempt to achieve a goal through intimidation, and Alkhabaz had no such goal of intimidation; rather, his goal was held to be a desire to "foster a friendship based on shared sexual fantasies." In contrast, Richard Machado, a student at UC-Irvine,

was convicted of a true threat. Machado sent—and re-sent when he got no immediate response—this email to fifty-nine Asian students:

> Subject: FUck you Asian Shit
>
> Hey Stupid Fucker,
>
> As you can see in the name, I hate Asians, including you. If it weren't for asias [*sic*] at UCI, it would be a much more popular campus. You are responsible for ALL the crimes that occur on campus. YOU are why I want you and your stupid ass comrades to get the fuck out ofUCI [*sic*], If you don't,I will hunt you down and kill your stupid asses. Do you hear me? I personally will make it my life carreer [*sic*] to find and kill everyone one of you personally. OK?????? That's how determined I am.
>
> Get the fuck out.
>
> MOther FUcker (Asian Hater)

After an initial trial ended with a hung jury, the retrial jury found Machado's email to be a true threat. One fact supporting the determination of a true threat was that it was targeted and sent directly to potential victims. A second fact was the email's unconditional and unequivocal threat to commit unlawful violence. A third fact was that even though not every recipient of the emails took them to be threats, many did, and ten students filed a complaint. A fourth fact was that the email was re-sent, which suggests a serious intent to carry out the threat. During the trial, jurors discovered numerous conduct elements further implicating Machado: he stole cash from his Asian roommate and used the roommate's credit card and car without authorization, he had a prior incident involving a threat, and he attempted to flee to Mexico. Machado claimed the email was merely an attempt to "scare" his targets, but the jury found that the totality of facts made his threat credible.

11. See, for example, Samuel Walker, *Hate Speech*, 1; and Timothy Shiell, *Campus Hate Speech on Trial*, 2nd ed. rev. (Lawrence: University Press of Kansas, 2009), 161–62.

12. I use the early 1980s as the dividing line not because of a difference in kind between the eras but because that is about when the sharp uptick in hate speech on universities and colleges was noticed. See, for example, Richard

Delgado, "Pressure Values and Bloodied Chickens: An Analysis of Paternalistic Objections to Hate Speech Regulation," *California Law Review* 82 (1994): 872.

13. M. Alison Kibler, *Censoring Racial Ridicule: Irish, Jewish, and African American Struggles over Race and Representation, 1890–1930* (Chapel Hill: University of North Carolina Press, 2015).

14. For example, the Dillingham Commission, a House–Senate commission chaired by Vermont senator William Paul Dillingham, published *The Dictionary of Races or Peoples* in 1911, which included a taxonomy of races for the purposes of immigration. Hebrews, Celts, and Slavs were considered separate races but were ranked above Asians and African Americans in the racial hierarchy. The commission concluded that immigration from Eastern and Southern Europe posed a serious threat to America.

15. Robert O'Neil, "Hate Speech, Fighting Words, and Beyond—Why American Law Is Unique," *Albany Law Review* 76 (2012/2013): n99.

16. Walker, *Hate Speech*, 24.

17. Walker, *Hate Speech*, 62–76.

18. Walker, *Hate Speech*, 76.

19. *Terminiello*, 337 at 4.

20. See, for example, *City of Little Falls v. Witucki*, 295 N.W.2d 243 (MN 1980); and *State v. Nelson*, A14-0356 (MN Ct. App. Dec. 22, 2014).

21. *Rosenfeld v. New Jersey*, 408 US 901 (1972) protected defendant's use of "motherfucker" four times at a school board meeting. *Lewis v. New Orleans*, 408 US 913 (1972), protected defendant's calling a police officer a "god damn mother fucker." *Brown v. Oklahoma*, 408 US 914 (1972), protected a defendant calling police officers at a meeting in a university chapel a "mother fucking fascist" and "black mother fucking pig."

22. Stephen Gard, "Fighting Words as Free Speech," *Washington University Law Quarterly* 58 (1980): 531. Similarly, Henry Louis Gates Jr. writes, "The young scholars at the *Harvard Law Review* also note, with others, that statutes prohibiting 'fighting words' have had discriminatory effects. An apparently not atypical conviction, upheld by the Louisiana state court, was occasioned by the following exchange between a white police officer and the black mother of a young suspect. He: 'Get your black ass in the goddamned car.' She: 'You goddamn mother ----ing police—I am going to [the superintendent of police] about this.' No prize for guessing who was convicted for 'fighting words.' As the legal scholar Kenneth Karst reports, 'Statutes proscribing abusive words are applied to members of racial and political minorities more frequently than can be wholly explained by any special proclivity of those people to speak abusively.' So much for the doctrine's political value." Gates, "Let Them Talk," 39.

23. O'Neil, "Hate Speech, Fighting Words," 482.

24. *Nuxoll ex rel. Nuxoll v. Indian Prairie Sch. Dist. # 204*, 523 F.3d 668, 672 (7th Cir. 2008); *Dworkin v. Hustler Magazine Inc.*, 867 F.2d 1188, 1200 (9th Cir. 1989); *Am. Booksellers Ass'n, Inc. v. Hudnut*, 771 F.2d 323, 331 n.3 (7th Cir. 1985); *Collin v. Smith*, 578 F.2d 1197, 1205 (7th Cir. 1978); and *Tollett v. United States*, 485 F.2d 1087, 1094 n.14 (8th Cir. 1973).

25. Walker, *Hate Speech*, 2.

26. Walker, *Hate Speech*, 15, 103–4.

27. See, for example, Richard Delgado, "Words That Wound: A Tort Action for Racial Insults, Epithets, and Name-Calling," *Harvard Civil Rights–Civil Liberties Review* 17 (1982): 133. Examples of cases include *Fisher v. Carrousel Motor Hotel, Inc.*, 424 S.W. 2d 627 (TX 1967); *Alcorn v. Ambro Engineering, Inc.*, 2 CA 3d 493 (1970); *Wiggs v. Courshon*, 355 F.Supp. 206 (1973); *Harris v. Harvey*, 605 F.2d 330 (7th Cir. 1976); *Contreras v. Crown Zellerbach, Inc.*, 88 WA 2d 735 (1977); *Haddix v. Port of Seattle*, No. 840149, King Co. (WA) Super. Ct. (1978); *Agarwal v. Johnson*, 25 CA 3d (1979); and *Imperial Diner, Inc. v. State Human Rights Appeal Board*, 52 NY 2d 72 (1980). Martin Denis discusses 1980s employment cases in "Race Harassment Discrimination: A Problem That Won't Go Away?," *Employee Relations Law Journal* 10 (Winter 1984–1985): 415.

28. See, for example, Herbert Marcuse, "Repressive Tolerance," in Robert Paul Wolff, Barrington Moore Jr. and Herbert Marcuse, *A Critique of Pure Tolerance* (Boston: Beacon Press, 1965). Marcuse argues that the liberal, democratic tradition is a lie employing subtle forms of domination whereby most people accept and even will their servitude. Under such conditions, tolerance (free speech) must be reinterpreted to mean only tolerance of revolutionary minorities. Since revolutionary minorities alone hold the truth, the false views of the majority must be suppressed, and they must be reeducated to the truth. April Kelly Woessner argues that "New Left" political intolerance is an inheritance from Marcuse's thought. See Woessner, "How Marcuse Made Today's Students Less Tolerant than Their Parents," *Heterodox Academy*, September 23, 2015, accessed 10-3-2017, https://heterodoxacademy.org/2015/09/23/how-marcuse-made-todays-students-less-tolerant-than-their-parents.

29. See, for example, Saul Alinsky, *Rules for Radicals* (New York: Random House, 1971). Notably, the alt-right has coopted Alinsky's rules for leftists. See, for example, Josh Harkinson, "How Ann Coulter and the Far Right Are Using the Lefty Playbook to Troll Berkeley," *Mother Jones*, April 26, 2017, accessed

9-11-2017, http://www.motherjones.com/politics/2017/04/ann-coulter-al t-right-berkeley-saul-alinsky-left-tactics-rules-for-radicals.

30. Gates, "Let Them Talk," 38.

31. SeeRichard Delgado, "Campus Antiracism Rules: Constitutional Narratives in Collision," *Northwestern University Law Review* 85 (1991): 343.

32. See Delgado, "Campus Antiracism Rules," 383–84.

33. See Matsuda, "Public Response," 2332.

34. See Matsuda, "Public Response," 2358, 2361–63.

35. See Mary Ellen Gale, "Reimagining the First Amendment: Racist Speech and Equal Liberty," *St. John's Law Review* 65 (1991): 119.

36. See Patricia Hodulik's defense of the (unconstitutional) UW System hate speech code: "The only burden it places on students is the burden of civility and respect for their peers." Hodulik, "Racist Speech on Campus," *Wayne State Law Review* 37 (1991): 1433.

37. *Overbreadth* is the legal term for a government policy that restricts protected speech. A policy can be overbroad on its face, in its application, or both. In cases of applied overbreadth, the plaintiff need only show that the government censored protected speech in the case at hand. In cases of facial overbreadth, the plaintiff must show (1) that the law restricts protected speech (not necessarily the speech in the case at hand) and (2) that the restriction is substantial. In determining whether the restriction is substantial, the court weighs the harm of invalidating a law that is constitutional in some applications against the real threat of chilling legitimate third-party speech. Courts do not consider a policy unconstitutional if it only minimally restricts protected speech, does not pose a realistic threat to protected speech, or can be saved through a narrowing construction.

38. A law is void for vagueness if it fails to define the crime "[1] with sufficient definiteness that ordinary people can understand what conduct is prohibited and [2] in a manner that does not encourage arbitrary and discriminatory enforcement." *Kolender v. Lawson*, 461 US 352, 357 (1983).

39. *Doe*, 721 at 863.

40. *UWM Post, et. al. v. Board of Regents of the University of Wisconsin*, 774 F. Supp. 1163 (E.D. WI 1991).

41. *Iota Xi Chapter of Sigma Chi Fraternity v. George Mason University*, 773 F. Supp. 792 (E.D. VA 1991).

42. *Dambrot v. Central Michigan University*, 839 F. Supp. 437 (E.D. MI 1993), *affirmed* 55 F.3d 1177 (6th Cir. 1995).

43. *Corry, et. al. v. Stanford University*, County of Santa Clara Supreme Court, Case no. 740309 (1995).

44. First Amendment protections can apply to private institutions as a matter of state law or institutional commitment. Examples of the First Amendment's relevance to private schools through state law are California's "Leonard Law" (*Corry v. Stanford University*) and the Massachusetts Civil Rights Act (*Abramowitz v. Trustees of Boston University*, C.A. No. 82680, Suffolk Superior Court, 1986). Examples of the First Amendment's relevance to private schools through school commitment are Harvard University (see Faculty of Arts and Sciences "Free Speech Guidelines," http://thefire.org/public/pdfs/0e06adc0b3cc0ccbcd96fc4b1c4ecea6.pdf?direct) and the University of Notre Dame (mission statement and Open Speaker Policy, http://thefire.org/article/10249.html).

45. The bill applied to private institutions receiving federal funds but exempted institutions with a religious mission inconsistent with the bill.

46. For a discussion of the Hyde-Craig bill and its California cousin, the Leonard Law, see Robert O'Neil, *Free Speech in the College Community* (Bloomington: Indiana University Press, 1997), 229–39.

47. For a discussion of the primary initial arguments for broad hate speech codes, see Shiell, *Campus Hate Speech on Trial*, chap. 2.

48. Robert O'Neil writes, "Quite simply, we in the United States approach hate speech very differently than do virtually all other western nations." O'Neil, "Hate Speech, Fighting Words. Samuel Walker points out that as the United States moved toward greater protections for hate speech from the 1940s to the 1970s, other countries were moving in the opposite direction. Walker, *Hate Speech*, 62–63. See also Scott J. Catlin, "A Proposal for Regulating Hate Speech in the United States: Balancing Rights under the International Covenant on Civil and Political Rights," *Notre Dame Law Review* 69 (1994): 771; Stephanie Farrior, "Molding the Matrix: The Historical and Theoretical Foundations of International Law Concerning Hate Speech," *Berkeley Journal of International Law* 14 (1996): 1; Friedrich Kubler, "How Much Freedom for Racist Speech? Transnational Aspects of a Conflict of Human Rights," *Hofstra Law Review* 27 (winter 1998): 335; Kevin Boyle, "Hate Speech—The United States versus the Rest of the World?," *Maine Law Review* 53 (2001): 485; Petal Nevella Modeste, "Race Hate Speech: The Pervasive Badge of Slavery That Mocks the Thirteenth Amendment," *Howard Law Journal* 44 (winter 2001): 311; Judge Helen Ginger Berrigan, "'Speaking Out' about Hate Speech," *Loyola Law Review* 48 (spring 2002):; Frederick Schauer, "The Exceptional First Amendment," in *American Exceptionalism and Human Rights*, ed. Michael Ignatieff (Princeton, NJ:

Princeton University Press, 2005), 29–56; Eduardo Bertoni, "War and Freedom of Expression: Hate Speech under the American Convention on Human Rights," *ILSA Journal of International and Comparative Law* 12 (spring 2006): 569; Robert Sedler, "An Essay on Freedom of Speech: The United States against the Rest of the World," *Michigan State Law Review* 2006 (2006): 377; and Winfried Brugger, "Ban on or Protection of Hate Speech?: Some Observations Based on German and American Law," *Tulane European and Civil Law Forum* 17 (2002): 1.

49. For example, see Kenneth Lasson, "Racial Defamation as Free Speech: Abusing the First Amendment," *Columbia Human Rights Law Review* 17 (1985): 11; Matsuda, "Public Response to Racist Speech"; Tsesis, *Destructive Messages*; Delgado and Stefancic, *Understanding Words That Wound*; and Jeremy Waldron, *The Harm in Hate Speech* (Cambridge: Harvard University Press, 2012).

50. See Tsesis, *Destructive Messages*, 180; and Delgado and Stefancic, *Understanding Words That Wound*, 198–99.

51. Section 130(1) states: "Whosoever, in a manner liable to disturb public peace, (1) incites hatred against parts of the population or invites violence or arbitrary acts against them, or (2) attacks the human dignity of others by insulting, maliciously degrading or defaming parts of the population shall be punished with imprisonment of no less than three months and not exceeding five years." Brugger, "Ban on or Protection of Hate Speech?," 5. Sections 185, 186, and 187 protect the honor of all humans as humans regardless of individual accomplishments, the honor necessary for civil public discourse, and the honor of a person necessary to reputation or standing in the community. Brugger, "Ban on or Protection of Hate Speech?," 8–10.

52. Specifically, "A person displays a placard on the steps of the national legislature stating, 'Wake up, you tired masses. I have four messages that you had better listen to, understand, and share! First, our president is a pig! I have painted two pictures to demonstrate my point. Here is one showing our clearly recognizable president as a pig engaged in sexual conduct with another pig in a judge's robe, and here is another, showing our President having a sexual encounter with his mother in an outhouse. Second, all our soldiers are murderers. Third, the Holocaust never happened. Fourth, African Americans use the slavery lie to extort money from the American government in the same way Jews use the Holocaust to extort money from Germany. Something should be done about this.'" Brugger, "Ban on or Protection of Hate Speech?," 3.

53. Tsesis, *Destructive Messages*, 195–96 and 173. Tsesis also argues that such laws are justified even if they are not effective. They are justified like laws against murder or theft are justified even if they do not reduce the number of murders

or thefts. Tsesis writes, "In a constitutional democracy each person's rights must be respected as intrinsically valuable . . . repudiating someone's personhood [as misethnic speech does] is in effect denying that reciprocal [moral] duty of humanity and the imperative to empathetic treatment are at all applicable to him or her." Tsesis, *Destructive Messages*, 173.

54. Delgado and Stefancic, *Understanding Words That Wound*, 199.

55. Richard Delgado, "Are Hate Speech Rules Constitutional Heresy? A Reply to Steven Gey," *Pennsylvania Law Review* 146 (1998): 874.

56. Delgado and Stefancic, *Understanding Words That Wound*, 199.

57. Waldron, *The Harm in Hate Speech*.

58. Nadine Strossen, *Hate: Why We Should Resist It with Free Speech, Not Censorship* (New York: Oxford University Press, 2018).

59. According to Osita Nwanevu, eighty-nine countries, including 84 percent of European countries, have broad hate speech bans. Nwanevu, "The Kids Are Right," *Slate*, March 12, 2017, accessed 9-11-2017, http://www.slate.com/articles/news_and_politics/cover_story/2017/03/there_s_nothing_outrageous_about_stamping_out_bigoted_speech.html.

60. Trevor Burrus, "Why Offensive Speech Is Valuable," Cato Institute Commentary, accessed 12-12-2017, http://www.cato.org/publications/commentary/why-offensive-speech-valuable.

61. Eric Heinze, "Nineteen Arguments for Hate Speech Bans—And Against Them," Free Speech Debate, March 31, 2014, accessed 8-14-2017, http://freespeechdebate.com/ru.

62. Gates, "Let Them Talk," 44.

63. The latter incident caused an astounded Jewish leader to say, "It stuns the mind that [they] would even remotely consider the need, much less the propriety of examining this pamphlet. . . . Is it incompetence, madness, mischief, or something more malign?" Stefan Braun, *Democracy Off Balance: Freedom of Expression and Hate Propaganda in Canada*, 2nd ed. (Toronto: University of Toronto Press, 2004), 105.

64. Braun, *Democracy Off Balance*, 97.

65. Tsesis, *Destructive Messages.* See also Anastaplo, *Campus Hate-Speech Codes*, and Frederickson, *Racism*.

66. For further criticism of *Destructive Messages*, see Anuj C. Desai, "Attacking *Brandenburg* with History: Does the Long-Term Harm of Biased Speech Justify a Criminal Statute Suppressing It?" *Federal Communications Law Journal* 55 (March 2003): 353; and W. Bradley Wendel, "The Banality of Evil and the First Amendment," *Michigan Law Review* 102 (May 2004): 1404.

67. Michael McConnell, "You Can't Say That," *New York Times*, June 22, 2012, accessed 9-4-2017, http://www.nytimes.com/2012/06/24/books/review/the-harm-in-hate-speech-by-jeremy-waldron.html?mcubz=3.

68. Richard Abel, *Speaking Respect, Respecting Speech* (Chicago: University of Chicago Press, 1998), 282.

69. Delgado and Stefancic, *Understanding Words That Wound*, 114–18.

70. Delgado and Stefancic, *Understanding Words That Wound*, 116.

71. Delgado and Stefancic, *Understanding Words That Wound*, 11.

72. For a detailed discussion of the philosophy of insults, including its fit or lack thereof with various areas of US speech law, see Jerome Neu, *Sticks and Stones: The Philosophy of Insults* (Oxford: Oxford University Press, 2008). Neu addresses insults in the campus hate speech context at 153–64 and concludes that the solution is "more speech" rather than legal bans.

73. Brugger, "Ban on or Protection of Hate Speech?," 2.

74. James Q. Whitman, "Enforcing Civility and Respect: Three Societies," *Yale Law Journal* 109 (January 1999): 1353–56.

75. Ronald Krotoszynski Jr., *The First Amendment in Cross Cultural Perspective* (New York: New York University Press, 2006).

76. Roger Alford, "Free Speech and the Case for Constitutional Exceptionalism," *Michigan Law Review* 106 (April 2008): 1087.

77. See, for example, Kubler, "How Much Freedom for Racist Speech?," 375; Boyle, "Hate Speech," 502; and Claudia Haupt, "Regulating Hate Speech: Damned If You Do and Damned If You Don't," *Boston University International Law Journal* 23 (fall 2005): 301.

78. Conor Friedersdorf, "A Civil Rights Icon Urges Law Grads to Defend Free Speech," *The Atlantic*, May 29, 2018, accessed 6-15-2018, https://www.theatlantic.com/education/archive/2018/05/a-civil-rights-icon-urges-law-grads-to-defend-free-speech/561380.

79. Hunter, "Escaping the Expression-Equality Conundrum."

80. Reliance on an immutable characteristic has some normative appeal (what is immutable is not the individual's fault) and provides a reliable basis for legal analysis, but it leads to the paradox of recognizing identity groups while attempting to make them irrelevant. Dan Danielsen and Karen Engle, *After Identity: A Reader in Law and Culture* (New York: Psychology Press, 1995), xiv.

81. See, for example, Delgado's influential "Campus Antiracism Rules," 387–88.

82. Hunter considers *Herndon v. Lowry* (1937) and *West Virginia Board of Education v Barnette* (1943) missed opportunities to doctrinally connect freedom

of expression to equality. *Police Dept. of Chicago v. Mosley*, 408 US 92 (1972) represents another missed opportunity: the decision made a strong connection when it struck down a local ordinance distinguishing labor picketing from other picketing based on the Equal Protection Clause rather than the "closely intertwined" First Amendment, but that ruling was followed by court opinions divorcing the speaker's expression from their group identity. *New York Times v. Sullivan* (1964) held for an individual right foremost that applied to groups only by extension.

83. Hunter, "Escaping the Expression-Equality Conundrum," 1712.

84. Hunter, "Escaping the Expression-Equality Conundrum," 1720.

85. john a. powell, "Worlds Apart: Reconciling Freedom of Speech and Equality," *Kentucky Law Journal* 85 (1996): 9.

86. Gates, "Let Them Talk," 44.

87. Consider a few examples from only the 2016–17 academic year: unsuccessful attempts to disinvite Arab American activist and feminist Linda Sarsour as a graduation speaker at the City College of New York; fire critical race theorist Tommy Curry from his tenured professorship at Texas A&M for allegedly advocating violence against whites; fire Boston University professor Saida Grundy for calling white college men a "problem population" and calling St. Patrick's Day a "white people's Kwanzaa"; fire Orange Coast College professor Olga Perez Stable Cox for criticizing President Donald Trump in class; fire Syracuse professor Dana Cloud for a pro–Muslim rally tweet; punish sociologist John Eric Williams of Trinity College in Connecticut for alleged racist remarks; intimidate classics professor Sarah Bond of the University of Iowa for explaining that ancient marble statues were often painted colors and do not represent "whiteness" as the classical ideal; and withhold funding from UW-Madison for offering a course on white privilege. Successful attempts including firing a Spalding University professor for asking why the university did not notify minority professors about a possible threat from an armed student, firing University of Tennessee at Knoxville instructor Judy Morelock for "mishandling" a dispute over a race-related quiz question; firing Essex County College adjunct Lisa Durden for defending a blacks-only Memorial Day event; intimidating Princeton African American scholar Keeanga-Yamahtta Taylor into canceling speaking engagements, watering down Lee Bebout's "problem of whiteness" course at Arizona State University; punishing a Southern Methodist student for posting satirical flyers about "why white women should date black men"; and canceling courses for instructor Kevin Allred at Rutgers University and Montclair State University for hyperbolic tweets criticizing President Trump.

88. Rmuse, "Racists Demand Punishment for African Americans Exercising First Amendment Rights," *Politicususa*, December 2, 2014, accessed 9-4-2017,

http://www.politicususa.com/2014/12/02/racists-demand-punishment-african-americans-exercising-amendment-rights.html. Steven Aggergaard, "Black Lives Matter and the Evolution of the First Amendment," *Minneapolis StarTribune*, December 23, 2015, accessed 6-25-2017, http://www.startribune.com/black-lives-matter-and-the-evolution-of-the-first-amendment/363428071. Joshua Kellem, " 'BLM' is an Expression of the First Amendment," *The Rocket*, October 27, 2016, accessed 6-27-2017. https://www.theonlinerocket.com/opinion/2016/10/27/blm-is-an-expression-of-the-first-amendment.

89. Thomas Peel, "Kaepernick Is a First Amendment Hero," *Mercury News*, September 2, 2016, accessed 6-17-2017, http://www.mercurynews.com/2016/09/02/thomas-peele-kaepernick-is-first-amendment-hero; Marc Tracy and Ashley Southall, "Black Football Players Lend Heft to Protests at Missouri," *New York Times*, November 8, 2015, accessed 6-17-2017, https://www.nytimes.com/2015/11/09/us/missouri-football-players-boycott-in-protest-of-university-president.html?mcubz=3; Scott Jaschik, "Backlash to Anthem Protests," *Inside Higher Education*, October 24, 2016, accessed 10-24-2016, https://www.insidehighered.com/news/2016/10/24/alabama-and-greenville-backlash-anthem-protests-black-students.

90. See, for example, Chuck Raasch, "Taking Down Student Painting Violated 1st Amendment, Clay Claims in Planned Lawsuit," *St. Louis Post-Dispatch*, February 21, 2017, accessed 6-17-2017, http://www.stltoday.com/news/local/govt-and-politics/taking-down-student-painting-violated-st-amendment-clay-claims-in/article_8ab33e1b-3a56-5b77-93fb-45ef7d06b628.html; Dwayne Wong, "Censoring Howard Zinn and Censoring American History," *Huffington Post*, May 15, 2017, accessed 9-12-2017, http://www.huffingtonpost.com/entry/censoring-howard-zinn-and-censoring-american-history_us_58bcb202e4b02b8b584dfd6a; Joy Garnett, "With NCAC Help, Artist Successfully Reverses Corporation's Objections to Black Lives Matter Artwork," National Coalition against Censorship, December 6, 2016, accessed 9-12-2017, http://ncac.org/blog/with-ncac-help-artist-successfully-overturns-corporations-objections-to-black-lives-matter-artwork; Jas Chana, "Free Speech Groups Defend Black History Month Exhibit Removed on Grounds of Offence," National Coalition against Censorship, February 10, 2017, accessed 9-12-2017, http://ncac.org/wp-content/uploads/2017/02/SanJosePR.pdf; Anna Silman, "10 Famous Comedians on How Political Correctness Is Killing Comedy," *Salon*, June 10, 2015, accessed 9-12-2017, http://www.salon.com/2015/06/10/10_famous_comedians_on_how_political_correctness_is_killing_comedy_we_are_addicted_to_the_rush_of_being_offended/; "African-American Classics Barred from Classrooms," slideshow, BET, September 26, 2013, accessed 9-12-2017,

http://www.bet.com/news/national/photos/2013/09/banned-book-week-african-american-classics-barred-from-classrooms.html#!092413-national-banned-books-the-color-purple-alice-walker.

91. Allia Malek and Wilson Dizard, "DOJ Says Ferguson Police Violated African-Americans' Free Speech Rights," *Al Jazeera America*, March 4, 2015, accessed 6-17-2017, http://america.aljazeera.com/articles/2015/3/4/Justice-says-Ferguson-police-violated-1st-amendment-rights.html; Taryn Finley, "6 N.W.A. Songs That Spoke about the Reality of Being Black in America," *Huffington Post*, August 13, 2015, accessed 9-12-2017, http://www.huffingtonpost.com/entry/nwa-songs-that-are-still-relevant-today_us_55cb6546e4b0923c12bece11; Rachel Bade, Kyle Cheney, and Heather Caygle, "CBC: 'We May Just Have to Kick Somebody's Ass' over Painting Removal," *Politico*, January 10, 2017, accessed 9-12-2017, http://www.politico.com/story/2017/01/congress-artwork-animals-cops-congressional-black-caucus-gop-233409.

92. Susan Herman, "ACLU President: We Didn't Always Have Free Speech," *Time*, November 20, 2015, accessed 10-20-2017, http://time.com/4120362/aclu-president-free-speech.

93. See, for example, Conor Friedersdorf, "The Most Shortsighted Attack on Free Speech in Modern History," *The Atlantic*, August 23, 2017, accessed 8-24-2017, https://www.theatlantic.com/politics/archive/2017/08/the-most-shortsighted-attack-on-free-speech-in-modern-history/537468.

94. Gara La Marche, "The Messy Business of Free Speech," *The Nation*, September 5, 2017, accessed 9-17-2017, https://www.thenation.com/article/the-messy-business-of-free-speech.

95. Anthony Romero, "Equality, Justice and the First Amendment," ACLU, August 15, 2017, https://www.aclu.org/blog/free-speech/equality-justice-and-first-amendment.

96. Andrew Lanham, "When W.E.B. Du Bois Was Un-American," *Boston Review*, January 13, 2017, accessed 12-8-2017, http://bostonreview.net/race-politics/andrew-lanham-when-w-e-b-du-bois-was-un-american.

97. Ernest Freeberg, "Inviting Controversy: When UT Students Demanded Their Free Speech Rights, a Half Century Ago," Knoxville History Project, August 28, 2017, http://knoxvillehistoryproject.org/2017/08/28/inviting-controversy-ut-students-demanded-free-speech-rights-half-century-ago.

98. Charles Murray, a fellow at the conservative American Enterprise Institute, spoke at Middlebury College in March 2017. Protesters shouted him down, and he was moved to another location to deliver his talk remotely. After Murray finished, he and Allison Stanger, a Middlebury professor and moderator

for the event, were assaulted and their car was blocked and damaged by approximately twenty persons, including eight masked ones the university believed used tactics indicating training in obstruction. The university eventually disciplined sixty-seven students for their roles in the mayhem.

99. Conservative advocate Heather Mac Donald of the Manhattan Institute spoke at Claremont McKenna College in April 2017. Nearly 200 students protested her talk due to her allegedly racist views. Some protesters blocked the entrance the building where she was speaking. After disciplinary hearings, the university suspended five students for breaching "institutional values of freedom of expression and assembly," but exonerated three others.

100. Speeches by conservative pundits Milo Yiannopolous and Ann Coulter were canceled due to protester violence (Yiannopolous) and the threat of protester violence (Coulter). Conor Friedersdorf, "UC Berkeley Declares Itself Unsafe for Ann Coulter," *The Atlantic*, April 20, 2017, accessed 9-12-2017, https://www.theatlantic.com/politics/archive/2017/04/uc-berkeley-declares-itself-unsafe-for-ann-coulter/523668.

101. Conservative pundit Ben Shapiro's talk at UW-Madison in November 2016 was repeatedly disrupted by shouting and obstructing protesters for about twenty minutes. Dana Kampa, "Conservative Pundit Ben Shapiro Lectures to Turbulent Crowd on Safe Spaces, Freedom of Speech," *Badger-Herald*, November 17, 2016, accessed 9-12-2017, https://badgerherald.com/news/2016/11/17/conservative-pundit-ben-shapiro-lectures-to-turbulent-crowd-on-safe-spaces-freedom-of-speech.

102. A student, Cameron Padgett, rented space at the university for alt-right leader and president of the National Policy Center Richard Spencer to speak. The university canceled the appearance, citing safety concerns. Padgett sued the university, claiming it violated his First Amendment rights. US District Court Judge W. Keith Watkins held in Padgett's favor. The case was dismissed when Spencer was cleared to speak. The student was awarded $29,900 in legal fees. Spencer's talk drew protesters from around the country and resulted in several arrests.

103. Associated Press, "U. of I. Cancels Talk by Nobel Laureate after Faculty Raises Concerns about His Views on Race, Intelligence," *Chicago Tribune*, May 17, 2017, accessed 9-12-2017, http://www.chicagotribune.com/news/ct-university-of-illinois-james-watson-talk-cancelled-20170517-story.html.

104. Ben Haller, "Professor Bret Weinstein Files $3.8 Million Claim against Evergreen State College," Reason.com, August 2, 2017, accessed 9-7-2017, http://reason.com/blog/2017/08/02/professor-bret-weinstein-files-38-millio.

105. Jacey Fortin, "Richard Dawkins Event Canceled over Past Comments about Islam," *New York Times*, July 24, 2017, accessed 9-4-2017, https://www.nytimes.com/2017/07/24/us/richard-dawkins-speech-canceled-berkeley.html?mcubz=3.

106. Jonathan Rauch, "In Defense of Prejudice," *Harper's Magazine* (May 1995): 43.

107. See, for example, Geoffrey Stone, "Political Conservatives Suddenly Embrace Free Speech on Campus," *Huffington Post*, May 1, 2017, accessed 12-8-2017, https://www.huffingtonpost.com/entry/political-conservatives-suddenly-embrace-free-speech_us_590745dee4b084f59b49fb07.

108. Clara Turnage, "Most Republicans Think Colleges Are Bad for the Country. Why?," *Chronicle of Higher Education*, July 10, 2017, accessed 12-8-2017, http://www.chronicle.com/article/Most-Republicans-Think/240587.

109. Scott Jaschik, "New Data Explain Republican Loss of Confidence in Higher Education," *Inside Higher Education*, August 17, 2017, accessed 8-23-2017, https://www.insidehighered.com/news/2017/08/17/new-data-explain-republican-loss-confidence-higher-education.

110. Carl Schurz, *Speeches, Correspondence and Political Papers of Carl Schurz*, vol. 1, ed. Frederic Bancroft (New York: Putnam, 1913), 227–30.

111. Burrus, "Why Offensive Speech Is Valuable."

112. Strossen, *Hate*, chapter 8.

113. See Timothy C. Shiell, "The Case of the Student Racist Face Book Message," *Journal of Academic Freedom* 5 (2014), https://www.aaup.org/sites/default/files/Shiell.pdf.

114. Courts have explicitly held that universities cannot enforce general policies requiring student speech be nonhateful, civil, tolerant, reasonable, or the like; they may only promote such speech as an aspiration. See, for example, *College Republicans v. Reed*, 523 F. Supp. 2d 1005 (N.D. CA 2007), and *Bair v. Shippensburg University*, 280 F. Supp. 2d 357 (M.D. PA 2003).

115. For example, the Foundation for Individual Rights in Education (FIRE) found that 85 percent of top institutions fail to provide students accused of serious misconduct the most basic elements of fair procedure. "Spotlight on Due Process," FIRE, September 5, 2017, accessed 9-12-2017, https://www.thefire.org/due-process-report-2017.

116. The relevant portions of the policies follow. Residence hall policy on harassment: "Harassing behavior, regardless of the method (written, verbal, via email or phone, online communities or other information technology resources, posting of inappropriate materials in any public area) is prohibited in the residence halls." Residence hall policy on disorderly conduct: "Disorderly conduct

within the residence halls is not permitted. This includes, but is not limited to, engaging in fighting, prank activities, using abusive language or acting in a manner so as to disturb or threaten the public peace." The computer use policy banned "distribution of any disruptive or offensive messages, including offensive comments about race, gender, hair color, disabilities, age, sexual orientation, pornography, religious beliefs and practice, political beliefs, or national origin." The discriminatory conduct policy: "Racist and other discriminatory conduct . . . will not be tolerated. Discrimination, discriminatory attitudes, and expressions that reflect discrimination are inconsistent with . . . efforts . . . to foster an environment of respect for the dignity and worth of all members of the university community and to eliminate all manifestations of discrimination within the university. [This] encompasses harassing conduct based upon the race, sex, gender identity or expression, religion, color, creed, disability, sexual orientation, national origin, ancestry, or age of an individual or individuals. . . . Institutions may wish to provide specific examples of racist and other discriminatory conduct, to further enhance understanding of the problem. Such examples might include: . . . 3. Verbal assaults based on ethnicity, such as name calling, racial slurs, or 'jokes' that demean a victim's color, culture or history."

117. For an argument, courts need to hold university officials more accountable, see Azhar Majeed, "Putting Their Money Where Their Mouth Is: The Case for Denying Qualified Immunity to University Administrators Who Violate Students' Speech Rights," *Cardozo Public Law, Policy and Ethics Journal* 8 (2010): 15.

118. Nicole Santa Cruz, Lauren Williams and Mike Anton, " 'Irvine 11': 10 students sentenced to probation, no jail time," *Los Angeles Times*, September 23, 2011, accessed 9-12-2017, http://latimesblogs.latimes.com/lanow/2011/09/irvine-11-sentenced-probation-no-jail-time.html.

119. See, for example, Stephanie Saul, "Dozens of Middlebury Students Are Disciplined for Charles Murray Protest," *New York Times*, May 24, 2017, accessed 9-7-2017, https://www.nytimes.com/2017/05/24/us/middlebury-college-charles-murray-bell-curve.html?mcubz=3.

120. See, for example, Andrew Beale and Sonner Kehrt, "Behind Berkeley's Semester of Hate," *New York Times*, August 4, 2017, accessed 9-7-2017, https://www.nytimes.com/2017/08/04/education/edlife/antifa-collective-university-california-berkeley.html?mcubz=3.

121. See, for example, Haller, "Weinstein Files $3.8 Million Claim," and Bari Weiss, "When the Left Turns on Its Own," *New York Times*, June 1, 2017, accessed 9-7-2017, https://www.nytimes.com/2017/06/01/opinion/when-the-left-turns-on-its-own.html?mcubz=3.

122. Scott Poole, "Free Speech and Black Speech in Charleston, South Carolina," *Huffington Post*, February 23, 2017, accessed 5-20-2017, http://www.huffingtonpost.com/entry/free-speech-and-black-speech-in-charleston-so uth-carolina_us_58af436be4b02f3f81e44521.

123. Scott Jaschick, "Protesters Tear Down Silent Sam," *Inside Higher Education*, August 21, 2018, accessed 8-21-2018, https://www.insidehighered.com/news/2018/08/21/protesters-tear-down-confederate-statue-unc-cha pel-hill.

124. Conor Friedersdorf, "The Lessons of Bygone Free Speech Fights," *The Atlantic*, December 10, 2015, accessed 9-17-2017, https://www.theatlantic.com/politics/archive/2015/12/what-student-activists-can-learn-from-bygone-fr ee-speech-fights/419178.

125. See note 28.

126. For example, Wendy Kaminer identifies three popular movements that contribute to the current campus climate suppressing offensive speech: the fe minist antipornography crusade, the pop-psychology recovery movement, and the push for campus multiculturalism. Kaminer, "The Progressive Ideas behind the Lack of Free Speech on campus," *Washington Post*, February 20, 2015, accessed 2-20-2018, https://www.washingtonpost.com/opinions/the-progr essive-ide
as-behind-the-lack-of-free-speech-on-campus/2015/02/20/93086efe-b0e7-11e 4-886b-c22184f27c35_story.html.

127. Popular critiques of Marcuse's repressive tolerance include Alex Callinicos, "Repressive Tolerance Revisited: Mill, Marcuse and MacIntyre," in *Aspects of Toleration: Philosophical Studies*, ed. John Norton and Susan Mendus (New York: Routledge 2010), 53–74; Maurice Cranston, "Herbert Marcuse," *Encounter* 32, no. 3 (1969): 38–50; Paul Eidelberg, "The Temptation of Herbert Marcuse," *Review of Politics* 31, no. 4 (1969): 442–58; Douglas Kellner, *Herbert Marcuse and the Crisis of Marxism* (Berkeley: University of California Press, 1984); Alasdair MacIntyre, *Marcuse* (London: Fontana/Collins, 1970); and Charles Taylor, "Marcuse's Authoritarian Utopia," *Canadian Dimension* 7, no. 3 (1970): 49–53.

128. Gates Jr. "Let Them Talk," 43.

129. For example, during the period September 2016 to August 2017, the Anti-Defamation League tracked nearly 200 cases of white supremacist propaganda on 126 campuses in thirty-nine states. Nick Roll, "ADL Says to Expect More White Supremacist Leaflets on Campuses," *Inside Higher Education*, September 11, 2017, accessed 9-11-2017, https://www.insidehighered.com/news/2017/09/11/adl-says-expect-more-white-supremacist-leaflets-campuses.

130. Delgado, "Pressure Valves and Bloodied Chickens," 881.

131. Bennett Carpenter, "Free Speech, Black Lives, and White Fragility," *Duke Chronicle*, January 19, 2016, accessed 9-7-2017, http://www.dukechronicle.com/article/2016/01/free-speech-black-lives-and-white-fragility.

132. Peter Salovey, "Free Speech, Personified," *New York Times: On Campus*, November 26, 2017, accessed 12-11-2017, https://www.nytimes.com/2017/11/26/opinion/free-speech-yale-civil-rights.html.

133. The Woodward Report, named after its chair, Comer Vann Woodward, was formally titled the Report of the Committee on Freedom of Expression. The report is available at https://yalecollege.yale.edu/deans-office/reports/report-committee-freedom-expression-yale.

134. See, for example, Cecelia Capuzzi Simon, "Fighting for Free Speech on America's Campuses," *New York Times*, August 1, 2016, accessed 6-21-2017, https://www.nytimes.com/2016/08/07/education/edlife/fire-first-amendment-on-campus-free-speech.html?mcubz=3.

BIBLIOGRAPHY

Abel, Richard. *Speaking Respect, Respecting Speech*. Chicago: University of Chicago Press, 1998.

Adelman, Lynn. "The Glorious Jurisprudence of Thurgood Marshall." *Harvard Law and Policy Review* 7 (winter 2013): 113–37.

Aggergaard, Steen. "Black Lives Matter and the Evolution of the First Amendment." *Minneapolis Star Tribune*, December 23, 2015. Accessed 6-25-2017. http://www.startribune.com/black-lives-matter-and-the-evolution-of-the-first-amendment/363428071/.

Alford, Roger. "Free Speech and the Case for Constitutional Exceptionalism." *Michigan Law Review* 106 (April 2008): 1071–88.

Alinsky, Saul. *Rules for Radicals*. New York: Random House, 1971.

Anastaplo, George. *Campus Hate-Speech Codes, Natural Rights, and Twentieth Century Atrocities*, rev. ed. Lewiston, NY: Edwin Mellen Press, 1999.

Anderson, Alexis. "The Formative Period of the First Amendment." *American Journal of Legal History* 24 (January 1980): 56–75.

Anderson, Karen. *Little Rock: Race and Resistance at Central High School*. Princeton, NJ: Princeton University Press, 2013.

Andre, Steven. "The Transformation of Freedom of Speech: Unsnarling the Twisted Roots of *Citizens United v. FEC*." *John Marshall Law Review* 44, no. 1 (2010): 69–127.

Apel, Dora. *Imagery of Lynching: Black Men, White Women, and the Mob*. New Brunswick, NJ: Rutgers University Press, 2004.

Arsenault, Raymond. *Freedom Riders: 1961 and the Struggle for Racial Justice*. New York: Oxford University Press, 2006.

Ash, Steven. *A Massacre in Memphis: The Race Riot that Shook the Nation One Year after the Civil War*. New York: Hill and Wang, 2013.

Associated Press. "U. of I. Cancels Talk by Nobel Laureate after Faculty Raises Concerns about His Views on Race, Intelligence." *Chicago Tribune*, May 17, 2017. Accessed 9-12-2017. http://www.chicagotribune.com/news/ct-university-of-illinois-james-watson-talk-cancelled-20170517-story.html.

Avery, Ron. "Late 1800s Bad for Blacks Only in Vice Was There Equal Job Opportunity." Philly.Com, February 16, 1998. Accessed 3-30-2016. http://

articles.philly.com/1998-02-16/news/25752508_1_black-customers-philadelphia-blacks-black-lawyer.

Bade, Rachel, Kyle Cheney, and Heather Caygle. "CBC: 'We May Just Have to Kick Somebody's Ass' over Painting Removal." Politico.com, January 10, 2017. Accessed 9-12-2017. http://www.politico.com/story/2017/01/congress-artwork-animals-cops-congressional-black-caucus-gop-233409.

Baer, Judith, and Leslie Friedman Goldstein. *The Constitutional and Legal Rights of Women: Cases in Law and Social Change*. Los Angeles: Roxbury Publishing, 2006.

Barber, Lucy. *Marching on Washington: The Forging of an American Political Tradition*. Berkeley: University of California Press, 2004.

Bass, S. Jonathan. "Transportation Discrimination." In *Encyclopedia of Civil Rights in America*, vol. 3, ed. David Bradley and Shelly Fisher Fishkin. Armonk: Sharpe Reference, 1998, 850–55.

Beale, Andrew, and Sonner Kehrt. "Behind Berkeley's Semester of Hate." *New York Times*, August 4, 2017. Accessed 9-7-2017. https://www.nytimes.com/2017/08/04/education/edlife/antifa-collective-university-california-berkeley.html?mcubz=3.

Belknap, Michael. *American Political Trials*, rev. ed. Westport, CT: Greenwood, 1994.

———. *Federal Law and Southern Order: Racial Violence and Constitutional Conflict in the Post-*Brown *South*. Athens: University of Georgia Press, 1987.

Bell, Derrick. *Race, Racism, and American Law*, 3rd ed. Boston: Little, Brown, 1992.

Berlin, Ira. *Slaves without Masters: The Free Negro in the Antebellum South*. New York: New Press, 2007.

Berman, Geoffrey. "A New Deal for Free Speech: Free Speech and the Labor Movement in the 1930s." *Virginia Law Review* 80 (February 1994): 291–322.

Berrigan, Judge Helen Ginger. " 'Speaking Out' about Hate Speech." *Loyola Law Review* 48 (spring 2002): 1–16.

Bertoni, Eduardo. "War and Freedom of Expression: Hate Speech under the American Convention on Human Rights." *ILSA Journal of International and Comparative Law* 12 (spring 2006): 569–74.

Blackstone, William. *Commentaries on English Law*. Oxford: Clarendon Press, 1765–1769. Available at http://avalon.law.yale.edu/subject_menus/blackstone.asp.

Blaustein, Albert, and Robert Zangrando, eds. *Civil Rights and the American Negro*. New York: Trident Press, 1968.

Bloom, Jack. *Class, Race and the Civil Rights Movement.* Bloomington: Indiana University Press, 1987.

Bollinger, Lee. *The Tolerant Society.* New York: Barnes & Noble, 1986.

Boyle, Kevin. "Hate Speech—The United States versus the Rest of the World?" *Maine Law Review* 53 (2001): 485–502.

Braden, Anne. "The Constitution and the Civil Rights Movement: The First Amendment and the Fourteenth." In *A Less Than Perfect Union: Alternative Perspectives on the U.S. Constitution*, ed. Jules Lobel. New York: Monthly Review Press, 1988.

Braun, Stefan. *Democracy Off Balance: Freedom of Expression and Hate Propaganda in Canada*, 2nd ed. Toronto: University of Toronto Press, 2004.

Breig, James. "Early American Newspapering." *Colonial Williamsburg Journal* (spring 2003). Accessed 3-24-2016. https://www.history.org/Foundation/journal/spring03/journalism.cfm

Browning, James. "Anti-Miscegenation Laws in the United States." *Duke Bar Journal* 1 (1951): 26–41.

Brugger, Winfried. "Ban on or Protection of Hate Speech?: Some Observations Based on German and American Law." *Tulane European and Civil Law Forum* 17 (2002): 1–21.

Burnham, Margaret. "Reflections on the Civil Rights Movement and the First Amendment." In *A Less Than Perfect Union: Alternative Perspectives on the U.S. Constitution*, ed. Jules Lobel. New York: Monthly Review Press, 1988.

Burrus, Trevor. "Why Offensive Speech Is Valuable." Cato Institute Commentary, March 23, 2015. Accessed 12-12-2017. http://www.cato.org/publications/commentary/why-offensive-speech-valuable.

Byrd-Chichester, Janell. "The Federal Courts and Claims of Discrimination in Higher Education." *Journal of Negro Education* 69, no. 1/2 (winter–spring 2000): 12–26.

Callinicos, Alex. "Repressive Tolerance Revisited: Mill, Marcuse and MacIntyre." In *Aspects of Toleration: Philosophical Studies*, ed. John Norton and Susan Mendus. New York: Routledge, 2010, 53–74.

Carpenter, Bennett. "Free Speech, Black Lives, and White Fragility." *Duke Chronicle*, January 19, 2016. Accessed 9-7-2017. http://www.dukechronicle.com/article/2016/01/free-speech-black-lives-and-white-fragility.

Carrigan, William, and Clive Web. "The Lynching of Persons of Mexican Origin or Descent in the United States, 1848–1928." *Journal of Social History* 37, no. 2 (winter 2003): 411–38.

Carroll, Thomas. "Freedom of Speech and Press during the Civil War." *Virginia Law Review* 9 (1923): 516–51.

Carter, William, Jr. "The Thirteenth Amendment and Pro-Equality Speech." *Columbia Law Review* 112 (2012): 1855–81.

Catlin, Scott J. "A Proposal for Regulating Hate Speech in the United States: Balancing Rights under the International Covenant on Civil and Political Rights." *Notre Dame Law Review* 69 (1994): 771–813.

Chafee, Zechariah, Jr. *Free Speech in the United States*. New York: Atheneum, 1941.

Chana, Jas. "Free Speech Groups Defend Black History Month Exhibit Removed on Grounds of Offence." National Coalition against Censorship, February 10, 2017. Accessed 9-12-2017. http://ncac.org/wp-content/uploads/2017/02/SanJosePR.pdf.

Chungchan, Gao. *African Americans in the Reconstruction Era*. New York: Routledge, 2000.

Cohen, Robert, and Reginald Zelnik, eds. *The Free Speech Movement: Reflections on Berkeley in the 1960s*. Berkeley: University of California Press, 2002.

Collins, Ann. *All Hell Broke Loose: American Race Riots from the Progressive Era through WWII*. Santa Barbara, CA: ABC-CLIO, 2012.

Congressional Research Services. *The Constitution of the United States, Analysis And Interpretation*. 2013 Supplement. Washington, DC: Congressional Research Services, 2013.

Conrad, Cecilia, John Whitehead, Patrick Mason, and James Stewart, eds. *African Americans in the U.S. Economy*. Lanham, MD: Rowman and Littlefield, 2005.

Cooley, Thomas. *A Treatise on Constitutional Limitations*. Boston: Little, Brown, 1868.

Corlett, J. Angelo, and Robert Francescotti. "Foundations of a Theory of Hate Speech." *Wayne State Law Review* 48 (fall 2002): 1071–100.

Corrigan, John, and Lynn Neal, eds. *Religious Intolerance in America: A Documentary History*. Chapel Hill: University of North Carolina Press, 2010.

Cover, Robert. "The Origins of Judicial Activism in the Protection of Minorities." *Yale Law Journal* 91 (June 1982): 1287–316.

Cranston, Maurice. "Herbert Marcuse." *Encounter* 32, no. 3 (1969): 38–50.

Crockett, Hasan. "The Incendiary Pamphlet: David Walker's Appeal in Georgia." *Journal of Negro History* 86, no. 3 (summer 2001): 305–18.

Curtis, Michael Kent. *Free Speech: The People's Darling Privilege: Struggles for Freedom of Expression in American History*. Durham, NC: Duke University Press, 2000.

Dalfiume, Richard. "The 'Forgotten Years' of the Negro Revolution." *Journal of American History* 55, no. 1 (June 1968): 90–106.

Dalin, David. "Jews, Nazis and Civil Liberties." In *American Jewish Yearbook 1980*. New York: American Jewish Committee and Jewish Publication Society of America, 1980. 3–28.

Danielsen, Dan, and Karen Engle. *After Identity: A Reader in Law and Culture*. New York: Psychology Press, 1995.

Dashev, Elian. "Economic Boycotts as Harassment: The Threat to First Amendment Protected Speech in the Aftermath of *Doe v. Reed*." *Loyola of Los Angeles Law Review* 45 (2011): 207–54.

Davis, Benjamin. *Communist Councilman from Harlem: Autobiographical Notes Written in a Federal Penitentiary*. New York: International, 1991.

Davis, Kenneth. "America's True History of Religious Tolerance." *Smithsonian Magazine*, October 2010. Accessed 3-4-2016. http://www.smithsonianmag.com/history/americas-true-history-of-religious-tolerance-61312684/.

Delfattore, Joan. *The Fourth R: Conflicts over Religion in America's Public Schools*. New Haven, CT: Yale University Press, 2004.

Delgado, Richard. "Are Hate Speech Rules Constitutional Heresy? A Reply to Steven Gey." *Pennsylvania Law Review* 146 (1998): 865–79.

———. "Pressure Values and Bloodied Chickens: An Analysis of Paternalistic Objections to Hate Speech Regulation." *California Law Review* 82 (1994): 871–92.

———. "Campus Antiracism Rules: Constitutional Narratives in Collision." *Northwestern University Law Review* 85 (1991): 343–87.

———. "Words That Wound: A Tort Action for Racial Insults, Epithets, and Name-Calling." *Harvard Civil Rights-Civil Liberties Review* 17 (1982): 133–84.

Delgado, Richard, and Jean Stefancic. *Understanding Words That Wound*. Boulder, CO: Westview Press, 2004.

Denis, Martin. "Race Harassment Discrimination: A Problem That Won't Go Away?" *Employee Relations Law Journal* 10 (winter 1984–1985): 415–36.

Desai, Anuj. "Attacking *Brandenburg* with History: Does the Long-Term Harm of Biased Speech Justify a Criminal Statute Suppressing It?" *Federal Communications Law Journal* 55 (March 2003): 353–94.

de Tocqueville, Alexis. *Democracy in America*. Trans. George Lawrence, ed. J. P. Mayer. New York: Harper, 1969.

DeVega, Chauncey. "White America's Racial Amnesia: The Sobering Truth about our Country's 'Race Riots.'" *Salon*, May 1, 2015. Accessed

9-21-2017. http://www.salon.com/2015/05/01/white_americas_racial_amnesia_the_sobering_truth_about_our_countrys_race_riots_partner/.

Diner, Hasia. *The Jews of the United States: 1654–2000*. Berkeley: University of California Press, 2004.

———. *In the Almost Promised Land*. Baltimore: Johns Hopkins University Press, 1995.

Dinnerstein, Leonard. *The Leo Frank Case*, rev. ed. Athens: University of Georgia Press, 2008.

Douglass, Frederick. "West India Emancipation." August 3, 1857, speech in Canandaigua, New York. Accessed 3-21-2016. http://www.blackpast.org/1857-frederick-douglass-if-there-no-struggle-there-no-progress.

Drake, Frederick, and Lynn Nelson, eds. *States' Rights and American Federalism: A Documentary History*. Westport, CT: Greenwood Press, 1999.

Dudziak, Mary. *Cold War Civil Rights: Race and the Image of American Democracy*. Princeton, NJ: Princeton University Press, 2000.

Ehrlich, Howard. *Campus Ethnoviolence and the Policy Options*. Report no. 4, National Institute Against Prejudice and Violence, 1990.

Eidelberg, Paul. "The Temptation of Herbert Marcuse." *Review of Politics* 31, no. 4 (1969): 442–58.

Eliot, Thomas. Book Reviews. *Harvard Law Review* 61 (1948): 899–903.

Emerson, Thomas. *The System of Free Expression*. New York: Random House, 1970.

———. *Toward a General Theory of the First Amendment*. New York: Random House, 1966.

Emmanuel, Anne. *Elbert Parr Tuttle: Chief Jurist of the Civil Rights Revolution*. Athens: University of Georgia Press, 2011.

Epps, Garret. "The Civil Rights Heroes the Court Ignored in *New York Times v. Sullivan*." *The Atlantic*, March 20, 2014. Accessed 9-27-2016. http://www.theatlantic.com/national/archive/2014/03/the-civil-rights-heroes-the-court-ignored-in-em-new-york-times-v-sullivan-em/284550/.

Fairclough, Adam. *Race and Democracy: The Civil Rights Struggle in Louisiana*. Athens: University of Georgia Press, 1995.

Farrior, Stephanie. "Molding the Matrix: The Historical and Theoretical Foundations of International Law Concerning Hate Speech." *Berkeley Journal of International Law* 14 (1996): 1–98.

Ferguson, Karen. *Black Politics in New Deal Atlanta*. Chapel Hill: University of North Carolina Press, 2002.

Fessenden, Tracy. "The Nineteenth-Century Bible Wars and the Separation of Church and State." *Church History* 74, no. 4 (December 2005): 784–811.

Finkelman, Paul. *The Supreme Court: Cases, Controversies, and Character from John Jay to John Roberts.* Santa Barbara, CA: ABC-CLIO, 2014.

———. "*Scott v. Sandford*: The Court's Most Dreadful Case and How It Changed History." *Chicago-Kent Law Review* 82 (2007): 3–48.

Finley, Taryn. "6 N.W.A. Songs That Spoke about the Reality of Being Black in America." *Huffington Post*, August 13, 2015. Accessed 9-12-2017. http://www.huffingtonpost.com/entry/nwa-songs-that-are-still-relevant-today_us_55cb6546e4b0923c12bece11.

Fiss, Owen. *The Irony of Free Speech*, 2nd ed. Cambridge, MA: Harvard University Press, 1996.

Foner, Eric. *The Story of American Freedom.* New York: Norton, 1998.

Foner, Philip. "The Rise of the Black Industrial Working Class, 1915–1918." In *African Americans and the U.S. Economy*, ed. Cecilia Conrad, John Whitehead, Patrick Mason, and James Stewart. Lanham, MD: Rowman and Littlefield, 2005.

Fortin, Jacey. "Richard Dawkins Event Canceled over Past Comments about Islam." *New York Times*, July 24, 2017. Accessed 9-4-2017. https://www.nytimes.com/2017/07/24/us/richard-dawkins-speech-canceled-berkeley.html?mcubz=3.

Franklin, John Hope, and Elizabeth Brooks Higginbotham. *From Slavery to Freedom*, 9th ed. New York: McGraw-Hill, 2009.

"Frederick Douglass." In *101 Changemakers: Rebels and Radicals Who Changed American History*, ed. Michelle Bollinger and Dao Tran. Chicago: Haymarket Books, 2012.

Frederickson, George. *Racism: A Short History.* Princeton, NJ: Princeton University Press, 2002.

Freeberg, Ernest. "Inviting Controversy: When UT Students Demanded Their Free Speech Rights, a Half Century Ago." Knoxville History Project, August 28, 2017. http://knoxvillehistoryproject.org/2017/08/28/inviting-controversy-ut-students-demanded-free-speech-rights-half-century-ago/.

Freund, Ernst. *The Police Power, Public Policy and Constitutional Rights.* Chicago: University of Chicago Press, 1904.

Friedersdorf, Conor. "A Civil Rights Icon Urges Law Grads to Defend Free Speech." *The Atlantic*, May 29, 2018. Accessed 6-15-2018. https://www.theatlantic.com/education/archive/2018/05/a-civil-rights-icon-urges-law-grads-to-defend-free-speech/561380.

———. "The Most Shortsighted Attack on Free Speech in Modern History." *The Atlantic*, August 23, 2017. Accessed 8-24-2017. https://www.the

atlantic.com/politics/archive/2017/08/the-most-shortsighted-attack-on-free-speech-in-modern-history/537468/.

———."UC Berkeley Declares Itself Unsafe for Ann Coulter." *The Atlantic*, April 20, 2017. Accessed 9-12-2017. https://www.theatlantic.com/politics/archive/2017/04/uc-berkeley-declares-itself-unsafe-for-ann-coulter/523668/.

———. "The Lessons of Bygone Free Speech Fights." *The Atlantic*, December 10, 2015. Accessed 9-17-2017. https://www.theatlantic.com/politics/archive/2015/12/what-student-activists-can-learn-from-bygone-free-speech-fights/419178/.

Friedman, Leon. *Southern Justice*. New York: Pantheon Books, 1965.

Fusfeld, Daniel, and Timothy Bates. "The Black Sharecropping System and Its Decline." In *African Americans and the U.S. Economy*, ed. Cecilia Conrad, John Whitehead, Patrick Mason, and James Stewart. Lanham, MD: Rowman and Littlefield, 2005.

Gale, Mary Ellen. "Reimagining the First Amendment: Racist Speech and Equal Liberty." *St. John's Law Review* 65 (1991): 119–85.

Gallay, Allan. *Indian Slavery in Colonial America*. Lincoln: University of Nebraska Press, 2009.

Gallup. "Free Expression on Campus: A Survey of U.S. College students and U.S. Adults." Gallup, 2016. Accessed 2-2-2017. https://www.knightfoundation.org/media/uploads/publication_pdfs/FreeSpeech_campus.pdf.

Gard, Stephen. "Fighting Words as Free Speech." *Washington University Law Quarterly* 58 (1980): 531–81.

Garnett, Joy. "With NCAC Help, Artist Successfully Reverses Corporation's Objections to Black Lives Matter Artwork." National Coalition against Censorship, December 6, 2016. Accessed 9-12-2017. http://ncac.org/blog/with-ncac-help-artist-successfully-overturns-corporations-objetions-to-black-lives-matter-artwork.

Gartner, Alan, and Christopher Ferreira. "A State of Action." *New York Law School Law Review* 59 (2014–2015): 95–109.

Gates, Henry Louis, Jr. "Let Them Talk." *New Republic*, September 20, 1993, 37–48.

Gellman, Eric. *Death Blow to Jim Crow: The National Negro Congress and the Rise of Militant Civil Rights*. Chapel Hill: University of North Carolina Press, 2014.

Gibson, Michael. "The Supreme Court and Freedom of Expression from 1791 to 1917." *Fordham Law Review* 55 (1986): 263–333.

Gilmore, Glenda Elizabeth. *Defying Dixie: The Radical Roots of Civil Liberty, 1919–1950*. New York: Norton, 2008.

Gordon, James. "Was the First Justice Harlan Anti-Chinese?" *Western New England Law Review* 36 (2014): 287–370.

Gottlieb, Robert, Mark Vallianatos, Regina M. Freer, and Peter Dreier, eds. *The Next Los Angeles: The Struggle for a Livable City*, 2nd ed. Berkeley: University of California Press, 2005.

Gottschalk, Peter. *American Heretics: Catholics, Jews, Muslims, and the History of Religious Intolerance*. New York: St. Martin's Press, 2013.

Gould, Jon. *Speak No Evil: The Triumph of Hate Speech Regulation*. Chicago: University of Chicago Press, 2005.

Greenberg, Jack. *Crusaders in the Courts: Legal Battles of the Civil Rights Movement*, anniversary ed. New York: Twelve Tables Press, 2004.

Greuning, Martha. Review of *Let Me Live*. *Journal of Negro History* 22, no. 3 (July 1937): 348–50.

Griffiths, Frederick. "Ralph Ellison, Richard Wright and the Angelo Herndon Case." *African American Review* 35 (winter 2001): 615–36.

Gussow, Mel. "Review/Theater; Black Leftist's Jail Ordeal in the South in the 1930's." *New York Times*, January 17, 1991. Accessed 9-4-2016. http://www.nytimes.com/1991/01/17/theater/review-theater-black-leftist-s-jail-ordeal-in-the-south-in-the-1930-s.html.

Hall, Kermit, ed. *A Nation of States: Federalism at the Bar of the Supreme Court*. New York: Garland, 2000.

Hall, Kermit, and Melvin Urofsky. *New York Times v. Sullivan: Civil Rights, Libel Law and the Free Press*. Lawrence: University Press of Kansas, 2011.

Haller, Ben. "Professor Bret Weinstein Files $3.8 Million Claim against Evergreen State College." Reason.com, August 2, 2017. Accessed 9-7-2017. http://reason.com/blog/2017/08/02/professor-bret-wein-stein-files-3
8-millio.

Harkinson, Josh. "How Ann Coulter and the Far Right Are Using the Lefty Playbook to Troll Berkeley." *Mother Jones*, April 26, 2017. Accessed 9-11-2017. http://www.motherjones.com/politics/2017/04/ann-coulter-alt-right-berkeley-saul-alinsky-left-tactics-rules-for-radicals/.

Harper, Kimberley. *White Man's Heaven: The Lynching and Expulsion of Blacks in the Ozarks 1894–1909*. Fayetteville: University of Arkansas Press, 2010.

Hartman, Chester, ed. *America's Growing Inequality: The Impact of Race and Poverty*. Lanham, MD: Lexington Books, 2014.

Haupt, Claudia. "Regulating Hate Speech: Damned If You Do and Damned If You Don't." *Boston University International Law Journal* 23 (fall 2005): 299–335.

Hawes, Ruth. "Slavery in Mississippi." *Sewanee Review* 21, no. 2 (April 1913): 223–34.

Heinze, Eric. "Nineteen Arguments for Hate Speech Bans—And Against Them." Free Speech Debate, March 31, 2014. Accessed 8-14-2017. http://freespeechdebate.com/ru.

Henderson, Nia-Malika. "The New Lynching Memorial Rewrites American History." CNN Travel, April 26, 2018. Accessed 5-12-2018. https://www.cnn.com/travel/article/lynching-memorial-montgomery-alabama/index.html.

Hentoff, Nat. "How Jazz Helped Hasten the Civil Rights Movement." *Wall Street Journal*, January 15, 2009. Accessed 10-22-2016. http://www.wsj.com/articles/SB123197292128083217.

———. *The First Freedom*. New York: Delacorte, 1980.

Herman, Susan. "ACLU President: We Didn't Always Have Free Speech." *Time*, November 20, 2015. Accessed 10-20-2017. http://time.com/4120362/aclu-president-free-speech/.

Herndon, Angelo. *Let Me Live*. New York: Random House, 1937. Reprint, New York: Arno Press, 1969. Reprint, Ann Arbor: University of Michigan Press, 2007.

———. "You Cannot Kill the Working Class." New York: International Labor Defense and League of Struggle for Negro Rights, 1937.

Hessler, Katherine. "Early Efforts to Suppress Protest: Unwanted Abolitionist Speech." *Boston University Public Law Journal* 7 (spring 1998): 185–217.

Hill, Robert. "Marcus Garvey, 'The Negro Moses.'" Schomberg Center for Research in Black Culture, n.d. Accessed 9-4-2016. http://exhibitions.nypl.org/africanaage/essay-garvey.html.

Hirschfeld, Fritz. *George Washington and Slavery: A Documentary Portrayal*. Columbia: University of Missouri Press, 1997.

History.com Staff. "Black Leaders during Reconstruction." 2010. Accessed 3-21-2016. http://www.history.com/topics/american-civil-war/black-leaders-during-reconstruction.

Hodulik, Patricia. "Racist Speech on Campus." *Wayne State Law Review* 37 (1991): 1433–50.

Homestead, Melissa. *American Women Authors and Literary Property, 1822–1869*. New York: Cambridge University Press, 2005.

Howard, John. *The Shifting Wind: The Supreme Court and Civil Rights from Reconstruction to Brown*. Albany: State University of New York Press, 1999.

Hoyt, Edwin. *The Palmer Raids 1919–1920: An Attempt to Suppress Dissent*. New York: Tor Books, 1993.

Hudson, David, Jr. "Civil Rights & First Amendment." First Amendment Center. Accessed 4-13-2016. http://www.firstamendmentcenter.org/civil-rights-first-amendment.

Hunter, Nan. "Escaping the Expression-Equality Conundrum: Toward Anti-Orthodoxy and Inclusion." *Ohio State Law Journal* 61 (2000): 1671–724.

Hunter, Robert. *Violence and the Labor Movement*. New York: Macmillan, 1919.

Huszar, George de. *Equality in America*. New York: H. W. Wilson, 1949.

Hutchins, Robert. "Foreword." In *Political and Civil Rights in the United States*, ed. Thomas Emerson and David Haber. Buffalo: Dennis, 1952.

Inglehart, Louise Edward. *Press and Speech Freedoms in America, 1619–1995*. Westport, CT: Greenwood Press, 1997.

Jackson, Robert. "Messages on the Launching of the 'Bill of Rights Review.'" *Bill of Rights Review* 1 (1940): 34–36.

Jacoby, Daniel. *Laboring for Freedom: A New Look at the History of Labor in America*. New York: Routledge, 2015.

Jacoway, Elizabeth. *Turn Away Thy Son: Little Rock, the Crisis That Shocked the Nation*. New York: Simon and Schuster, 2007.

James, Portia. "New Negro Opinion Newspaper." Smithsonian Collections blog, May 20, 2011. Accessed 9-27-2017. http://si-siris.blogspot.com/2011/05/new-negro-opinion-newspaper.html.

Jaschik, Scott. "Protesters Tear Down Silent Sam." *Inside Higher Education*, August 21, 2018. Accessed 8-21-2018. https://www.insidehighered.com/news/2018/08/21/protesters-tear-down-confederate-statue-unc-chapel-hill.

———. "New Data Explain Republican Loss of Confidence in Higher Education." *Inside Higher Education*, August 17, 2017. Accessed 8-23-2017. https://www.insidehighered.com/news/2017/08/17/new-data-explain-republican-loss-confidence-higher-education.

———. "Backlash to Anthem Protests." *Inside Higher Education*, October 24, 2016. Accessed 10-24-2016. https://www.insidehighered.com/news/2016/10/24/alabama-and-greenville-backlash-anthem-protests-black-students.

Jay, Stewart. "The Creation of the First Amendment Right to Free Expression: From the Eighteenth Century to the Mid-Twentieth Century." *William Mitchell Law Review* 34 (2008): 773–1020.

Jordan, William. "African-American Accommodation and Protest during World War I." *Journal of American History* 81, no. 4 (March 1995): 1562–83.

Kaminer, Wendy. "The Progressive Ideas behind the Lack of Free Speech on Campus." *Washington Post*, February 20, 2015. Accessed 2-20-2018. https://www.washingtonpost.com/opinions/the-progressive-ideas-behind-th

e-lack-of-free-speech-on-campus/2015/02/20/93086efe-b0e7-11e4-886b-c22184f27c35_story.html.

Kalven, Harry, Jr. *The Negro and the First Amendment*. Chicago: University of Chicago Press, 1966.

Kampa, Dana. "Conservative Pundit Ben Shapiro Lectures to Turbulent Crowd on Safe Spaces, Freedom of Speech." *Badger-Herald*, November 17, 2016. Accessed 9-12-2017. https://badgerherald.com/news/2016/11/17/conservative-pundit-ben-shapiro-lectures-to-turbulent-crowd-on-safe-spaces-freedom-of-speech/.

Katz, William Loren. *Black Indians: A Hidden Heritage*. New York: Atheneum, 1996.

Kellem, Joshua. "'BLM' Is an Expression of the First Amendment." *The Rocket*, October 27, 2016. Accessed 6-27-2017. https://www.theonlinerocket.com/opinion/2016/10/27/blm-is-an-expression-of-the-first-amendment/.

Kelley, Blair. *Right to Ride: Streetcar Boycotts and African American Citizenship in the Era of* Plessy v. Ferguson. Chapel Hill: University of North Carolina Press, 2010.

Kellner, Douglas. *Herbert Marcuse and the Crisis of Marxism*. Berkeley: University of California Press, 1984.

Kesselman, Mark, Joel Krieger, and William Joseph. *An Introduction to Comparative Politics: Political Challenges and Changing Agendas*. Boston: Cengage Learning, 2015.

Kibler, M. Alison. *Censoring Racial Ridicule: Irish, Jewish, and African American Struggles over Race and Representation, 1890–1930*. Chapel Hill: University of North Carolina Press, 2015.

King, Martin Luther, Jr. *The Papers of Martin Luther King, Jr.*, vol. 3. Ed. Clayborne Carson et al. Berkeley: University of California Press, 1997.

Kindred, Kay. "When First Amendment Values and Competition Policy Collide: Resolving the Dilemma of the Mixed-Motive Boycott." *Arizona Law Review* 34 (1992): 709–42.

King, Shannon. *Whose Harlem Is This Anyway?: Community Politics and Grassroots Activism in the New Negro Era*. New York: New York University Press, 2015.

Kirwan, Albert. *Revolt of the Rednecks: Mississippi Politics, 1876–1925*. Lexington: University of Kentucky Press, 1951.

Kiuchi, Yuya, ed. *Race Still Matters: The Reality of African American Lives and the Myth of Postracial Society*. Albany: State University of New York Press, 2016.

Klarman, Michael. "Rethinking the Civil Rights and Liberties Revolution." *Virginia Law* 82 *Review* (February 1996): 1–67.

Klement, Frank. "President Lincoln, The Civil War, and the Bill of Rights." *Lincoln Herald* 94, no. 1 (1992): 10–23.

———. *The Copperheads in the Middle West.* Gloucester, MA: Peter Smith, 1972.

Kluger, Richard. *Indelible Ink: The Trials of John Peter Zenger and the Birth of America's Free Press.* New York: Norton, 2016.

Krotoszynski, Ronald, Jr. *The First Amendment in Cross Cultural Perspective.* New York: New York University Press, 2006.

Kubler, Friedrich. "How Much Freedom for Racist Speech? Transnational Aspects of a Conflict of Human Rights." *Hofstra Law Review* 27 (winter 1998): 335–76.

Kuersten, Ashland. *Women and the Law: Leaders, Cases and Documents.* Santa Barbara, CA: ABC-CLIO, 2003.

Kujovich, Gil. "Equal Opportunity in Higher Education and the Black Public College: The Era of Separate but Equal." *Minnesota Law Review* 72 (1987): 29–172.

Kuo, Joyce. "Excluded, Segregated and Forgotten: A Historical View of the Discrimination of Chinese Americans in Public Schools." *Asian American Law Journal* 5 (1998): 181–212.

Laidler, Harry Wellington. *Boycotts and the Labor Struggle: Economic and Legal Aspects.* New York: Columbia University Press, 1914.

La Marche, Gara. "The Messy Business of Free Speech." *The Nation*, September 5, 2017. Accessed 9-17-2017. https://www.thenation.com/article/th e-messy-business-of-free-speech/.

Lanham, Andrew. "When W.E.B. Du Bois Was Un-American." *Boston Review*, January 13, 2017. Accessed 12-8-2017. http://bostonreview.net/race-po litics/andrew-lanham-when-w-e-b-du-bois-was-un-american.

Lasson, Kenneth. "Racial Defamation as Free Speech: Abusing the First Amendment." *Columbia Human Rights Law Review* 17 (1985): 11–55.

Latham, Frank. *The Rise and Fall of Jim Crow, 1865–1964.* Danbury, CT: Franklin Watts, 1969.

Lauber, Almon Wheeler. *Indian Slavery in Colonial Times within the Present Limits of the United States. 1913; reprint Williamstown, MA: Corner House, 1970.*

Lawrence, Charles, III. "If He Hollers Let Him Go: Regulating Racist Speech on Campus." *Duke Law Journal* 1990 (1990): 431–83.

Lee, Erika. *At America's Gates: Chinese Immigration during the Exclusion Era, 1882–1943.* Chapel Hill: University of North Carolina Press, 2003.

Levy, Leonard. *Emergence of a Free Press.* New York: Oxford University Press, 1985.

———. *Legacy of Suppression*. Cambridge, MA: Harvard University Press, 1960.

Lewis, Anthony. *Make No Law: The Sullivan Case and the First Amendment*. New York: Random House, 1991.

Lindquist, Stefanie, and Frank Cross. *Measuring Judicial Activism*. New York: Oxford University Press, 2009.

Linfield, Michael. *Freedom under Fire: U.S. Civil Liberties in Times of War*. Boston: South End Press, 1991.

Logan, Rayford. *The Betrayal of the Negro: From Rutherford B. Hayes to Woodrow Wilson*. Boston: Da Capo Press, 1965.

Lord, Robert, John Sexton, and Edward Harrington. *History of the Archdiocese of Boston in the Various Stages of Its Development, 1604–1943*, vol. 2. New York: Sheed and Ward, 1944.

Lorence, James. *The Unemployed People's Movement*. Athens: University of Georgia Press, 2011.

Lynch, Matthew, ed. *Before Obama: A Reappraisal of Black Reconstruction Era Politicians*. Santa Barbara, CA: Praeger, 2012.

MacIntyre, Alasdair. *Marcuse*. London: Fontana/Collins, 1970.

Mack, Kenneth. "Law and Mass Politics in the Making of the Civil Rights Lawyer, 1931–1941." *Journal of American History* 93, no. 1 (June 2006): 37–62.

MacKinnon, Catharine. *Only Words*. Cambridge, MA: Harvard University Press, 1993.

Majeed, Azhar. "Putting Their Money Where Their Mouth Is: The Case for Denying Qualified Immunity to University Administrators Who Violate Students' Speech Rights." *Cardozo Public Law, Policy and Ethics Journal* 8 (2010): 515–72.

Malek, Allia, and Wilson Dizard. "DOJ Says Ferguson Police Violated African-Americans' Free Speech Rights." *Al Jazeera America*, March 4, 2015. Accessed 6-17-2017. http://america.aljazeera.com/articles/2015/3/4/Justice-says-Ferguson-police-violated-1st-amendment-rights.html.

Malone, Christopher. *Between Freedom and Bondage: Race, Party and Voting Rights in the Antebellum North*. New York: Routledge, 2008.

Marcuse, Herbert. "Repressive Tolerance." In Robert Paul Wolff, Barrington Moore Jr., and Herbert Marcuse, *A Critique of Pure Tolerance*. Boston: Beacon Press, 1965.

Martin, Charles. "Communists and Blacks: The ILD and the Angelo Herndon Case." *Journal of Negro History* 64, no. 2 (spring 1979): 131–41.

———. *The Angelo Herndon Case and Southern Justice*. Baton Rouge: Louisiana State University Press, 1976.

Maslow, Will, and Joseph Robison. "Civil Rights Legislation and the Fight for Equality, 1862–1952." *University of Chicago Law Review* 20 (1953): 363–413.

Massey, Douglas, and Nancy Denton. *American Apartheid: Segregation and the Making of the Underclass*. Cambridge, MA: Harvard University Press, 1998.

Matsuda, Mari. "Public Response to Racist Speech: Considering the Victims Story." *Michigan Law Review* 87 (1989): 2320–81.

McCluskey, Neil, S.J. *Catholic Viewpoint on Education*. Garden City, NY: Image Books, 1962.

McConnell, Michael. "You Can't Say That." *New York Times*, June 22, 2012. Accessed 9-4-2017. http://www.nytimes.com/2012/06/24/books/review/the-harm-in-hate-speech-by-jeremy-waldron.html?mcubz=3.

McGovern, James. *Anatomy of a Lynching: The Killing of Claude Neal*. Baton Rouge: Louisiana State University Press, 1982.

McLaughlin, Jim, and Rob Schmidt. "National Undergraduate Study." McLaughlin and Associates, October 26, 2015. Accessed 11-12-2016. https://www.dropbox.com/s/sfmpoeytvqc3cl2/NATL%20College%20 10-25-15%20Presentation.pdf?dl=0.

McWilliams, Carey. "The Witch Hunt and Civil Rights." *The Nation*, June 28, 1952, 651–53.

Modeste, Petal Nevella. "Race Hate Speech: The Pervasive Badge of Slavery That Mocks the Thirteenth Amendment." *Howard Law Journal* 44 (winter 2001): 311–48.

Moore, John Hammond. "The Angelo Herndon Case, 1932–1937." *Phylon* 32, no. 1 (1971): 60–71.

Moore, Peter. "Half of Democrats Support a Ban on Hate Speech." YouGov, May 20, 2015. Accessed 9-19-2017. https://today.yougov.com/news/2015/05/20/hate-speech/.

Murphy, Paul. *World War I and the Origin of Civil Liberties in America*. New York: Norton, 1979.

———. *The Meaning of Free Speech: First Amendment Freedom from Wilson to FDR*. Santa Barbara, CA: Praeger, 1972.

Mustard, David. *Racial Justice in America*. Santa Barbara, CA: ABC-CLIO, 2003.

Neu, Jerome. *Sticks and Stones: The Philosophy of Insults*. Oxford: Oxford University Press, 2008.

Newsom, Michael deHaven. "Common School Religion: Judicial Narratives in a Protestant Empire." *Southern California Interdisciplinary Law Journal* 11 (spring 2002).

Nichols, David. *A Matter of Justice: Eisenhower and the Beginning of the Civil Rights Revolution*. New York: Simon and Schuster, 2007.

Nielsen, Laura Beth. *License to Harass: Law, Hierarchy, and Offensive Public Speech*. Princeton, NJ: Princeton University Press, 2004.

———. "Subtle, Pervasive, Harmful: Racist and Sexist Remarks in Public as Hate Speech." *Journal of Social Issues* 58, no. 2 (2002): 265–80.

Nord, Warren. *Religion and American Education: Rethinking a National Dilemma*. Chapel Hill: University of North Carolina Press, 1995.

"Note: The Void-for-Vagueness Doctrine in the Supreme Court." *University of Pennsylvania Law Review* 109 (November 1960): 67–116.

"Note: Recent Cases." *University of Pennsylvania Law Review and American Law Register* 91 (January 1943): 473–82.

"Note: The Negro Citizen in the Supreme Court." *Harvard Law Review* 52 (March 1939): 823–32.

"Note: Supreme Court as Protector of Political Minorities." *Yale Law Journal* 46 (1937): 862–66.

"Note: Recent Cases." *University of Pennsylvania Law Review* 84 (1935–1936): 256–57.

Nwanevu, Osita. "The Kids Are Right." *Slate*, March 12, 2017. Accessed 9-11-2017. http://www.slate.com/articles/news_and_politics/cover_story/2017/03/there_s_nothing_outrageous_about_stamping_out_bigoted_speech.html.

O'Neil, Robert. "Hate Speech, Fighting Words, and Beyond—Why American Law Is Unique." *Albany Law Review* 76 (2012/2013): 467–98.

———. *Free Speech in the College Community*. Bloomington: Indiana University Press, 1997.

Parten, Bennett. "Communism and Race in the 1930s Deep South." *History Is Now Magazine*, July 15, 2015. Accessed 9-2-2016. http://www.historyisnowmagazine.com/blog/2015/7/5/communism-and-race-in-the-1930s-deep-south#.V8i9cpgrLIU.

Pascoe, Peggy. "Miscegenation Law, Court Cases, and Ideologies of 'Race' in Twentieth Century America." *Journal of American History* 83, no. 1 (June 1996): 44–69.

Peel, Thomas. "Kaepernick Is a First Amendment Hero." *Mercury News*, September 2, 2016. Accessed 6-17-2017. http://www.mercurynews.com/2016/09/02/thomas-peele-kaepernick-is-first-amendment-hero/.

Perdue, Theda, and Michael D. Green. *The Cherokee Nation and the Trail of Tears*. New York: Penguin, 2007.

Perkins, Haven. "Religion for Slaves: Difficulties and Methods." *Church History* 10, no. 3 (September 1941): 228–45.

Perloff, Richard. "The Press and Lynchings of African Americans." *Journal of Black Studies* 30, no. 3 (January 2000): 315–30.

Perry, Lewis. *Civil Disobedience: An American Tradition*. New Haven, CT: Yale University Press, 2013.

Policinski, Gene. "Civil Rights Movement Rode Assembly, Petition to Greater Freedom." First Amendment Center, January 31, 2013. Accessed 9-9-2016. http://www.firstamendmentcenter.org/civil-rights-movement-rode-assembly-petition-to-greater-freedom.

Poole, Scott. "Free Speech and Black Speech in Charleston, South Carolina." *Huffington Post*, February 23, 2017. Accessed 5-20-2017. http://www.huffingtonpost.com/entry/free-speech-and-black-speech-in-charleston-south-carolina_us_58af436be4b02f3f81e44521.

Pound, Roscoe. "Interests of Personality and Honor." *Harvard Law Review* 28 (1915): 343–65.

Poushter, Jacob. "40% of Millennials OK with Limiting Speech Offensive to Minorities." Pew Research Center, November 20, 2015. Accessed 10-12-2017. http://www.pewresearch.org/fact-tank/2015/11/20/40-of-millennials-ok-with-limiting-speech-offensive-to-minorities/.

powell, john a. "Worlds Apart: Reconciling Freedom of Speech and Equality." *Kentucky Law Journal* 85 (1996): 9–95.

Prakash, Saikrishna, and John Yoo. "The Origins of Judicial Review." *University of Chicago Law Review* 70 (2003): 887–982.

———. "Origins of Judicial Review: Questions for the Critics of Judicial Review." *George Washington Law Review* 72 (2003): 354–80.

Raasch, Chuck. "Taking Down Student Painting Violated 1st Amendment, Clay Claims in Planned Lawsuit." *St. Louis Post-Dispatch*, February 21, 2017. Accessed 6-17-2017. http://www.stltoday.com/news/local/govt-and-politics/taking-down-student-painting-violated-st-amendment-clay-claims-in/article_8ab33e1b-3a56-5b77-93fb-45ef7d06b628.html.

Rabban, David. *Free Speech in Its Forgotten Years, 1870–1920*. New York: Cambridge University Press, 1997.

Rael, Patrick. *Black Identity and Black Protest in the Antebellum North*. Chapel Hill: University of North Carolina Press, 2002.

Rauch, Jonathan. "The Unknown Supreme Court Decision that Changed Everything for Gays." *Washington Post*, February 5, 2014. Accessed 10-20-2016. https://www.washingtonpost.com/news/volokh-conspiracy/

wp/2014/02/05/the-unknown-supreme-court-decision-that-changed-everything-for-gays/?utm_term=.8d744be0c80b.

———. "In Defense of Prejudice." *Harper's Magazine* (May 1995): 37–39 and 42–46.

Raymond, Emilie. *Stars for Freedom: Hollywood, Black Celebrities, and the Civil Rights Movement*. Seattle: University of Washington Press, 2015.

Rmuse. "Racists Demand Punishment for African Americans Exercising First Amendment Rights." *Politicususa*, December 2, 2014. Accessed 9-4-2017. http://www.politicususa.com/2014/12/02/racists-demand-punishment-african-americans-exercising-amendment-rights.html.

Roll, Nick. "ADL Says to Expect More White Supremacist Leaflets on Campuses." *Inside Higher Education*, September 11, 2017. Accessed 9-11-2017. https://www.insidehighered.com/news/2017/09/11/adl-says-expect-more-white-supremacist-leaflets-campuses.

Romero, Anthony. "Equality, Justice and the First Amendment." ACLU, August 15, 2017. Accessed 10-12-2017.https://www.aclu.org/blog/free-speech/equality-justice-and-first-amendment.

Rosenberg, Gerald. *The Hollow Hope: Can Courts Bring About Social Change?*, 2nd ed. Chicago: University of Chicago Press, 2008.

Rudwick, Elliot. "W.E.B. DuBois: Protagonist of the African-American Protest." In *Black Leaders of the Twentieth Century*, ed. John Hope Franklin and August Meier. Urbana-Champaign: University of Illinois Press, 1982.

Ruether, Rosemary Radford. *Christianity and Social Systems: Historical Constructions and Ethical Challenges*. Lanham, MD: Rowman and Littlefield, 2008.

Salmon, Marylynn. "The Legal Status of Women 1776–1830." *History Now: The Journal of the Gilder Lehrman Institute of American History* 7 (spring 2006).

Salovey, Peter. "Free Speech, Personified." *New York Times: On Campus*, November 26, 2017. Accessed 12-11-2017. https://www.nytimes.com/2017/11/26/opinion/free-speech-yale-civil-rights.html.

Santa Cruz, Nicole, Lauren Williams, and Mike Anton. "'Irvine 11': 10 Students Sentenced to Probation, No Jail Time." *Los Angeles Times*, September 23, 2011. Accessed 9-12-2017. http://latimesblogs.latimes.com/lanow/2011/09/irvine-11-sentenced-probation-no-jail-time.html.

Sargentich, Lewis. "The First Amendment Overbreadth Doctrine." *Harvard Law Review* 83 (1970): 844–927.

Saul, Stephanie. "Dozens of Middlebury Students Are Disciplined for Charles Murray Protest." *New York Times*, May 24, 2017. Accessed 9-7-2017.

https://www.nytimes.com/2017/05/24/us/middlebury-college-charles-murray-bell-curve.html?mcubz=3.

Schauer, Frederick. "The Exceptional First Amendment." In *American Exceptionalism and Human Rights*, ed. Michael Ignatieff. Princeton, NJ: Princeton University Press, 2005.

Schlesinger, Arthur. *The Vital Center: The Politics of Freedom*. Boston: Houghton-Mifflin, 1949.

Schmidt, Christopher. "The Civil Rights–Civil Liberties Divide." *Stanford Civil Rights and Civil Liberties* 12 (February 2016): 1–41.

———. "*New York Times v. Sullivan* and the Legal Attack on the Civil Rights Movement." *Alabama Law Review* 66 (2014): 293–335.

Schurz, Carl. *Speeches, Correspondence and Political Papers of Carl Schurz*, vol. 1. Ed. Frederic Bancroft. New York: Putnam, 1913.

Schwartz, Bernard. *A Book of Legal Lists: A List of the Best and Worst Law*. New York: Oxford University Press, 1997.

Sedler, Robert. "An Essay on Freedom of Speech: The United States against the Rest of the World." *Michigan State Law Review* 2006 (2006): 377–84.

Seybert, Tony. "Slavery and Native Americans in British North America and the United States: 1600 to 1865." Slavery in America, n.d. Accessed 3-4-2016. https://web.archive.org/web/20040804001522/http:/www.slaveryinamerica.org/history/hs_es_indians_slavery.htm.

Shiell, Timothy. *Campus Hate Speech on Trial*, 2nd ed. Lawrence: University Press of Kansas, 2009.

———. "The Case of the Student Racist Face Book Message." *Journal of Academic Freedom* 5 (2014). https://www.aaup.org/sites/default/files/Shiell.pdf.

Silman, Anna. "10 Famous Comedians on How Political Correctness Is Killing Comedy." *Salon*, June 10, 2015. Accessed 9-12-2017. http://www.salon.com/2015/06/10/10_famous_comedians_on_how_political_correctness_is_killing_comedy_we_are_addicted_to_the_rush_of_being_offended/.

Simon, Cecelia Capuzzi. "Fighting for Free Speech on America's Campuses." *New York Times*, August 1, 2016. Accessed 6-21-2017. https://www.nytimes.com/2016/08/07/education/edlife/fire-first-amendment-on-campus-free-speech.html?mcubz=3.

Simpkin, John. "Education of Slaves." Spartacus Educational, updated January 2015. Accessed 3-25-2016. http://spartacus-educational.com/USASeducation.htm.

Singer, Joseph William. "No Right to Exclude: Public Accommodations and Private Property." *Northwestern University Law Review* 90 (summer 1996): 1283–497.

Sitkoff, Harvard. *A New Deal for Blacks: The Emergence of Civil Rights as a National Issue: The Depression Decade*. New York: Oxford University Press, 1978.

Sklar, Richard. "The Fiction of the First Amendment." *Western Political Quarterly* 6, no. 2 (June 1953): 302–19.

Smith, J. Clay, and Scott Burrell. "Justice Thurgood Marshall and the First Amendment." *Arizona State Law Journal* 26 (summer 1994): 461–78.

Smith, Robert Michael. *From Blackjacks to Briefcases—A History of Commercialized Strikebreaking and Unionbusting in the United States*. Athens: Ohio University Press, 2003.

Snyder, Christina. *Slavery in Indian Country: The Changing Face of Captivity in Early America*. Cambridge, MA: Harvard University Press, 2010.

Spivak, John. "Foreword." In Angelo Herndon, *You Cannot Kill the Working Class*. New York: International Labor Defense and League of Struggle for Negro Rights, 1937, 3.

Steele, Richard W. "Fear of the Mob and Faith in Government in Free Speech Discourse, 1919–1941." *American Journal of Legal History* 38 (January 1994): 55–83.

Stevens, Doris. *Jailed for Freedom: American Women Win the Vote*. Troutdale, OR: New Sage Press, 1995.

Stewart, James. "The Critical Role of African-Americans in the Development of the Pre–Civil War U.S. Economy." In *African Americans and the U.S. Economy*, ed. Cecilia A. Conrad, John Whitehead, Patrick Mason, and James Stewart. Lanham, MD: Rowman and Littlefield, 2005.

Stockley, Grif. *Blood in Their Eyes: The Elaine Massacres of 1919*. Fayetteville: University of Arkansas Press, 2001.

Stone, Geoffrey. "Political Conservatives Suddenly Embrace Free Speech on Campus." *Huffington Post*, May 1, 2017. Accessed 12-8-2017. https://www.huffingtonpost.com/entry/political-conservatives-suddenly-embrace-free-speechus_590745dee4b084f59b49fb07.

———. *Perilous Times: Free Speech during Wartime*. New York: Norton, 2004.

Strossen, Nadine. *Hate: Why We Should Resist It with Free Speech, Not Censorship*. New York: Oxford University Press, 2018.

Sturgis, Amy. *The Trail of Tears and Indian Removal*. Westport, CT: Greenwood Press, 2007.

Taft, Philip. "Workers of a New Century." US Department of Labor, n.d. Accessed 3-8-2016. http://www.dol.gov/general/aboutdol/history/chapter4.

Taylor, Charles. "Marcuse's Authoritarian Utopia." *Canadian Dimension* 7, no. 3 (1970): 49–53.

Thomas, Kendall. "Rouge et Noir Reread: A Popular Constitutional History of the Angelo Herndon Case." *Southern California Law Review* 65 (September 1992): 2599–704.

Tillman, Lynne. "Kendall Thomas by Lynne Tillman." *BOMB—Artists in Conversation* 59 (spring 1997). Accessed 4-26-2016. http://bombmagazine.org/article/2059/kendall-thomas.

Touchstone, Blake. *Master and Slaves in the House of the Lord: Race and Religion in the American South 1740–1870*. Lexington: University Press of Kentucky, 1988.

Tracy, Marc, and Ashley Southall. "Black Football Players Lend Heft to Protests at Missouri." *New York Times*, November 8, 2015. Accessed 6-17-2017. https://www.nytimes.com/2015/11/09/us/missouri-football-players-boycott-in-protest-of-university-president.html?mcubz=3.

Trotter, Joe. "Impact of the Great Depression on African Americans." In *Encyclopedia of the Great Depression*, vol. 1, ed. Robert McElvaine. New York: Macmillan, 2004.

Tsesis, Alexander. *Destructive Messages: How Hate Speech Paves the Way for Harmful Social Movements*. New York: New York University Press, 2002.

Turnage, Clara. "Most Republicans Think Colleges Are Bad for the Country. Why?" *Chronicle of Higher Education*, July 10, 2017. Accessed 12-8-2017. http://www.chronicle.com/article/Most-Republicans-Think/240587.

Tushnet, Mark. "The Hughes Court and Radical Political Dissent: The Case of Dirk De Jonge and Angelo Herndon." *Georgia State University Law Review* 28 (winter 2012): 333–77.

———. *Making Civil Rights Law: Thurgood Marshall and the Supreme Court, 1936–1961*. New York: Oxford University Press, 1994.

Tygiel, Jules. *Baseball's Great Experiment: Jackie Robinson and His Legacy*, expanded ed. New York: Oxford University Press, 1997.

Van Tuyll, Debra Reddin. "Freedom of the Press in a Slave Society at War." In *An Indispensable Liberty: The Fight for Free Speech in Nineteenth-Century America*, ed. Mary Cronin. Carbondale: Southern Illinois Press, 2016, 61–89.

Vann Woodward, Comer. *The Strange Career of Jim Crow*, 3rd rev. ed. New York: Oxford University Press, 1974.

Villasenor, John. "Views among College Students Regarding the First Amendment: Results from a New Survey." Brookings Institution,

September 18, 2017. Accessed 9-19-2017. https://www.brookings.edu/blog/fixgov/2017/09/18/views-among-college-students-regarding-the-first-amendment-results-from-a-new-survey/.

Waldron, Jeremy. *The Harm in Hate Speech*. Cambridge, MA: Harvard University Press, 2012.

Walker, Anders. "'Neutral' Principles: Rethinking the Legal History of Civil Rights, 1934–1964." *Loyola University Chicago Law Journal* 40 (2009): 385–436.

Walker, Juliet. *The History of Black Business in America: Capitalism, Race, Entrepreneurship*, vol. 2, 2nd ed. Chapel Hill: University of North Carolina Press, 2009.

Walker, Samuel. *Hate Speech: The History of an American Controversy*. Lincoln: University of Nebraska Press, 1994.

———. *In Defense of American Liberties: A History of the ACLU*. New York: Oxford University Press, 1990.

Ware, Leland. "Brown at 50: School Desegregation from Reconstruction to Resegregation." *University of Florida Journal of Law and Public Policy* 16 (August 2005): 267–98.

Warren, Charles. *The Supreme Court in United States History*, 2nd ed., vol. 1. Boston: Little, Brown, 1926.

Warren, Joyce. *Women, Money, and the Law: Nineteenth-Century Fiction, Gender, and the Courts*. Iowa City: University of Iowa Press, 2005.

Washburn, Patrick. *The African American Press: Voice of Freedom*. Evanston, IL: Northwestern University Press, 2006.

Watson, Tom. "This Is What a Movement Looks Like: Civil Rights, Civil Liberties, and Feet on the Ground." *Forbes*, August 24, 2013. Accessed 9-21-2016. http://www.forbes.com/sites/tomwatson/2013/08/24/this-is-what-a-movement-looks-like-civil-rights-civil-liberties-and-feet-on-the-ground/#3a652bae4109.

Weiss, Bari. "When the Left Turns on Its Own." *New York Times*, June 1, 2017. Accessed 9-7-2017. https://www.nytimes.com/2017/06/01/opinion/when-the-left-turns-on-its-own.html?mcubz=3.

Wells, N. Douglas. "Thurgood Marshall and 'Individual Self-Realization' in First Amendment Jurisprudence." *Tennessee Law Review* 61 (fall 1993): 237–87.

Wendel, W. Bradley. "The Banality of Evil and the First Amendment." *Michigan Law Review* 102 (May 2004): 1404–22.

West, Emily. *Family or Freedom: People of Color in the Antebellum South*. Lexington: University Press of Kentucky, 2012.

White, G. Edward. "The First Amendment Comes of Age: The Emergence of Free Speech in Twentieth-Century America." *Michigan Law Review* 95 (November 1996): 299–392.

Whitman, James Q. "Enforcing Civility and Respect: Three Societies." *Yale Law Journal* 109 (January 1999): 1279–398.

Williams, Heather Andrea. *Self-Taught: African American Education in Slavery and Freedom*. Chapel Hill: University of North Carolina Press, 2005.

Woessner, April Kelly. "How Marcuse Made Today's Students Less Tolerant than Their Parents." *Heterodox Academy*, September 23, 2015. Accessed 10-3-2017. https://heterodoxacademy.org/2015/09/23/how-mar cuse-made-todays-students-less-tolerant-than-their-parents/.

Woliver, Laura. "Dissent Is Patriotic: Disobedient Founders, Narratives, and Street Battles." *Tulsa Law Review* 50 (winter 2015): 381–95.

Wong, Dwayne. "Censoring Howard Zinn and Censoring American History." *Huffington Post,* May 15, 2017. Accessed 9-12-2017. http://www.huf fingtonpost.com/entry/censoring-howard-zinn-and-censoring-ame rican-history_us_58bcb202e4b02b8b584dfd6a.

Wright, Gavin. *Sharing the Prize*. Cambridge, MA: Harvard University Press, 2013.

———. *Slavery and American Economic Development*. Baton Rouge: Louisiana State University Press, 2006.

Yarbrough, Fay. *Race and the Cherokee Nation: Sovereignty in the Nineteenth Century*. Philadelphia: University of Pennsylvania Press, 2008.

Yassky, David. "Eras of the First Amendment." *Columbia Law Review* 91 (November 1991): 1699–755.

Zhang, Ai-min. *Origins of the African American Civil Rights Movement, 1865–1956*. New York: Routledge, 2014.

Zinn, Howard. *A People's History of the American States: 1492 to the Present. New York: Harper Collins, 2003.*

CASES

Abernathy v. Alabama, 380 US 447 (1965)

Abbington v. Louisville, Case No. 243 (W.D. KY 1941)

Abington v. Schempp, 374 US 203 (1963)

Abramowitz v. Trustees of Boston University, C.A. No. 82680, Suffolk Superior Court, 1986

Abrams v. United States, 250 US 616 (1919)

Adair v. United States, 208 US 161 (1908)
Agarwal v. Johnson, 25 CA 3d (1979)
Alcorn v. Ambro Engineering, Inc., 2 CA 3d 493 (1970)
Alexander v. Holmes County Board of Education, 396 US 19 (1969)
Alston v. Norfolk, 112 F.2d 992 (4th Cir. 1940)
Amalgamated Food Employees Union v. Logan Valley Plaza, 391 US 496 (1968)
Am. Booksellers Ass'n, Inc. v. Hudnut, 771 F.2d 323, 331 n.3 (7th Cir. 1985)
Anderson v. Dunn, 19 US 204 (1821)
Bair v. Shippensburg University, 280 F. Supp. 2d 357 (M.D. PA 2003)
Barnette v. West Virginia, 319 US 624 (1943)
Barron v. Baltimore, 32 US 243 (1833)
Barrows v. Jackson, 346 US 249 (1953)
Bates v. Little Rock, 361 US 516 (1960)
Bayard v. Singleton, 1 NC (Mart.) 48 (1787)
Beauharnais v. Illinois, 343 US 250 (1952)
Bell v. Maryland, 378 US 226 (1964)
Benton v. Maryland, 395 US 784, 1969
Berea College v. Kentucky, 211 US 45 (1908)
Bethel School District No. 403 v. Fraser, 478 US 675 (1986)
Blake v. McClung, 172 US 239 (1898)
Blyew v. United States, 80 US 581 (1872)
Board of Education v. Minor, 23 OH 211 (1872)
Boynton v. Virginia, 364 US 454 (1960)
Bradwell v. Illinois, 83 US 130 (1873)
Brandenburg v. Ohio, 395 US 444 (1969)
Breedlove v. Suttles, 302 US 277 (1937)
Browder v. Gayle, 352 US 903 (1956)
Brown v. Board of Education, 347 US 483 (1954) (*Brown* I)
Brown v. Board of Education, 349 US 294 (1955) (*Brown* II)
Brown v. Louisiana, 383 US 131 (1966)
Brown v. Mississippi, 297 US 278 (1936)
Brown v. Oklahoma, 408 US 914 (1972)
Bryant v. New York, 278 US 63 (1928)
Buchanan v. Warley, 245 US 60 (1917)
Burns v. United States, 274 US 328 (1927)
Cantwell v. Connecticut, 310 US 296 (1940)
Carr v. State, 176 GA 55 (1932) (*Carr v. State* I)
Carr v. State, 176 GA 747 (1933) (*Carr v. State* II)

Carroll v. Princess Anne, 393 US 175 (1968)
Chambers v. Florida, 309 US 227 (1940)
Chaplinsky v. New Hampshire, 315 US 568 (1941)
Cherokee Nation v. Georgia, 30 US 1 (1831)
Citizens United v. FEC, 558 US 310 (2010)
Chicago Police Dept. v. Mosley, 408 US 92 (1972)
City of Little Falls v. Witucki, 295 N.W.2d 243 (MN 1980)
Civil Rights Cases, 109 US 3 (1883)
Clark v. Community for Creative Non-Violence, 468 US 288 (1984)
Cohen v. California, 403 US 15 (1971)
Cohen v. San Bernardino Community College, 92 F.968 (1996)
College Republicans v. Reed, 523 F. Supp. 2d 1005 (N.D. CA 2007)
Collin v. Smith, 578 F.2d 1197, 1205 (7th Cir. 1978)
Commonwealth v. Brown, 309 PA 515 (1933)
Commonwealth v. Caton, 8 VA (4 Call) 5 (1782)
Commonwealth v. Davis, 167 US 43 (1897)
Commonwealth v. Morris, 3 VA 176 (1811)
Contreras v. Crown Zellerbach, Inc., 88 WA 2d 735 (1977)
Cooper v. Aaron, 358 US 1 (1958)
Coppage v. Kansas, 236 US 1 (1915)
Corrigan v. Buckley, 271 US 323 (1926)
Corry, et. al. v. Stanford University, County of Santa Clara Supreme Court, Case no. 740309 (1995)
Cox v. Louisiana, 379 US 536 (1965)
Cox v. New Hampshire, 312 US 569 (1941)
Craig v. Harney, 331 US 367 (1947)
Crown v. John Peter Zenger (1735)
Cumming v. Board of Education of Richmond County, 175 US 528 (1899)
Dambrot v. Central Michigan University, 839 F. Supp. 437 (E.D. MI 1993), *affirmed* 55 F.3d 1177 (6th Cir. 1995)
Davis v. Monroe County Board of Education, 526 US 629 (1999)
Debs v. United States, 249 US 211 (1919)
DeJohn v. Temple University, 537 F. 3d 301 (3rd Cir. 2008)
De Jonge v. Oregon, 299 US 353 (1937)
Dennis v. United States, 341 US 494 (1951)
Doe v. University of Michigan (E.D. MI 1989)
Donahoe v. Richards, 38 ME 379 (1854)
Dred Scott v. Sandford, 60 US 393 (1857)

Drews v. Maryland, 378 US 547 (1964)
Dworkin v. Hustler Magazine Inc., 867 F.2d 1188, 1200 (9th Cir. 1989)
Edwards v. South Carolina, 377 US 229 (1963)
Elonis v. United States, 575 US — (2015)
Everson v. Board of Education, 330 US 1 (1947)
Ex parte Jackson, 96 US 727 (1878)
Feiner v. New York, 340 US 315 (1951)
Fikes v. Alabama, 352 US 191 (1957)
First National Bank of Boston v. Bellotti, 435 US 765 (1978)
Fiske v. Kansas, 274 US 380 (1927)
Fisher v. Carrousel Motor Hotel, Inc., 424 S.W. 2d 627 (TX 1967)
Fontana v. United States, 262 F. 283 (8th Cir. 1919)
Ford v. State, 53 AL 150 (1875)
Fox v. North Carolina, 378 US 587 (1964)
Fox v. Washington, 236 US 273 (1915)
Frohwerk v. United States, 249 US 204 (1919)
Gantt v. Clemson, 320 F.2d 611 (4th Cir. 1963)
Garner v. Louisiana, 368 US 157 (1961)
Garrison v. Louisiana, 379 US 64 (1964)
Gibson v. Florida Legislative Investigative Committee, 372 US 539 (1963)
Gitlow v. New York, 268 US 652 (1925)
Gober v. Birmingham, 373 US 374 (1963)
Gomillion v. Lightfoot, 364 US 339 (1960)
Gooding v. Wilson, 405 US 518 (1972)
Grayned v. Rockford, 408 US 104 (1972)
Green v. Virginia, 378 US 550 (1964)
Greer v. Spock, 424 US 828 (1976)
Gregory v. Chicago, 394 US 111 (1969)
Griggs v. Duke Power Company, 401 US 424 (1971)
Grubl v. United States, 264 F. 44 (8th Cir. 1920)
Guinn and Beal v. United States, 238 US 347 (1915)
Haddix v. Port of Seattle, No. 840149, King Co. (WA) Super. Ct. (1978)
Hague v. CIO, 307 US 496 (1939)
Hall v. DeCuir, 95 US 485 (1877)
Hamm v. Rock Hill, 379 US 306 (1964)
Harris v. Harvey, 605 F.2d 330 (7th Cir. 1976)
Harris v. Virginia, 378 US 552 (1964)
Harshfield v. United States, 260 F. 659 (8th Cir. 1919)

Hartzell v. United States, 322 US 680 (1944)
Henderson v. United States, 339 US 816 (1950)
Herndon v. Lowry, 301 US 242 (1937)
Herndon v. Georgia, 295 US 441 (1935)
Herndon v. The State, 178 GA 597 (1934)
Herndon v. The State, 178 GA 832 (1934)
Hess v. Indiana, 414 US 105 (1973)
Holmes v. Danner, 191 F. Supp. 385 (M.D. GA 1961)
Holmes v. Walton (NJ 1780)
Hoover v. State, 59 AL 57 (1877)
Hudgens v. NLRB, 424 US 507 (1976)
Hylton v. United States, 3 US 171 (1796)
Imperial Diner, Inc. v. State Human Rights Appeal Board, 52 NY 2d 72 (1980)
In re Wood, 140 US 278 (1891)
International Harvester Co. v. Kentucky, 234 US 216 (1914)
Iota Xi Chapter of Sigma Chi Fraternity v. George Mason University, 773 F. Supp. 792 (E.D. VA 1991)
Iron Crow v. Ogalala Sioux Tribe, 231 F.2d 89 (8th Cir. 1956)
Johnson v. Kentucky, 83 F. Supp. 707 (E.D. KY 1949)
Johnson v. M'Intosh, 21 US 543 (1823)
Josiah Philip's Case (VA 1778)
Kampmann v. United States, 259 F. 192 (7th Cir. 1919)
Kirchberg v. Feenstra, 450 US 455 (1981)
Kennedy v. State, 76 NC 251 (1877)
Kolender v. *Lawson*, 461 US 352 (1983)
Lane v. Wilson, 307 US 268 (1939)
Late Corporation of the Church of Jesus Christ of Latter-Day Saints v. United States, 136 US 1 (1890)
Lewis v. New Orleans, 408 US 913 (1972)
Linmark Associates v. Willingboro, 431 US 85 (1977)
Lochner v. New York, 198 US 45 (1905)
Lombard v. Louisiana, 373 US 267 (1963)
Louisiana v. NAACP, 366 US 293 (1961)
Loving v. Virginia, 388 US 1 (1967)
Lovell v. City of Griffin, 303 US 444 (1938)
Lucy v. Adams, 350 US 1 (1955)
Lum v. Rice, 275 US 78 (1927)
Mapp v. Ohio, 367 US 643 (1963)

Marbury v. Madison, 5 US 137 (1803)
Marsh v. Alabama, 326 US 501 (1946)
Marshall v. Gordon, 243 US 521 (1917)
Masses Publishing Co. v. Patten, 244 F. 535 (S.D. NY 1917), reversed 246 F. 24 (2nd Cir. 1917)
McCabe v. Atchison, Topeka & Santa Fe Railway Co., 235 US 151 (1914)
McCauley v. University of the Virgin Islands, 618 F.3d 232 (3rd Cir. 2010)
McCormick v. Burt, 95 IL 263 (1880)
McLaurin v. Oklahoma, 339 US 637 (1950)
M'Cutchen v. Marshall, 33 US 220 (1834)
Mendez v. Westminster, 161 F.2d 774 (9th Cir. 1947) (en banc) (1947)
Meredith v. Fair, 313 F.2d 532 (5th Cir. 1962)
Merrion v. Jicarilla Apache Tribe, 455 US 130 (1982)
Meyer v. Nebraska, 262 US 390 (1923)
Milliken v. Bradley, 418 US 717 (1974)
Milwaukee Social Democratic Pub. Co. v. Burleson, 255 US 407 (1921)
Minersville v. Gobitis, 310 US 586 (1940)
Minor v. Happersett, 88 US 163 (1875)
Missouri ex. rel. Gaines v. Canada, 305 US 337 (1938)
Mitchell v. Charleston, 378 US 551 (1964)
Mitchell v. United States, 313 US 80 (1941)
Moore v. Dempsey, 261 US 86 (1923)
Moore v. Monroe, 64 IA 367 (1884)
Morgan v. Virginia, 328 US 373 (1946)
Murray v. Pearson, 169 MD 478 (1936)
Mutual Film Corporation v. Industrial Commission of Ohio, 236 US 230 (1915)
Myers v. Anderson, 238 US 368 (1915)
NAACP v. Alabama, 357 US 449 (1958)
NAACP v. Alabama, 377 US 288 (1964)
NAACP v. Button, 371 US 415 (1963)
NAACP v. Claiborne Hardware, 458 US 886 (1982)
National Socialist Party of America v. City of Skokie, 432 US 43 (1977)
Near v. Minnesota, 283 US 697 (1931)
New Negro Alliance v. Sanitary Grocery, 303 US 552 (1938)
New York Times v. Sullivan, 376 US 254 (1964)
Nixon v. Condon, 286 US 73 (1932)
Nixon v. Herndon, 273 US 536 (1927)
Norris v. Alabama, 294 US 587 (1935)

Nuxoll ex rel. Nuxoll v. Indian Prairie Sch. Dist. # 204, 523 F.3d 668, 672 (7th Cir. 2008).
One, Inc. v. Oleson, 355 US 371 (1958)
Organization for a Better Austin v. Keefe, 402 US 415 (1971)
Ozawa v. United States, 260 US 178 (1922)
Pace v. Alabama, 106 US 583 (1883)
Palko v. Connecticut, 302 US 314 (1937)
Parker v. Franklin, 331 F.2d 841 (5th Cir. 1964)
Patterson v. Alabama, 294 US 600 (1935)
Patton v. Mississippi, 332 US 463 (1947)
Pennekamp v. Florida, 328 US 331 (1946)
People v. Croswell, 3 Johns. Cas. 337 NY 1804
People v. Hall, 4 CA 399 (1854)
People v. Lloyd, 304 IL 23 (1922)
People v. Malone, 29 NY Crim. Rpts. 325 (NY S.Ct. 1913)
Permoli v. Municipality No. 1 of New Orleans, 44 US 589 (1845)
Peterson v. Greenville, 373 US 244 (1963)
Pickering v Board of Education, 391 US 563 (1968)
Pierce v. United States, 252 US 239 (1920)
Plessy v. Ferguson, 163 US 537 (1896)
Pope v. Williams, 193 US 621 (1904)
Powell v. Alabama, 287 US 45 (1932)
Queen v. Hepburn, 11 US 290 (1813)
Rankin v. McPherson, 483 US 378 (1987)
R.A.V. v. St. Paul, 505 US 377 (1992)
Reynolds v. United States, 98 US 145 (1878)
Roberts v. City of Boston, 59 MA 198 (1850)
Roberts v. Haragan, 346 F. Supp. 2d 853 (N.D. TX 2004)
Rosenfeld v. New Jersey, 408 US 901 (1972)
Roth v. United States, 354 US 476 (1957)
Rutgers v. Maddington (NY City Mayor's Ct. 1784)
Sandberg v. United States, 257 F. 643 (9th Cir. 1919).
Schaefer v. United States, 251 US 466 (1920)
Schenk v. United States, 249 US 47 (1919)
Schneider v. New Jersey, 308 US 147 (1939)
Scott v. Negro Ben, 10 US 3 (1810)
Scott v. Negro London, 7 US 324 (1806)
Scott v. State, 39 GA 321 (1869)

Shelley v Kraemer, 334 US 1 (1948)
Shelton v. Tucker, 364 US 479 (1960)
Shilter v. United States, 257 F. 724 (9th Cir. 1919)
Shuttlesworth v. City of Birmingham, 394 US 147 (1969)
Silva v. University of New Hampshire, 888 F. Supp. 293 (D. NH 1994)
Sipuel v. Oklahoma, 332 US 631 (1948)
Slaughter-House Cases, 83 US 36 (1873)
Smith v. Allwright, 321 US 649 (1944)
Snyder v. Milwaukee, 308 US 147 (1939)
Snyder v. Phelps, 56 US 443 (2011)
Spies v. Illinois, 123 US 131 (1887)
Spiller v. Inhabitants of Woburn, 94 MA 127 (1866)
Stanley v. Georgia, 394 US 557 (1969)
State ex rel Finger v. Weedman, et. al., 55 SD 343 (1929)
State ex rel. Gaines v. Canada, 305 US 337 (1938)
State ex rel Weiss v. District Board, 76 WI 177 (1890)
State v. Nelson, A14-0356 (MN Ct. App. Dec. 22, 2014)
State v. Pierce, 163 WI 615 (1916)
State v. Thrasher, 3 TX App. 262 (1877)
Steele v. Louisville and Nashville Railroad, 323 US 192 (1944)
Strauder v. West Virginia, 100 US 303 (1880)
Street v. New York, 394 US 576 (1969)
Stromberg v. California, 283 US 359 (1931)
Sweatt v. Painter, 339 US 629 (1950)
Symsbury Case, 1 Kirby 444 (CT Super. Ct. 1785)
Talley v. California, 362 US 60 (1960)
Tapes v. Hurley, 66 CA 473 (1885)
Taylor v. Louisiana, 370 US 154 (1962)
Taylor v. Mississippi, 319 US 583 (1943)
Ten Pound Act Cases (NH 1786)
Terminiello v. Chicago, 337 US 1 (1949)
Thomas v. Collins, 323 US 516 (1945)
Thomas v. Mississippi, 380 US 524 (1965)
Thornhill v. Alabama, 310 US 88 (1940)
Tinker v. Des Moines School District, 303 US 593 (1969)
Tollett v. United States, 485 F.2d 1087 (8th Cir. 1973)
Trevett v. Weeden (RI 1786)
Truax v. Raich, 239 US 33 (1915)

Tunstall v. Brotherhood of Locomotive Firemen and Engineers, 323 US 210 (1944)
United States v. Alkhabaz, 104 F. 3d 1492 (6th Cir. 1997)
United States v. Berrigan, 2 AK 442 (D. AK 1905)
United States v. Carolene Products, 304 US 144 (1938)
United States v. Cruikshank, 92 US 542 (1875)
United States v. Hall, 248 Fed. 150 (D. MT 1918)
United States v. Harris, 106 US 629 (1882)
United States v. Machado, 195 F. 3d 454 (9th Cir. 1999)
United States v. Morrison, 529 US 598 (2000)
United States v. Reese, 92 US 214 (1876)
United States v. Schutte, 252 F. 212 (D. ND 1918)
United States v. Schwimmer, 279 US 644 (1929)
Updegraph v. Commonwealth, 11 Serg. & Rawle 394 PA (1824)
UWM Post, et. al. v. Board of Regents of the University of Wisconsin, 774 F. Supp. 1163 (E.D. WI 1991)
Virginia v. Black, 583 US 343 (2003)
Ward v. Rock Against Racism, 491 US 781 (1989)
Watkins v. United States, 354 US 178 (1957)
Watson v. Memphis, 373 US 526 (1963)
West Virginia v. State Board of Ed. v. Barnette, 319 US 624 (1943)
Whitney v. California, 274 US 357 (1927)
Wiggs v. Courshon, 355 F.Supp. 206 (1973)
Williams v. North Carolina, 378 US 548 (1964)
Willis v. Pickwick Restaurants, 231 F. Supp. 396 (1964)
Wood v. Davis, 11 US 271 (1812)
Worcester v. Georgia, 31 US 515 (1832)
Yates v. United States, 354 US 298 (1957)
Yick Wo v. Hopkins, 118 US 356 (1886)

INDEX

www.ingramcontent.com/pod-product-compliance
Lightning Source LLC
Chambersburg PA
CBHW030326270326
41926CB00010B/1518

* 9 7 8 1 4 3 8 4 7 5 8 2 0 *